Optimizing Student Success in School With the Other Three Rs

Reasoning, Resilience, and Responsibility

a volume in
Research in Educational Productivity

Series Editor:
Herbert J. Walberg, *Stanford University, Hoover Institution*

Research in Educational Productivity

Herbert J. Walberg, Series Editor

Optimizing Student Success in School With the Other Three Rs

Reasoning, Resilience, and Responsibility

edited by

Robert J. Sternberg
Tufts University

and

Rena F. Subotnik
Center for Psychology in Schools and Education,
American Psychological Association

INFORMATION AGE
PUBLISHING

Greenwich, Connecticut • www.infoagepub.com

Library of Congress Cataloging-in-Publication Data

Optimizing student success in school with the other three rs :
reasoning, resilience, and responsibility / edited by Robert J. Sternberg and
Rena F. Subotnik.
    p. cm. — (Research in educational productivity)
 Includes bibliographical references and index.
 ISBN 1-59311-430-3 (pbk.) — ISBN 1-59311-431-1
 1. Thought and thinking—Study and teaching. 2. Reasoning—Study and
teaching. 3. Resilience (Personality trait)—Study and teaching. 4.
Responsibility—Study and teaching. 5. Academic achievement. I.
Sternberg,
Robert J. II. Subotnik, Rena Faye. III. Series.
 LB1590.3.O68 2005
 378.1'734--dc22
                            2005029946

Printed in the United States of America

CONTENTS

CHAPTER 1

INTRODUCTION

Rena F. Subotnik and Gregory White

Schools are under enormous pressure to boost student achievement. Under the No Child Left Behind legislation (2002), schools are faced with unprecedented demands to document improvements for all populations that make up their student bodies. Many schools may even be forced to close if annual yearly progress goals are not met, leaving their students to be dispersed to other institutions. With schools busy preparing their students to meet these mandated competencies, the idea of introducing additional variables for teachers and administrators to incorporate into the curriculum may seem counterproductive. The authors in this volume argue, however, that the "Other Three Rs," *reasoning, resilience*, and *responsibility*, when taught and modeled appropriately, can enhance student achievement and help to create an atmosphere in schools more conducive for learning. After school graduation, the Other 3 Rs (or TOTR) can also provide the learning and interpersonal skills that are valued in the workplace. As stated in the federal report "21st Century Skills for 21st Century Jobs": Future employees will require a portfolio of problem-solving, analytical and creative thinking skills, as well as skills in interpersonal communication, negotiation and self-management (U.S. Department of Commerce et al., 1999, as cited in Carnegie 2003, p. 13).

Optimizing Student Success in School With the Other Three Rs:
Reasoning, Resilience, and Responsibility, 1–16
Copyright © 2006 by Information Age Publishing

Fostering TOTRs can create productive contexts for learning and improve students' capacity to learn. For example, skills of *reasoning* can offer students a toolbox of strategies to solve problems; learning *resilience* can aid student motivation by focusing on overcoming learning obstacles rather than despairing over failure; and integrating skills of *responsibility* can help students to associate achievement with effort and good organization. The Other 3 Rs can also be instrumental to success in nonacademic dimensions of life, not only during childhood, but also during employment, civic life, and in the course of human relationships.

OVERCOMING OBSTACLES TO STUDENT ACHIEVEMENT

Despite increased spending and efforts at reform since the Elementary and Secondary Education Act of 1965, wide achievement gaps persist between students from different economic classes and racial backgrounds (U.S. Department of Education, 2005). In addition, results from the 2003 National Assessment of Educational Progress reveal that only 32% of U.S. eighth graders are reading proficiently at or above grade level, and more than a quarter of U.S. students cannot read at the basic level (U.S. Department of Education National Center for Education Statistics, 2005). Obstacles to student achievement can be found at home and at school. These obstacles lead to achievement gaps between students, and these gaps increase with each year of schooling. This volume argues that the TOTRs can promote achievement and the realization of full academic potential, especially for students who are labeled as underperformers.

Home Factors

Parental involvement in school and a home environment focused on academics are critical influences on academic achievement. Parental involvement in schools is not only related to higher academic achievement, but also to higher educational aspirations, higher motivation to achieve, lower rates of disciplinary problems, higher rates of extracurricular involvement, and higher rates of school completion (Child Trends, 2004; Epstein & Dauber, 1991; Henderson & Beria, 1994; Nord & West, 2001; Wentzel, 1999; Zill & Nord, 1994, as cited in Barton, 2003). However, lower socioeconomic status (SES) parents are less likely to be involved or feel welcomed in schools; therefore, schools need to conduct more directed outreach to low-SES parents (Gerwertz, 2003, as cited in Barton, 2003). In a review of 29 experimental studies, efforts to promote an academically stimulating home environment by parents and teachers was more predictive of academic learning than was family SES. Positive attributes of a student's home environment include homework supervision, discussion of school and current events, encouragement of reading, screening of television viewing and peer activities, delayed gratification, and setting long-term goals (Walberg, 2005). In contrast, unstable homes, financial hardship, emotional or physical abuse, substance abuse, or other family problems can create a distraction from learning and produce children at risk of school failure (Wang, Haertel, & Walberg, 1998).

Children living in poverty and who come from unstable homes start out behind academically in preschool and learn at a slower rate compared to others, resulting in a cumulative disadvantage over time (Walberg, 2005). Furthermore, factors such as poor health and nutrition, low birth weight, exposure to lead, and frequent relocation compound the risk for lower academic achievement (Barton, 2003). In addition, the effect of television on academic achievement deserves special mention. Eighth graders who watched more than 5 hours of television per night had the lowest average mathematics scores recorded on the Third International Mathematics and Science Study. The opportunity cost of lower achievement is evident for students who do not spend time doing homework, reading, or being involved in extracurricular activities (Child Trends, 2003, as cited in Barton, 2003; Walberg, 2005).

School Factors

Along with home background factors, several school-related factors also influence student achievement. These factors include teacher quality, class size, school safety, peer group, and school leadership, as well as how summer breaks are utilized (Mayer, Mullens, & Moore, 2000; Walberg, 2005).

Teacher Quality. Among school factors, teacher quality is the most important influence on student achievement. The added value of good teaching for 3 consecutive years has been shown to improve student achievement dramatically. Conversely, poor teaching year after year not only impedes achievement but retards students' academic development (Rivkin, Hanushek, & Kain, 2002; Sanders & Rivers, 1996). Factors related to teaching quality include strong academic preparation, in-field teaching, and years of experience (Mayer et al., 2000). Students learn more from teachers with strong academic abilities, and the field of teaching needs to attract more candidates with higher academic skills (Ballou, 1996; Ehrenberg & Brewer, 1994, 1995; Ferguson, 1991; Ferguson & Ladd, 1996; Gitamer, Latham, & Ziomek, 1999; Henke, Chen, & Geis, 2000; Henke, Geis, & Giambattista, 1996; Mosteller & Moynihan, 1972;

Murnane et al., 1991; Vance & Schlechty, 1982, as cited in Mayer et al., 2000). Moreover, students learn more from teachers holding bachelor's or master's degrees in the subjects that they teach, especially in mathematics and science (Darling-Hammond, 2000; Goldhaber & Brewer, 1997; Monk & King, 1994, as cited in Mayer et al., 2000). Instructional experience is also related to increases in student achievement, at least for the first 5 years of teaching, with the effect leveling off after 5 years (Darling-Hammond, 2000; Murnane & Phillips, 1981; Rivkin, Hanushek, & Kain, 1998, as cited in Mayer et al., 2000).

Teacher quality varies across communities. Out-of-field teachers are employed more widely in high poverty schools and in schools with higher numbers of minority students (Jerald & Ingersol, 2002, as cited in Barton, 2003). In addition, low-income, African American, and Hispanic students are more likely to have less experienced teachers, greater teacher turnover, and higher rates of teacher absence (Mayer et al., 1998, 2000, as cited in Barton, 2003).

High Expectations. Holding high expectations also leads to high achievement. Data from the "High School and Beyond" longitudinal study show that academic achievement is closely related to a rigorous curriculum for all students (Bryk, Lee, & Holland, 1993; Chubb & Moe, 1990, as cited in Mayer et al., 2000). Experimental and field studies show that: (1) setting specific, challenging goals leads to higher performance than setting easy goals, no goals, or simply encouraging students to do their best (Lock, Shaw, Saari, & Lantham, 1981, as cited in Walberg, 2005). (2) The amount of homework that teachers require is also important (Betts & Costrell, 2001, as cited in Walberg, 2005), as is (3) increased instructional time for reading and mathematics (Education Trust, 2001, as cited in Walberg, 2005). Although academic expectations have increased over the years, a 2001 Harris Interactive poll conducted with Walberg (2005) reveals that principals, teachers, and students differ in their perceptions regarding academic expectations. When asked whether teachers have high expectations for their students, 56% of principals responded affirmatively, compared to 39% of teachers and only 25% of students themselves. In addition, not every student who is capable or willing to pursue college preparatory coursework does so, as white and Asian students enroll in rigorous academic courses at higher rates than other groups of students (Wirt et al., 2000, as cited in Mayer et al., 2000).

School Organization. In addition to teaching and learning factors, the organizational characteristics of schools such as class size, school safety, and leadership influence on student success. Meta-analyses reveal gains in academic achievement in classes with an optimal class size of 13–20 students, especially for low-income and minority students. It must be noted, however, that it would be counterproductive to reduce class size by hiring lower quality teachers (Bohrnstedt & Stecher, 1999; Krueger, 1998; Mosteller, Light, & Sachs, 1996; Robinson & Wittebols, 1986, as cited in Mayer et al., 2000).

A safe school with shared norms for learning is also important to foster student achievement. Research has concluded that a positive disciplinary environment is linked to: (1) higher achievement (Barton, Coley, & Wenglinsky, 1998; Bryk, Lee, & Holland, 1993; Chubb & Moe, 1990, as cited in Mayer et al., 2000), (2) student respect for teachers, regular attendance, avoidance of substance use, and the absence of fighting/bullying and carrying weapons (Mayer et al., 2000), (3) a stable professional community with shared high expectations, values, and goals, as well as openness to new ideas (Louis, Kruse, & Marks, 1996, as cited in Mayer et al., 2000).

Peer Group Factors

Peer group attitudes toward school are related to academic grades, academic goals, and perceived competence. Peers' influence can be negative and lead to anti-intellectual attitudes, higher dropout rates, higher pregnancy rates, gang involvement, and substance abuse. Alternatively, having peers with high academic motivation can positively enhance the school experience for students at risk of academic failure (Wang et al., 1998).

OPTIMIZING STUDENT ACHIEVEMENT WITH THE OTHER 3 Rs

Although negative family and school factors impact on achievement, the psychological attributes of learners themselves can mitigate these factors and lead to school success. Abilities, motivation, and prior achievement, as well as attributions for success and failure, all affect learning. The Other 3 Rs, *reasoning, resilience*, and *responsibility*, are skills for learning that engender the persistence and determination to achieve academic and life success and are not limited by innate ability or background. The Other 3 Rs promote a mindset of "what can be" rather than one of lowered expectations. The Other 3 Rs, especially as they interact with one another, provide powerful learning tools for all students to reach their academic potential. These learning strategies provide skills for students to reason well and to develop as educationally resilient, self-directed learners.

Reasoning

Reasoning is the ability to draw conclusions from evidence, and often entails the use of metacognitive strategies, or internal dialogue and self-monitoring activities, to improve learning. Research reveals that children can be taught metacognitive strategies, including ways to use past experience and background knowledge to predict future outcomes, examine new information to build comprehension, and allocate learning resources such as time and memory (Bransford, Brown, & Cocking, 2000).

In an environment of increased testing and accountability, schools today are heavily focused on teaching and assessing analytical and memory skills (Sternberg, 2003a). However, according to Sternberg (1999), practical and creative skills are also important for success in school and in life. Halpern (2005) also affirms that critical thinking and problem solving are essential skills that help students to assess information, formulate inferences, and make decisions.

In addition to learning how to analyze information critically, creatively, and practically, students also need to harness problem-solving skills. Together, such analyses can be used to set and achieve desired goals, generate and answer difficult questions, and move through and overcome obstacles that are barriers to learning and achievement. Schools can help students choose, adapt, and create tools for problem solving as a means to transfer learning to new situations (Bransford et al., 2000). The importance of problem-solving skills for later life success is shown in Werner and Smith's (2001) Kauai Longitudinal Study. Measures of problem-solving skills at age 10 had a significant positive association with successful adaptation at age 40.

Instruction and assessment can be tailored for students with different academic abilities to promote the development of advanced reasoning skills (Wang, 1992, as cited in Wang et al., 1998). With a foundation of such skills, and the opportunity to expand learning through teacher-led activities that promote active inquiry and experimentation, students progress from novices to expert learners and problem solvers. Furthermore, multiple methods of assessment such as special assignments, exhibitions, portfolios, and performances, as well as multiple-choice tests, may better allow students with different abilities and prior knowledge to demonstrate their learning (McCombs & Whistler, 1997, as cited in Wang et al., 1998).

Resilience

Resilience can be defined as overcoming adversity to achieve good developmental outcomes. (Masten & Coatsworth, 1998). Wang and colleagues (1998) reveal that two of the most important characteristics of resilient children are a high level of engagement in activities and belief in self-determination. Resilient children are also able to identify and engage relationships and environments that promote their growth, and have the ability to screen out negative messages. Other characteristics of resilient children include healthy expectations, a clear sense of purpose, a sense of competence, resourcefulness, flexibility, even temper, openness to new experiences, humor, and good interpersonal skills (Wang et al., 1998).

Educational resilience describes a child's ability to achieve academic and social success in the classroom despite early and ongoing personal vulnerabilities and adversities (Wang et al., 1998). Schools can employ the following factors to cultivate resilience: (1) teacher expectations and actions that model caring but high expectations; (2) curriculum and instruction that builds on student knowledge and diversity; (3) school organization and climate that promotes active student participation and sense of small learning communities; and (4) peer learning programs, mentoring, and extracurricular activities (Bernard, 2004; Wang et al., 1998). Results indicate that children in schools implementing resiliency-building strategies have higher standardized test scores in reading and mathematics, higher aspirations for academic learning, and improved academic self-concepts (Wang & Oates, 1996, as cited in Wang et al., 1998).

Responsibility

Responsibility involves being accountable for one's actions and inactions. Responsibility entails understanding and having empathy for others' opinions as well as concern for the common good. Schools can develop a sense of responsibility that can be exercised in personal, civic, and academic domains.

Personal responsibility is grounded in an individual sense of morality that is not influenced unduly by peer perspectives. Personal responsibility not only relates to being accountable for one's own actions, but also includes the wisdom to be responsible for others (Sternberg, 2003b). Personal responsibility can be developed by participation in leadership development activities that are challenging and engaging. Schools, families, and communities can provide opportunities for students to develop and voice their opinions, make decisions, hold responsible positions, express creativity, work as part of a team, and help others. These opportunities help students to develop autonomy, a positive identity, and self-awareness (Bernard, 2004).

Civic responsibility involves employing critical thinking and commitment of one's talents to solve community problems (Carnegie, 2003).

Civic responsibility can be cultivated through student involvement in school governance as well as in-depth service learning activities. Within schools, teachers can involve students in creating classroom rules, and schools can design disciplinary policies with student input aimed at restorative not punitive justice (i.e.: mediation, peace making circles, etc.) (Benard, 2004; Wang, Haertel, & Walberg, 1998) Policies can also encourage student bystanders to prevent bullying behavior in schools. (Slaby, Wilson-Brewer, & Dash, 1994). In addition to classroom learning, service learning that is linked to the curriculum is also an effective way to develop civic responsibility in students (Carnegie, 2003).

Academic responsibility involves learners taking an active role in their academic success. Teachers can encourage *academic* responsibility in students by developing self-regulation skills and a sense of personal agency through strategies that allow students to become increasingly responsible for their own learning. Learners develop self-regulation skills by actively setting learning goals, managing their time wisely, identifying and organizing learning resources, seeking assistance when needed, accomplishing learning goals, and assessing what they learn (Wang et al., 1998; Zimmerman & Martinez-Pons, 1988).

Motivation, perceived self-efficacy, and a sense of mastery are key psychological attributes necessary for the development of responsibility. In academic learning, achievement motivation involves determination, persistence, goal direction and intention, and is linked to increased school completion and increased reading and math scores, as well as improved mental health and interpersonal skills (Larson, 2000; Ryan & Deci, 2000; Scales & Leffert, 1999; Werner & Smith, 1992, as cited in Benard, 2004). Self-efficacy, another dimension of responsibility, is the belief that one has the personal power and ability to succeed. Perceived self-efficacy may in fact be more important than innate ability. Experimental studies consistently show that perceived self-efficacy increases effort and persistence, and leads to higher achievement (Bandura, 1995, 1997; Maddox, 2002; Multon, 1991; Shunk, 1989, 1991; Zimmerman, 1995, as cited in Bernard, 2004).

IMPLICATIONS

Teacher preparation should incorporate knowledge of the Other Three Rs, as well as their impact on student achievement and how they can be incorporated into practice. TOTRs are universal learning skills available to all students, and cultivating all three of these skills can boost student performance, especially for underachievers. Although each of TOTRs is related to school and life success, they are most effective when they are used together. In the course of problem solving, reasoning skills offer the ability to judge which strategies best address the needs of a particular situation. Responsibility provides understanding of the consequences (for oneself and others) of employing or not employing different problem-solving strategies, and taking ownership of the results. And resilience produces the patience to work through the problem-solving process by capitalizing on lessons learned until achieving desired outcomes.

CHAPTER SUMMARIES

Reasoning, Resilience and Responsibility

Robert Sternberg begins his chapter with a comparison of contemporary and more desirable school practices. The central feature of both conceptions is the way that intelligence is conceived and assessed. The contemporary system of schooling is dependent on tests to measure a narrow range of memory and analytical skills. According to Sternberg, a more optimal setting for school and life success incorporates analytic, creative, and practical thinking, as well as wisdom. Sternberg builds connections between reasoning and intelligence (including analytic and practical thinking), creative thinking and resilience, and wisdom and responsibility. The resulting structure is the theory entitled "WICS," for wisdom, intelligence, and creativity synthesized.

For each component of the theory Sternberg presents compelling examples and arguments. The theory is evolved from a large and historic body of work that began with the Triarchic Theory of Intelligence and evolved through the Theory of Successful Intelligence to WISC. Each iteration is more comprehensive and offers more opportunities to apply the evidence-based practices that have emerged from the research on WISC. This chapter sets the stage for the themes that emerge in Parts II–IV of the book.

Catherine Good and *Carol Dweck* present a well-documented and tightly argued discussion connecting student motivation, by way of reasoning, resilience, and responsibility, with academic achievement. Their logic path begins with students' views of their own intelligence. Those students who subscribe to the belief that their abilities are fixed approach every challenge as a reflection of their innate gifts or deficits. Those who ascribe their abilities to incremental learning and experience are more likely to consider challenges as difficult but natural components of their intellectual growth process.

Students with incremental views of their abilities are more able to transfer knowledge into reasoning strategies that allow for solving novel problems. Students with incremental views of their abilities are also more prepared to be resilient in the face of challenges because successes and failures are associated with effort and reasoning skills rather than predetermined abilities. Resilience also serves as a form of inoculation from diminished performance due to stereotype threat. Good and Dweck show that students who hold incremental views of their intelligence are likely to take responsibility for their learning and behaviors. The authors provide readers with three evidence-based instructional strategies designed to improve student achievement. The first instructional method employs direct instruction on incremental versus entity theories of intelligence. Next, instructors can use praise strategically to reinforce incremental learning goals. The third approach is to tie discussions of stereotype threat to students' views of their own intelligence.

Reasoning

Students often have difficulty reasoning through word problems because of missing pieces in their knowledge base. Success in solving word problems is no trivial matter, especially since eighth-grade mathematics achievement influences access to advanced courses in high school and choice of majors in college. According to *Richard Mayer*, student gaps can be categorized into five strands, including factual, conceptual, strategic, procedural, and attitudinal knowledge.

Mayer deftly analyzes all the potential errors that could be made by a student in one simple word problem. He then goes on to provide methods for optimizing students' ability to reason by removing their knowledge deficiencies. Mayer argues that students are poorly served by the standard mathematics curriculum, which focuses exclusively on procedural knowledge at the expense of factual, conceptual, strategic, and attitudinal knowledge. Access to important knowledge and the opportunity to exercise mathematical reasoning is an immediate and accessible antidote to poor mathematics achievement. With appropriate training, teachers could explicate mathematical problems in ways that elicit understanding and the ability to reason that can generalize to the solution of problems in other domains as well.

Terezinha Nunes provides readers with insights on mathematical reasoning from her work with deaf pupils. Deaf children, and now most children who are not successful in the early grades, are deeply involved in language comprehension and achievement. Learning mathematics takes a secondary role. Nunes shows us through her research that with appropriate teaching strategies and opportunities, deaf children can be successful mathematical thinkers.

One key feature of Nunes's argument is the fact that deaf children tend to prefer visual–spatial rather than serial information processing, not only in mathematics but in most arenas. When information is presented to them in visual spatial form, they can be more successful than hearing children. However, even if all teaching could rely more heavily on visual cues and presentations, gaps in informal mathematical experience and exposure result in deficits for deaf children. Nunes describes such informal exposure as the kind of talking aloud one does when one is counting how many minutes are left on a journey or estimating costs of shopping. In order to provide deaf children with such modeling, Nunes and her colleagues designed an intervention program for promoting everyday exposure to money counting and counting strings. The chapter's focus on deaf children is not only interesting in and of itself but has many potential applications to other students who are not exposed to rich aural language associated with mathematics.

Tom Luce and *Lee Thompson* remind us of how valuable data and evidence-based best practices can be to educators, parents, and policymakers hoping to raise student achievement in U.S. schools. In order to be successful at closing achievement gaps, we need to document knowledge and skills already attained by various subgroups of students as well as assess the achievement level students can attain with excellent instruction and curriculum content. Luce and Thompson argue that reform efforts should be founded on detailed longitudinal student performance information and modeled on educational best practices that have been successful with underachieving populations. They provide readers with descriptions of their methodology for tracking individual student progress in individual schools and determining which educational practices are proven to work in even the most challenging of circumstances. This method provides a detailed road map for longitudinal researchers and reformers desiring to spur excellence in schools.

The rationale for the work conducted by The National Center for Educational Accountability, where Luce formerly served as chairman (and its affiliate *Just for the Kids*), is embedded in the chapter's cogent review of school reform efforts since the Effective School Movement, including long-standing disconnects between high-quality research and practice in education. Luce and Thompson also stress the need for analyses that take into account the complex interplay of evidence-based interventions within local contexts. With such efforts in place, the quality of student learning should be sufficient to meet the demands of postsecondary reasoning skills. This work is part of a larger framework discussed in *Do What Works: How Proven Practices Can Improve America's Public Schools,* published by Ascent Education Press in 2005.

Resilience

Mary Walsh and *Mary Brabeck* present a chapter focused on the detrimental effects of poverty on student success. They further identify personal, school, and community factors that are likely to enhance the resilience of children living in poverty. According to Walsh and Brabeck, meeting the academic and mental health needs of low SES requires a careful analysis of risks and a concurrent assessment of strengths to guide appropriate prevention and intervention strategies. Their main argument is that the factors that lead to addressing poverty and engendering resilience are complex and require coordination among various stakeholders.

Walsh and Brabeck highlight a few key variables associated with resiliency, including school engagement, family engagement, and socioemotional functioning. Each of these variables is gravely affected by poverty, yet coordinated, systemic approaches to prevention and intervention can improve resiliency on the part of low SES. The evidence-based model presented by Walsh and Brabeck for personal, family, school, and community collaboration is developmental and draws from work they have conducted in the Boston Public Schools as well as policy developed by the Centers for Disease Control. These comprehensive approaches promote health education, physical education, health services, nutrition services, counseling, psychological and social services, healthy school environment, health promotion for staff, and parent/community involvement.

Rather than focusing on resilience as a passive state, *Edmund Gordon* and *Brenda Mejia* prefer the conception of "defiance," or constructive resistance to academic and career barriers. The authors identify four systemic constraints on academic achievement, particularly on the part of minority youth. Two constraints can be addressed by communities in which students live (community and family support for learning, changing student behaviors and attitudes toward learning), and two require political leadership, financial support, and intensive organization (better selection and preparation of teachers, better distribution of relevant resources).

The authors' studies of "defiant" African American men provide the following characteristics: willingness to stand out from their peers, active cultivation of a meaningful relationship with a mentor, realistic attributions for success and failure that reflect control over one's experiences, and the ability to view challenges as opportunities. Gordon and Mejia propose a policy of "affirmative development" by which education stakeholders enhance opportunities for minority youth in homes, schools, communities, and school systems to raise academic achievement, expand career goals, and support "defiance."

Responsibility

Barry Zimmerman draws our attention to the relationship between academic responsibility, student achievement, and student self-concept. According to Zimmerman, students must take responsibility for their academic successes and failures in order to maximize their achievement. In unstructured classrooms and homes, however, many students learn that taking responsibility for mistakes or failures can lead to unpleasant consequences, which can reinforce blaming academic failure on uncontrollable outside forces. In this chapter, Zimmerman provides readers with theory, research, and practice designed to increase student academic responsibility.

Some successful interventions include modeling by instructors of effective learning strategies. In addition to modeling, instructors offer feedback to students that reaffirms their ability to complete the work if effort is expended on appropriate problem-solving strategies. The aim of the intervention is to promote student self-regulation, and self-regulation is best learned when students view their academic lives as controllable. The best setting for enhancing student views of controllability are structured in ways in which students have clearly delineated roles in the classroom, and consequences for their actions are understood and experienced. If we heed Zimmerman's arguments, today's students will enter their adulthood as more responsible citizens and problem solvers.

Jacquelynne Eccles focuses her chapter on the role of motivation in the development of academic responsibility. She explores how student motivation is affected by many factors, including how gender and ethnic groups view academic achievement and school engagement. Resilience comes into play as well when young people encounter discrimination and low expectations. Eccles provides readers with an elegant Expectancy–Value Model of Academic Achievement Motivation, including its development and relation to optimizing student success.

Expectations for academic success depend on the importance students place on the task, subject, or general school performance. Expectations also depend on the likelihood students think they can be successful at those tasks. Furthermore, school expectations may or may not be related to an individual's long-range career and life goals. All goals, short and long, intellectual and social, are embedded in issues of cultural, gender, social class, and identity. The implications for teaching the model include (1) focusing on successful mastery of material rather than on performance comparisons, and (2) including a variety of carefully selected explanatory examples of concepts designed to increase students' sense of ownership of the material. Eccles argues that we need to understand far more about what motivates students to undertake academic tasks in order to develop effective interventions that enhance student responsibility.

A Classroom Model for Reasoning, Resilience, and Responsibility

Jeanine Cogan and colleagues report on a professional development project developed at the American Psychological Association (APA) designed to "help teachers convey three key skills applicable to their students' academic and general life pursuits: how to *reason* well, be *resilient* in the face of challenges, and take *responsibility* for one's own learning." This project began as an initiative under the leadership of former APA President Robert Sternberg and developed into a collaboration of researchers, teachers, and other education professionals focused on integrating the Other Three Rs into the elementary school curriculum.

The chapter describes the basis on which the Other Three Rs were selected as a focus for the project and their transformation into a professional development curriculum being piloted in the Montgomery County (Maryland) Public Schools. The three underlying assumptions of the project are (1) that the Other Three Rs are teachable and learnable, (2) that once they are learned, they lead to increased academic achievement and improved life skills, and (3) that the Other Three Rs derive their greatest power by way of interaction, most specifically in the form of the ABC Problem-Solving Model.

Susan Goldman provides readers with an analysis of policy and research implications derived from the strategies and research lines proposed by the authors of this volume. She grounds her commentary in a concern for integrating cognitive, social, and emotional development with learning.

Goldman offers three recommendations for ensuring the quality of policy-based research on the Other Three Rs. One suggestion is to continue conducting studies of reasoning, resilience, and responsibility widely in challenging school environments so as to address the important concerns of practitioners. A second proposal is to include a longitudinal component in research designs in order to assess the effects of interventions beyond a cross-sectional analysis. Third, Goldman urges us to work together to define our terms carefully and consistently. Without precise, agreed-upon definitions of reasoning, resilience, and responsibility, researchers, and policymakers will have difficulty generalizing from research.

The authors of this volume present in detail their evidence-based arguments for promoting TOTRs in schools as a way to optimize student success. As a result of this outstanding display of scholarship, we look forward to a burgeoning interest in the application of TOTRs to school curriculum and to teacher education.

ACKNOWLEDGMENT

Many thanks to Ashley Edmiston for her able assistance in managing the prepublication editing of this book.

REFERENCES

Barton, P. E. (2003). *Parsing the achievement gap: Baselines for tracking progress.* Princeton, NJ: Educational Testing Service.

Bernard, B. (2004). *Resiliency: What we have learned.* San Francisco: WestEd.

Bransford, J. D., Brown, A. L., & Cocking, R. R. (2000). *How people learn: Brain, mind, experience, and school.* Washington, DC: National Academy Press.

Carnegie Corporation of New York and CIRCLE (The Center for Information and Research on Civic Learning and Engagement). (2003). *The civic mission of schools.* Retrieved June, 6, 2004, from http://www.civicmissionofschools.org/public_html/CivicMissionofSchools.pdf

Halpern, D. F. (2005). The enhancement of critical thinking: With decades of converging evidence, meta-analyses with large effect sizes, and societal need, would you allow your child to be assigned to a control group? In H. J. Walberg & R. F. Subotnik (Eds.), *The scientific basis of educational productivity.* Greenwich, CT: Information Age.

Masten, A. S., & Coatsworth, J. D. (1998). The development of competence in favorable and unfavorable environments: Lessons from research on successful children. *American Psychologist, 53*(2), 205–220.

Mayer, D. P., Mullens, J. E., & Moore, M. T. (2000). *Monitoring school quality: An indicators report* (NCES 2001-030). Washington, DC: U.S. Department of Education, National Center for Education Statistics.

No Child Left Behind Act of 2001. (2002). (Public Law 107-110).

Rivkin, S. G., Hanushek, E. A., & Kain, J. F. (2002). *Teachers, schools and academic achievement.* Washington, DC: National Bureau of Economic Research.

Sanders, W. L., & Rivers, J. C. (1996). *Cumulative and residual effects of teachers on future academic achievement.* Knoxville: University of Tennessee Value Added Research and Assessment Center.

Slaby, R. G., Wilson-Brewer, R., & Dash, K. (1994). *Aggressors, victims, and bystanders: Thinking and acting to prevent violence.* Newton, MA: Education Development Center, Inc.

Sternberg, R. J. (1999). The theory of successful intelligence. *Review of General Psychology, 3*(4), 292–316.

Sternberg, R. J. (2003a). The Other 3 Rs: part two: reasoning. *Monitor, 34*(4), 5.

Sternberg, R. J. (2003b). Responsibility: One of The Other Three Rs. *Monitor, 34*(3), 5.

United States Department of Education. (2005). *No Child Left Behind: Introduction.* Retrieved January 6, 2005, from http://www.ed.gov/nclb/overview/intro/index.html

United States Department of Education National Center for Education Statistics. (2005). *2003 National Assessment of Education Progress: Reading.* Retrieved January 7, 2005, from http://nces.ed.gov/nationsreportcard/reading/results2003/natachieve-g8.asp

Walberg, H. J. (2005). Improving educational productivity: An assessment of extant research. In H. J. Walberg & R. F. Subotnik (Eds.), *The scientific basis of educational productivity.* Greenwich, CT: Information Age.

Wang, M. C., Haertel, G. D., & Walberg, H. J. (1998). *Building educational resilience.* Bloomington, IN: Phi Delta Kappa Educational Foundation.

Werner, E. E., & Smith, R. S. (2001). *Journeys from childhood to midlife: Risk, resilience and recovery.* Ithaca, NY: Cornell University Press.

Zimmerman, B. J., & Martinez-Pons, M. (1988). Construct validation of a strategy model of student self-regulated learning. *Journal of Educational Psychology, 80*(3), 284–290.

CHAPTER 2

REASONING, RESILIENCE, AND RESPONSIBILITY FROM THE STANDPOINT OF THE WICS THEORY OF HIGHER MENTAL PROCESSES

Robert J. Sternberg

Many of us believe that the system of schooling we have is not quite the one we want. But what is lacking in it? And how should it be changed? These are the two major questions addressed in this chapter. I first consider the system we have, and then, the system toward which I believe we should aspire.

THE SYSTEM WE HAVE

In order to contemplate the kind of educational system we would like to have, it helps to contemplate the system we currently have. Only in this way can we become sensitive to needed changes. So what kind of system have we created?

Optimizing Student Success in School With the Other Three Rs:
Reasoning, Resilience, and Responsibility, 17–37

The Societal System Created by Tests

We have created a system of schooling that is driven by tests. Tests of intelligence-related cognitive and academic skills define success in many cultures. People with higher test scores seem to be more successful in a variety of ways and those with lower test scores seem to be less successful (Herrnstein & Murray, 1994; Hunt, 1995). Why are scores on intelligence-related tests closely related to societal success? Consider two points of view.

The Received Point of View. According to Herrnstein and Murray (1994), Wigdor and Garner (1982), and others, conventional tests of intelligence account for about 10–20% of the variation, on average, in various kinds of real-world outcomes. This figure increases if one makes various corrections to it (e.g., for attenuation in measures or for restriction of range in particular samples). Although this percentage is not particularly large, it is not trivial either. Indeed, it is difficult to find any other kind of predictor that fares as well. Clearly, the tests have some value (Hunt, 1995; Schmidt & Hunter, 1981, 1998). They predict success in many jobs, and predict success even better in schooling for jobs. Rankings of jobs by prestige usually show higher-prestige jobs associated with higher levels of intelligence-related skills. Theorists of intelligence differ as to why the tests have some success in prediction of job level and competency.

Some theorists believe that the role of intelligence in society emerges along the lines of some kind of natural law. In their book, Herrnstein and Murray (1994) refer to an "invisible hand of nature" guiding events such that people with high IQs tend to rise toward the top socioeconomic strata of a society and people with low IQs tend to fall toward the bottom strata. Jensen (1969, 1998) has made related arguments, as have many others (see, e.g., [largely unfavorable] reviews by Gould, 1981; Lemann, 1999; Sacks, 1999; Zenderland, 1998). Herrnstein and Murray present data to support their argument, although many aspects of their data and their interpretations of these data are arguable (Fraser, 1995; Gould, 1995; Jacoby & Glauberman, 1995; Sternberg, 1995).

This point of view has a certain level of plausibility to it. First, more complex jobs almost certainly do require higher levels of intelligence-related skills. Presumably, lawyers need to do more complex mental tasks than do street cleaners. Second, reaching the complex jobs via the educational system almost certainly requires a higher level of mental performance than does reaching less complex jobs. Finally, there is at least some heritable component of intelligence (Plomin, DeFries, McClearn, & Rutter, 1997), so that nature must play some role in who gets what mental skills. Despite this plausibility, there is an alternative point of view.

An Alternative Point of View. An alternative point of view is that the sorting influence of intelligence in society is more a societal invention than a discovery of an invisible hand of nature (Sternberg, 1997). The United States and some other societies have created societies in which test scores matter profoundly. High test scores may be needed for placement into higher tracks in elementary and secondary school. They may be needed for admission to selective undergraduate programs. They may be needed again for admission to selective graduate and professional programs. Test scores help individuals gain the access routes to many of the highest-paying and most prestigious jobs if one did not test well. Low GRE scores, for example, may exclude one not only from one selective graduate school, but from many others as well. To the extent that there is error of measurement, it will have comparable effects in many schools.

According to this point of view, there are many able people who may be disenfranchised because the kinds of abilities they have, although these abilities may be important for job performance, are not important for test performance. For example, the kinds of creative and practical skills that matter to success on the job typically are not measured on the tests used for admissions to educational programs. At the same time, society may be overvaluing those who have a fairly narrow range of skills, and a range of skills that may not serve these individuals particularly well on the job, even if they do lead to success in school and on the tests.

On this view, it is scarcely surprising that ability tests predict school grades, because the tests originally were explicitly designed for this purpose (Binet & Simon, 1916). In effect, the United States and other societies have created closed systems: Certain abilities are valued in instruction, for example, memory and analytical abilities. Ability tests are then created that measure these abilities and thus predict school performance. Then assessments of achievement are designed that also assess for these abilities. Little wonder that ability tests are more predictive in school than in the workplace. Within the closed system of the school, a narrow range of abilities leads to success on ability tests, in instruction, and on achievement tests. But these same abilities are less important later on in life.

According to the societal-invention view, closed systems can be and have been constructed to value almost any set of attributes at all. In some societies, caste is used. Members of certain castes are allowed to rise to the top; members of other castes have no chance. Of course, the members of the successful castes believe they are getting their due, much as did the nobility in the Middle Ages when they rose to the top and subjugated their serfs. Even in the United States, if one were born a slave in the early 1800s, one's IQ would make little difference: One would die a slave. Slave owners and others rationalized the system, as social Darwinists always have, by believing that the fittest were in the roles they rightfully belonged in.

The general conclusion is that societies can and do choose a variety of criteria to sort people. Some societies have used or continue to use caste systems, whether explicit, as in India, or implicit, as in the United States. Others use or have used race, religion, or wealth of parents as bases for sorting people. Many societies use a combination of criteria. Once a system is in place, those who gain access to the power structure, whether via their passage through elite education or elsewhere, are likely to look for others like themselves to enter into positions of power. The reason, quite simply, is that there probably is no more powerful basis of interpersonal attraction than similarity, so that people in a power structure look for others similar to themselves. The result is a potentially endlessly looping closed system that keeps replicating itself.

As a society, we can create a closed system that advantages only certain types of children and that disadvantages other types. Children who excel in memory and analytical abilities may end up doing well on ability tests and achievement tests, and hence find the doors of opportunity open to them. Children who excel in other abilities may end up doing poorly on the tests, and find the doors shut. By treating children with alternative patterns of abilities as losers, we may end up creating harmful self-fulfilling prophecies.

What kind of system might we wish to have? This is the topic of the next section of this chapter.

THE SYSTEM WE MIGHT HAVE: THE OTHER THREE Rs

Together with my colleagues Cynthia Belar and Rena Subotnik in the Education Directorate at the American Psychological Association (APA), in 2003, I formed and met with an APA presidential task force on education. This task force proposed a number attributes that schools should develop that currently are not being sufficiently developed. The most important can be characterized as "the Other Three R's," that is, the three R's beyond reading, 'riting, and 'rithmetic. They are reasoning, resilience, and responsibility. In this section, I discuss each of the Other Three Rs (TOTRs) in turn. I discuss them in close relation to a theory of higher mental processes I have proposed, WICS, which deals with wisdom, intelligence, and creativity, synthesized (Sternberg, 2003). My argument is that reasoning is closely related to intelligence, resilience to creativity, and responsibility to wisdom. This argument is elaborated below.

Reasoning

Reasoning can be defined narrowly in terms of inductive and deductive reasoning skills. The latter is used, in general, to go from specific information to general conclusions. It is, by its nature, uncertain, in that one can never know for sure whether an inductive conclusion is correct. For example, the fact that I have, in my life, only seen robins with red breasts does not mean that all robins have red breasts. I may, eventually, encounter one that does not. So in concluding that all robins have red breasts, I can draw a conclusion that is inductively strong, but by no means certain. In contrast, in deductive reasoning, one can draw conclusions with logical certainty. If I assert that all robins have red breasts, and that this particular bird is a robin, I can be logically assured that this bird is a robin. Of course, I cannot be certain that my conclusion, in addition to be logically valid, is also factually true.

These kinds of analytical reasoning skills are important to success in school and in life, and hence it makes sense that most tests of cognitive and academic skills would measure these skills in a variety of different ways. Yet I have argued in my work for a broader conception of reasoning, in particular, and of intelligence, in general. Hence, when I speak of reasoning as one of the Other Three Rs, I am speaking of it in its broadest sense. Reasoning in its narrow sense comprises the inductive and deductive kinds. But research suggests, for example, that people who excel in abstract reasoning do not necessarily excel in practical reasoning, and vice versa (Sternberg et al., 2000). It may therefore be important to look beyond narrow measures to understand how people reason in their everyday lives.

According to my theory of successful intelligence (Sternberg, 1997, 1999), (successful) intelligence is (1) the ability to succeed in life according to your own definition of success within your sociocultural context; (2) by capitalizing on your strengths and correcting or compensating for your weaknesses; (3) in order to adapt to, shape, and select environments; and (4) through a combination of analytical, creative, and practical skills

Consider the first component of the theory: most schools do not attempt to specify precisely what students eventually should do with their lives. Rather, they seek people who will formulate or who have formulated a meaningful and coherent set of goals, and have shown the ability to reach those goals. One student may wish to be a statesperson, another to be a scientist, and another to be an artist. The question typically is not so much what goals students have chosen, but rather, what the students have done to show that they can realize those goals in a distinguished way. Thus, this item actually includes three subitems: (a) identifying meaningful goals, (b) coordinating those goals in a meaningful way so that they form a coherent story of what one is seeking in life, and (c) moving a substantial distance along the path toward reaching those goals. Reasoning can be applied to abstract problems. But in the theory of successful intelligence, one emphasis is on reasoning for choosing one's goals in life.

This first item recognizes that "intelligence" means a somewhat different thing to each individual. The student who wishes to become a Supreme Court judge will be taking a different path from the student who wishes to become a distinguished novelist—but both will have formulated a set of coherent goals toward which to work. An educational program should care less what goal is chosen than that the individual has chosen a worthwhile set of goals and shown the ability to achieve them.

The second component recognizes that although psychologists sometimes talk of a "general" factor of intelligence (Jensen, 1998; Spearman, 1927; see Sternberg & Grigorenko, 2002), really, virtually no one is good at everything or bad at everything. People who are the future leaders of society are people who can apply their reasoning skills to their own lives. They have reasoned about themselves, identifying their strengths and weaknesses, and found ways to work within that pattern of abilities.

There is no single way to succeed in a job that works for everyone. For example, some lawyers are successful by virtue of their very strong analytical reasoning skills. They may never argue in a courtroom, but they can put together an airtight legal argument. Another lawyer may have a commanding presence in the courtroom, but be less powerful in analytical reasoning. The legal profession in the United Kingdom recognizes this distinction by having separate roles for the solicitor and the barrister. In the United States, successful lawyers find different specializations that allow them to make the best use of their talents. Unsuccessful lawyers may actually attempt to capitalize on weaknesses, for example, litigating cases when their legal talent lies elsewhere. However, their reasoning may be in abstract cases; they are unable to apply it to the use of their own talents.

This same general principle applies in any profession. Consider, for example, teaching. Educators often try to distinguish characteristics of expert teachers (see Sternberg & Williams, 2001), and indeed, they have distinguished some such characteristics. But the truth is that teachers can excel in many different ways. Some teachers are better in giving large lectures, others in small seminars, others in one-on-one mentoring. There is no one formula that works for every teacher. Good teachers figure out their strengths and try to arrange their teaching so that they can capitalize on their strengths and at the same time either compensate for or correct their weaknesses. Team teaching is one way of doing so, in that one teacher can compensate for what the other does not do well.

People have very different patterns of abilities. Sometimes selection committees for gifted programs, independent schools, or undergraduate or graduate programs will have feelings of discomfort, recognizing that they are having to choose between "oranges and apples"—that is, evaluate people whose strengths are very different on a single scale that does not seem to apply across all applicants. When the committee looks at their task from the standpoint of the theory of successful intelligence, their job becomes easier. The question is not how well people do on some common scale, but rather, how well they do on whatever scales are relevant to their making the most of their own aspirations—in other words, how well they capitalize on their strengths without letting their weaknesses get in their way.

The third component recognizes that intelligence broadly defined refers to more than just "adapting to the environment," which is the mainstay of conventional definitions of intelligence. The theory of successful intelligence distinguishes among adapting, shaping, and selecting. Reasoning is applied to decide which of these three options best fits one's needs at a given time.

In adaptation to the environment, one modifies oneself to fit an environment. The ability to adapt to the environment is important in life. People who are not adaptable may not be able to transfer the skills they showed in the previous environment to a new one. Over the course of a lifetime, environmental conditions change greatly. A kind of work that at one point in time may be greatly valued (e.g., forming a start-up company) may, at another point in time, be valued little, if at all. In research, the problems change, and sometimes, people who were effective in solving the problems of one decade are relatively ineffective in solving the problems of another decade. In governmental leadership, some elected leaders prove to be dinosaurs—people who were able to lead the country effectively under one set of conditions but not under another set of conditions (such as when the national or world economy tanks). Clearly, adaptability is a key skill in any definition of intelligence. An intelligent individual ought to be able to show the ability to adapt to a variety of environments.

In life, adaptation is not enough, however. Adaptation needs to be balanced with shaping. In shaping, one modifies the environment to fit what one seeks of it, rather than modifying oneself to fit the environment. Truly great people in any field are not just adaptors, they are also shapers. They recognize that they cannot change everything, but that if they want to have an impact on the world, they have to change some things. Part of successful intelligence is deciding what to change, and then how to change it.

For example, I was recently president of the American Psychological Association. The association is an extremely complex organization comprising 155,000 individuals who represent many constituencies and interest groups. It is difficult to effect change because almost without regard to what one does, there will be some special-interest group that will be offended by the change. Yet an effective president must not just try to adapt to all the special-interest groups, but to shape the environment in which they work. This means effecting change even though some groups will not want it. Effectiveness also requires, however, recognizing what changes plausibly can be made, and what changes cannot be made.

When an individual goes to an institution, one hopes that the individual will not only adapt to the environment, but shape it in a way that makes it a better place than it was before. I often tell my own students that a career is about having an impact—about making a field or a place better, more interesting, or more enriched for one's having been there. Shaping is how one has this kind of impact.

Sometimes, one attempts unsuccessfully to adapt to an environment and then also fails in shaping that environment. No matter what one does to try to make the environment work out, nothing in fact seems to work. In such cases, the appropriate action may be to select another environment.

Many of the greatest people in any one field are people who started off in another field and found that the first field was not really the one in which they had the most to contribute. Rather than spend their lives doing something that turned out not to match their pattern of strengths and weaknesses, they found something else to do where they really had a contribution to make. Again, they apply reasoning reflexively—to their own lives in order to make their lives more personally meaningful and satisfying.

The fourth component points out that successful intelligence involves a broader range of abilities than is typically measured by tests of intellectual and academic skills. Most of these tests measure primarily or exclusively memory and analytical abilities. With regard to memory, they assess the abilities to recall and recognize information. With regard to analytical abilities, they measure the skills involved when one analyzes, compares and contrasts, evaluates, critiques, and judges. These are important skills during the school years and in later life. But they are not the only skills that matter for school and life success. One needs not only to remember and analyze concepts; one needs also to be able to generate and apply them.

Intelligence is not, as Edwin Boring (1923) once suggested, merely what intelligence tests test. Intelligence tests and other tests of cognitive and academic skills measure part of the range of intellectual skills; they do not measure the whole range. One should not conclude that a person who does not test well is not smart. Rather, one should merely look at test scores as one indicator among many of a person's intellectual skills.

This definition of successful intelligence suggests that there is no single unidimensional measure of intelligence, such as the IQ, that fully captures all aspects of intelligence. Similarly, there is no one method of teaching that works for everyone. In our work at the Center for the Psychology of Abilities, Competencies, and Expertise at Yale University, we develop curricula that teach standard school subjects and assess achievement in these subjects in ways that enable students to capitalize on creative and practical as well as memory and analytical skills (Sternberg & Grigorenko, 2000). Our research suggests that students learn better when they are taught for successful intelligence than when they are taught by commonly used alternative methods (Grigorenko, Jarvin, & Sternberg, 2002; Sternberg, Torff, & Grigorenko, 1998). In other words, students learn best when they can capitalize on their strengths and also correct or compensate for their weaknesses (Sternberg, Grigorenko, Ferrari, & Clinkenbeard, 1999).

If we, as a society, begin to teach and assess achievement more broadly than we have in the past, we also need to assess abilities more broadly than we have. In a collaboration called the "Rainbow Project," funded by the College Board, we at Yale have worked with faculty at a total of 15 institutions to pilot a test we developed for predicting college success. The test measures creative and practical as well as analytical skills. Our pilot data, based on just over 1,000 students at these institutions, indicate that the Rainbow Test significantly and substantially improves prediction of college success (Sternberg & the Rainbow Project Collaborators, 2004). Interestingly, it simultaneously increases diversity, because students excelling on creative and practical tests tend to be more ethnically diverse than those excelling on narrow memory and analytical-reasoning tests.

Resilience

The second of the Other Three Rs is resilience. When I was just starting out learning to be a psychologist, I remember sitting around with two colleagues—graduate students like myself—wondering what it takes to become really great in the field. None of us had the foggiest idea. After 30 years in the field, I have concluded that a set of skills we first learn as children but can continue to learn as adults is key—namely, the skills needed for resilience.

Dr. Laura Barbanel, a former member of the APA Board of Directors, commented to me one day that, in her experience, the first memories most children had of their school experiences were, for the most part, memories of humiliation and pain. For me, such experiences are not limited to my first memory. They continued from elementary school onward.

What I did not realize when I entered a career as a psychologist was that they were not over. I cannot even begin to recount the repeated humiliations of rejected articles and grant proposals, less than stellar course-critique ratings from students, verbal jabs from colleagues, and less than favorable responses to some of my ideas from the field. I have recounted some of these experiences in a book of advice for young (and even not so young) psychologists (Sternberg, 2004).

The conclusion I have reached is that what distinguishes those who are highly successful from others is, in large part, resilience in the face of humiliations, defeats, and setbacks of various kinds. Without resilience, we risk watching the world go by instead of actively participating in it. What we do not realize when we are younger is that almost *all* of us go through these periods of staggering defeat or, at least, uncertainty. The question is not whether you will go through it; it is how you will come out of it.

If there is one piece of advice I needed when I was starting out, it was that no matter how much success you have, the path along the way is strewn with difficult obstacles, of which, at the time, seem insurmountable (Sternberg, 2004). If one can only persevere, they will not look nearly so monstrous when one looks back on them years later.

I once was talking to Steven Yussen, a psychologist and Dean of the School of Education at the University of Minnesota. I asked him how he found his job as dean and he commented to me that a major part of it was dealing for several hours a day with essentially insoluble problems—ones that needed to be addressed, but that would never truly be solved. I realized that much of life is that way. Our expectation is that things normally should go fine and that, every once in a while, there will be a problem to face, which we should quickly solve so we can return to a state of normalcy. Perhaps others' lives have gone this way. Mine never has. Difficult and sometimes insoluble problems are, for better or worse, part of the state of normalcy.

Hence we need to prepare our children with the skills they need to cope with a world that is uncertain, sometimes seemingly capricious, and often extremely difficult. They need to learn the coping skills that form the backbone of resilience (Sternberg, 1997; Sternberg & Grigorenko, 2000).

In order to make a novel and meaningful contribution to the world, one must be creative. But in order to be creative, one must be resilient. According to the investment theory of creativity, creative thinkers are like good investors: They buy low and sell high (Sternberg, 2003; Sternberg & Lubart, 1995, 1996). Whereas investors do so in the world of finance, creative people do so in the world of ideas. Creative people generate ideas that are like undervalued stocks (stocks with a low price-to-earnings ratio), and both the stocks and the ideas are generally rejected by the public. When creative ideas are proposed, they often are viewed as bizarre, useless, and even foolish, and are summarily rejected. The person proposing them often is regarded with suspicion and perhaps even with disdain and derision. If the person is not resilient, he or she simply gives up on the idea.

Creative ideas are both novel and valuable. They potentially have impact (Sternberg, 2004). But, they are often rejected because the creative innovator stands up to vested interests and defies the crowd. The crowd does not maliciously or willfully reject creative notions. Rather, it does not realize, and often does not want to realize, that the proposed idea represents a valid and advanced way of thinking. Society generally perceives opposition to the status quo as annoying, offensive, and reason enough to ignore innovative ideas. Resilience provides the way to advancing one's agenda, despite opposition from the crowd.

Evidence abounds that creative ideas are often rejected (Sternberg, 2003; Sternberg & Lubart, 1995). Initial reviews of major works of literature and art are often negative. Toni Morrison's *Tar Baby* received negative reviews when it was first published, as did Sylvia Plath's *The Bell Jar.* The first exhibition in Munich of the work of Norwegian painter Edvard Munch opened and closed the same day because of the strong negative response from the critics. Some of the greatest scientific papers have been rejected not just by one journal, but even by several journals before being published. For example, John Garcia, a distinguished biopsychologist, was immediately denounced when he first proposed that a form of learning called classical conditioning could be produced in a single trial of learning (Garcia & Koelling, 1966). Without resilience, none of these and other creators would have produced the large volume of significant work for which they became known.

From the investment view, then, the creative person buys low by presenting a unique idea and then attempting to convince other people of its value. After convincing others that the idea is valuable, which increases the perceived value of the investment, the creative person sells high by leaving the idea to others and moving on to another idea. People typically want others to love their ideas, but immediate universal applause for an idea usually indicates that it is not particularly creative.

Creativity is as much a decision about and an attitude toward life as it is a matter of ability. Creativity is often obvious in young children, but it is harder to find in older children and adults because their creative potential has been suppressed by a society that encourages intellectual conformity. What are the resilience skills needed in order to make the kind of meaningful contribution to society at least some people would like to make?

1. *Redefining problems.* Redefining a problem means taking a problem and turning it on its head. Many times in life individuals have a problem and they just don't see how to solve it. They are stuck in a box. Redefining a problem essentially means extricating oneself from the box. This process is the synthetic part of creative thinking.

The resilient individual will encounter many kinds of novel situations that resist easy definition in terms of past experience. The more flexible the individual is in redefining these situations so that they make sense to him or her, the more likely the individual is to succeed.

2. *Questioning and analyzing assumptions.* Everyone has assumptions. Often one does not know he or she has these assumptions because they are widely shared. Resilient people question assumptions and eventually lead others to do the same. Questioning assumptions is part of the analytical thinking involved in creativity. When Copernicus suggested that Earth revolves around the sun, the suggestion was viewed as preposterous because everyone could see that the sun revolves around Earth. Galileo's ideas, including the relative rates of falling objects, caused him to be banned as a heretic.

Sometimes it is not until many years later that society realizes the limitations or errors of their assumptions and the value of the creative person's thoughts. The impetus of those who question assumptions allows for cultural, technological, and other forms of advancement.

Schools in particular, and society in general, tend to make a pedagogical mistake by emphasizing the answering and not the asking of questions. The good student is perceived as the one who rapidly furnishes the right answers. The expert in a field thus becomes the extension of the expert student—the one who knows and can recite a lot of information. As John Dewey (1933) recognized, *how* one thinks is often more important than *what* one thinks. Schools need to teach students how to ask the right questions (questions that are good, thought-provoking, and interesting) and lessen the emphasis on rote learning. Institutions perhaps do not wish to identify as talented those who merely are experts in spitting back what others have previously said.

3. *Realizing that creative ideas do not sell themselves.* Everyone would like to assume that their wonderful, creative ideas will sell themselves. But as Galileo, Edvard Munch, Toni Morrison, Sylvia Plath, and millions of others have discovered, they do not. On the contrary, creative ideas are usually viewed with suspicion and distrust. Moreover, those who propose such ideas may be viewed with suspicion and distrust as well. Because people are comfortable with the ways they already think, and because they probably have a vested interest in their existing way of thinking, it can be extremely difficult to dislodge them from their current way of thinking. One needs resilience in the face of the fact that one's ideas will not be

accepted easily, and the more creative they are, the harder they will be to sell.

4. *Recognizing that knowledge is a double-edged sword.* On the one hand, one cannot be creative without knowledge. Quite simply, one cannot go beyond the existing state of knowledge if one does not know what that state is. Many students have ideas that are creative with respect to themselves, but not with respect to the field because others have had the same ideas before. Those with a greater knowledge base can be creative in ways that those who are still learning about the basics of the field cannot be.

At the same time, those who have an expert level of knowledge can experience tunnel vision, narrow thinking, and entrenchment. Experts can become so stuck in a way of thinking that they become unable to extricate themselves from it (Frensch & Sternberg, 1989). Learning must be a lifelong process, not one that terminates when a person achieves some measure of recognition. When a person believes that he or she knows everything there is to know, he or she is unlikely to ever show truly meaningful creativity again. Novices need to be resilient in the face of the feedback they are likely to get that, because they are novices, they are unable to contribute meaningfully to the world's store of knowledge.

The upshot of this is that the teaching–learning process is a two-way process. Just as students have to learn from teachers, teachers have much to learn from students. Teachers have knowledge students do not have, but students have flexibility teachers often do not have—precisely because the students do not know as much as the teachers do. By learning from, as well as teaching to, one's students, one opens up channels for creativity that otherwise would remain closed.

5. *Willingness to surmount obstacles.* Buying low and selling high means defying the crowd. And people who defy the crowd—people who think creatively—almost inevitably encounter resistance. The question is not whether one will encounter obstacles; that obstacles will be encountered is a fact. The question is whether the creative thinker has the resilience to persevere. I have often wondered why so many people start off their careers doing creative work and then vanish from the radar screen. Here is at least one reason why: Sooner or later, they decide that being creative is not worth the resistance and punishment. The truly creative thinkers pay the short-term price because they recognize that they can make a difference in the long term. But often it is a long while before the value of creative ideas is recognized and appreciated. One needs to be resilient while waiting for one's ideas to be recognized.

Creative individuals will encounter many obstacles in their lives. Some of them have led "charmed" lives. But sooner or later, the obstacles start to present themselves. The ones who go on to greatness will be those who are prepared to surmount rather than succumb to these obstacles. In other words, they are not just creative, but resilient.

6. *Willingness to take sensible risks.* When creative people defy the crowd by buying low and selling high, they take risks in much the same way as do people who invest. Some such investments simply may not pan out. Moreover, defying the crowd means risking the crowd's wrath. But there are levels of sensibility to keep in mind when defying the crowd. Creative people take sensible risks and produce ideas that others ultimately admire and respect as trendsetting. In taking these risks, creative people sometimes make mistakes, fail, and fall flat on their faces. Such failures can destroy people who lack resilience.

Nearly every major discovery or invention entailed some risk. When a movie theater was the only place to see a movie, someone created the idea of the home video machine. Skeptics questioned if anyone would want to see videos on a small screen. Another initially risky idea was the home computer. Many wondered if anyone would have enough use for a home computer to justify the cost. These ideas were once risks that are now ingrained in our society.

Willingness to take risks is especially important for students. Many of them got to where they are by *not* taking risks. They played the academic game with consummate gamesmanship, doing what needed to be done and playing it safe so that they would not get "burned." But there is a transition in the life of every great contributor. He or she needs to start taking risks. It is important, therefore, to select people who are willing to risk.

7. *Tolerance of ambiguity.* People like things to be in black and white. They like to think that a country is good or bad (ally or enemy) or that a given idea in education works or does not work. The problem is that there are a lot of grays in creative work. Artists working on new paintings and writers working on new books often report feeling scattered and unsure in their thoughts. They often need to figure out whether they are even on the right track. Scientists often are not sure whether the theory they have developed is exactly correct. These creative thinkers need to tolerate the ambiguity and uncertainty until they get the idea just right. They need to be resilient in the face of what can be crushing ambiguity that they would like nothing more than to resolve.

A creative idea tends to come in bits and pieces and develops over time. However, the period in which the idea is developing tends to be uncomfortable. Without time or the ability to tolerate ambiguity, many may jump to a less than optimal solution. Creative individuals often will be undertaking major projects in their graduate years. They should be individuals who are willing to tolerate ambiguity long enough to make these projects not just good, but great.

8. *Self-efficacy.* People often reach a point where they feel as if no one believes in them. We reach this point frequently, feeling that no one values or even appreciates what we are doing. Because creative work often doesn't get a warm reception, it is extremely important that the creative people believe in the value of what they are doing. Part of resilience, then, is maintaining a basic belief in the value of what one has to offer. This is not to say that individuals should believe that every idea they have is a good idea. Rather, individuals need to believe that, ultimately, they have the ability to make a difference. In the course of their studies, there will come times when high-achieving individuals will doubt themselves. To succeed in life, one has to believe not in each and every thing one does, but in one's ability to get done what needs to get done, and to have the resilience to recover from the inevitable setbacks that life throws at one.

9. *Finding what one loves to do.* Teachers must help students find what excites them to unleash their students' best creative performances. Teachers need to remember that this may not be what really excites them. People who truly excel creatively in a pursuit, whether vocational or avocational, almost always genuinely love what they do. Certainly, the most creative people are intrinsically motivated in their work (Amabile, 1996). Less creative people often pick a career for the money or prestige and are bored with or loathe their career. Most often, these people do not do work that makes a difference in their field.

One often meets students who are pursuing a certain field not because it is what they want to do, but because it is what their parents or other authority figures expect them to do. One may feel sorry for such students, knowing that although they may do good work in that field, they almost certainly will not do great work. It is hard for people to do great work in a field that simply does not interest them.

10. *Willingness to delay gratification.* Part of being resilient means being able to work on a project or task for a long time without immediate or interim rewards. Students must learn that rewards are not always immediate and that there are benefits to delaying gratification. The fact of the matter is that, in the short term, people are often ignored when they do creative work or even punished for doing it. The question then is whether they have the resilience to endure in the face of such punishment.

Hard work often does not bring immediate rewards. Students do not immediately become expert baseball players, dancers, musicians, or sculptors. And the reward of becoming an expert can seem very far away. Students often succumb to the temptations of the moment, such as watching television or playing video games. The people who make the most of their abilities are those who wait for a reward and recognize that few serious challenges can be met in a moment.

The short-term focus of most school assignments does little to teach children the value of delaying gratification. Projects are clearly superior in meeting this goal, but it is difficult for teachers to assign home projects if they are not confident of parental involvement and support. By working on a task for many weeks or months, students learn the value of making incremental efforts for long-term gains.

Because much of schooling is about short-term rewards, many of students will not truly have learned the importance of delaying gratification. Yet it is a lesson they need to learn, because the great contributions to the world are rarely made quickly. My undergraduate mentor, Endel Tulving, once commented that "Young people end up being surprised by the amount of time it takes for work to make a difference." Tulving was right, of course. And because of the time lapse, students need to learn that good things can come to those who actively seek them, and then wait.

11. *Courage.* Defying the crowd takes, above all, courage. Those who do not have courage may be many things—they will not be creative. A potentially creative individual can be many things. If he or she is not courageous, the other things may not matter.

Perhaps the best role model I have seen, oddly enough, is Nancy Drew, the young detective in the series by Carolyn Keene. No matter what difficult situation Nancy finds herself in, she coolly and calmly applies problem-solving skills to work her way out of it. Most children will not come from the privileged environment that Nancy came from, but they can apply the same skills she did to solving their life problems. So can we all.

Responsibility

I view responsibility, the third of the 3 Rs, as very closely linked to wisdom. I believe in this link because I define wisdom as the application of intelligence, creativity, and knowledge for a common good. In other words, wisdom is about using one's intelligence, creativity, and knowledge in a responsible way. My full definition of wisdom is the use of one's intelligence, creativity, and knowledge toward a common good by balancing one's own interests, other people's interests, and institutional interests (such as of community or country) over the short and long terms through the infusion into action of moral and ethical values.

How does this conception of wisdom apply to schools? Well, it emphasizes the fact that students need to think in a responsible way. But this is not what our current system of accountability stresses. I have no argument with holding schools accountable. Quite the contrary. But many of the tests that are now being used in the accountability movement are extremely narrow in what they measure. Our concern is that the current emphasis on narrow accountability may inadvertently strait-jacket teachers and schools in what and how they teach, and implicitly devalue wisdom, creativity, and responsibility because these constructs are not measured on the tests.

In our own work at the Center for the Psychology of Abilities, Competencies, and Expertise at Yale, we teach for wisdom in the context of already existing curricula so that teachers need not teach yet another course. We emphasize the importance of understanding issues from other people's points of view. What one group in U.S. history might call "American settlers," for example, another group might call "foreign invaders."

Wisdom and responsibility should be taught to children from an early age so that they will not get in the habit of thinking foolishly and of considering only their own interests. Wisdom is something we all can and should acquire throughout our lifetimes.

The former top officers of Enron, Arthur Andersen, WorldCom, and other corporations that have generated egregious scandals are nothing if not smart and well educated. Similarly, some of our smartest and most knowledgeable politicians have brought about their own downfalls through ugly scandals. How can smart people be so foolish? In large part, because they succumb to irresponsibility.

Five fallacies permeate the thinking of foolish people who succumb to irresponsibility in their thought and actions.

The what-me-worry (unrealistic optimism) fallacy. This fallacy, named after *Mad Magazine* protagonist Alfred E. Neuman's favorite line and renamed by Jennifer Jordan as the "unrealistic-optimism fallacy," occurs when one believes one is so smart or powerful that it is pointless to worry about the outcomes, and especially the long-term ones, of what one does because everything will come out all right in the end—there is nothing to worry about, given one's brains or power. If one simply acts, the outcome will be fine. Bill Clinton tended to repeat behavior that, first as Governor and then as President, was likely to come to a bad end. He seemed not to worry about it. Consider as another example a corrupt business executive at a company such as Enron, the former monolith that went bankrupt because of mismanagement and corruption. The "what-me-worry" fallacy is exemplified by the formation and execution of code-named schemes to sequester assets that would have embarrassed all but the most brazen of scamsters.

The egocentrism fallacy. This fallacy arises when one comes to think that one's own interests are the only ones that are important. One starts to ignore one's responsibilities to other people or to institutions. Sometimes, people in positions of responsibility may start off with good intentions, but then become corrupted by the power they yield and their seeming unaccountability to others for it. A prime minister, for example, might use his office in part or even primarily to escape prosecution, as has appeared to happen in some European countries in recent years. The "egocentrism" fallacy was exemplified by Enron executives showing a complete disregard of anyone but themselves in their unending attempts to enrich themselves at the expense of employees, stockholders, and consumers.

The omniscience fallacy. This fallacy results from having available at one's disposal essentially any knowledge one might want that is, in fact, knowable. With a phone call, a powerful leader can have almost any kind of knowledge made available to him or her. At the same time, people look up to the powerful leader as extremely knowledgeable or even close to all-knowing. The powerful leader may then come to believe that he or she really is all-knowing. So may his or her staff, as illustrated by Janis (1972) in his analysis of victims of groupthink. In case after case, brilliant government officials made the most foolish of decisions, in part because they believed they knew much more than they did. People who believe they are omniscient are unable to learn from their mistakes, in part because they typically are unwilling to admit to them. After all, how can someone who is omniscient make a mistake? One can argue about whether the current administration in the United States in 2004 has made any mistakes, say, in Iraq. What is unarguable is that the president, the top leader, has so far not admitted to having made any. The "omniscience" fallacy was also shown by Enron executives acting like they had financial acumen and genius that they clearly did not have.

The omnipotence fallacy. This fallacy results from the extreme power one wields, or believes one wields. The result is overextension, and often, abuse of power. Sometimes, leaders create internal or external enemies in order to demand more power for themselves to deal with the supposed enemies (Sternberg, 2005). In the United States, the central government has arrogated more power after September 11, 2001, than has been the case for any government in recent history on the grounds of alleged terrorist threats. In Zimbabwe, Robert Mugabe has turned one group against another, as has Hugo Chavez, each with appears to be the similar goal of greatly expanding and maintaining his own power.

The "omnipotence" fallacy was shown by Enron executives believing that the assets of the corporation were their own personal piggybank with which they could do whatever they chose.

The invulnerability fallacy. This fallacy derives from the presence of the illusion of complete protection, such as might be provided by a large staff. People, and especially leaders, may seem to have many friends ready to protect them at a moment's notice. The leaders may shield themselves from individuals who are anything less than sycophantic.

The "invulnerability" fallacy was shown by Enron executives' confidence that they could behave in utterly outrageous ways and not get caught.

Of course, these same patterns of behavior have been shown in many outside the corporate world. The list is long. Saddam Hussein is said to have squirreled away billions of dollars. Charles Taylor in Liberia or Idi Amin in Uganda make the corporate thieves look like Boy Scouts, and both managed to get asylum in countries that, for one reason or another, perhaps financial, were willing to forget their multitudinous sins. As has been said: If one murders one person, one goes to jail for life; if one murders a million, one gets political asylum.

Smart people may be particularly susceptible to these fallacies because, at least in some of our societies, they have been so rewarded for their intelligence that they lose sight of their humanity. They are at risk for irresponsibility of the kind that has brought down so many corporations, governments, and, for that matter, families.

Schools need to pay more attention not just to what students know, but to *how they use* what they know. Intelligence and knowledge are not enough. At the extreme, many of today's terrorists are smart and well educated, but are using their intelligence and education toward reprehensible ends. Schools should develop students who are not only smart and knowledgeable, but also wise. We must teach for wisdom (Sternberg, 1998, 2001). In doing so, we teach students to use their knowledge responsibly.

Some people might believe that the introduction of values renders wisdom somehow a "relativistic" construct, but there are certain values that seem to be universal across the world's great religions and ethical systems, such as those of sincerity, honesty, compassion, reciprocity, and courage. These are, ultimately, the bases of responsibility.

CONCLUSION

In this chapter, I have discussed the roles of reasoning, resilience, and responsibility, and have related them to my WICS theory (Sternberg, 2003). I have suggested that reasoning is linked to intelligence, resilience to creativity, and responsibility to wisdom. And I have argued that The Other Three Rs provide an expanded basis for schooling. We are working, at the American Psychological Association and the PACE Center at Yale, toward the infusion of at least some of these ideas into the U.S. educational system. Will you join us?

REFERENCES

Amabile, T.M. (1996). *Creativity in context*. Boulder, CO: Westview Press.
Binet, A., & Simon, T. (1916). *The development of intelligence in children*. Baltimore: Williams & Wilkins. (Original work published 1905)
Boring, E. G. (1923, June 6). Intelligence as the tests test it. *New Republic*, pp. 35–37.

Dewey, J. (1933). *How we think*. Boston: Heath.

Fraser, S. (Ed.). (1995). *The bell curve wars: Race, intelligence and the future of America*. New York: Basic Books.

Frensch, P. A., & Sternberg, R. J. (1989). Expertise and intelligent thinking: When is it worse to know better? In R. J. Sternberg (Ed.), *Advances in the psychology of human intelligence* (Vol. 5, pp. 157–188). Hillsdale, NJ: Erlbaum.

Garcia, J., & Koelling, R. A. (1966). The relation of cue to consequence in avoidance learning. *Psychonomic Science, 4*, 123–124.

Gould, S. J. (1981). *The mismeasure of man*. New York: Norton.

Gould, S. J. (1995). Curveball. In S. Fraser (Ed.), *The bell curve wars* (pp. 11–22). New York: Basic Books.

Grigorenko, E. L., Jarvin, L., & Sternberg, R. J. (2002). School–based tests of the triarchic theory of intelligence: Three settings, three samples, three syllabi. *Contemporary Educational Psychology, 27*, 167–208.

Herrnstein, R. J, & Murray, C. (1994). *The bell curve*. New York: Free Press.

Hunt, E. (1995). The role of intelligence in modern society. *American Scientist, 83*, 356–368.

Jacoby, R., & Glauberman, N. (Eds.). (1995). *The bell curve debate*. New York: Times Books.

Janis, I. L. (1972). *Victims of groupthink*. Boston: Houghton Mifflin.

Jensen, A. R. (1969). Intelligence, learning ability and socioeconomic status. *Journal of Special Education. 3*, 23–35.

Jensen, A. R. (1998). *The g factor: The science of mental ability*. Westport, CT: Praeger/Greenwoood.

Lemann, N. (1999). *The big test: The secret history of the American meritocracy*. New York: Farrar, Straus & Giroux.

Plomin, R., DeFries, J. C., McClearn, G. E., & Rutter, M. (1997). *Behavioral genetics* (3rd ed.). New York: Freeman.

Sacks, P. (1999). *Standardized minds: The high price of America's testing culture and what we can do to change it*. Cambridge, MA: Perseus Books.

Schmidt, F. L., & Hunter, J. E. (1981). Employment testing: Old theories and new research findings. *American Psychologist, 36*, 1128–1137.

Schmidt, F. L., & Hunter, J. E. (1998). The validity and utility of selection methods in personnel psychology: practical and theoretical implications of 85 years of research findings. *Psychological Bulletin, 124*, 262–274.

Spearman, C. (1927). *The abilities of man*. London: Macmillan.

Sternberg, R. J. (1995). *For whom does the bell curve toll? It tolls for you*. Washington, DC: EdPress.

Sternberg, R. J. (1997). *Successful intelligence*. New York: Plume.

Sternberg, R. J. (1998). A balance theory of wisdom. *Review of General Psychology, 2*, 347–365

Sternberg, R. J. (1999). The theory of successful intelligence. *Review of General Psychology, 3*, 292–316.

Sternberg, R. J. (2001). Why schools should teach for wisdom: The balance theory of wisdom in educational settings. *Educational Psychologist, 36*(4), 227–245.

Sternberg, R. J. (2003). *Wisdom, intelligence, and creativity synthesized*. New York: Cambridge University Press.

Sternberg, R. J. (2004). *Psychology 101½: The unspoken rules for success in academia.* Washington, DC: American Psychological Association.

Sternberg, R. J. (2005). Foolishness. In R. J. Sternberg & J. Jordan (Eds.), *Handbook of wisdom: Psychological perspectives* (pp. 331-352). New York: Cambridge University Press.

Sternberg, R. J., Forsythe, G. B., Hedlund, J., Horvath, J., Snook, S., Williams, W. M., Wagner, R. K., & Grigorenko, E. L. (2000). *Practical intelligence in everyday life.* New York: Cambridge University Press.

Sternberg, R. J., & Grigorenko, E. L. (2000). *Teaching for successful intelligence.* Arlington Heights, IL: Skylight Training and Publishing.

Sternberg, R. J., & Grigorenko, E. L. (Eds.). (2002). *The general factor of intelligence: How general is it?* Mahwah, NJ: Erlbaum.

Sternberg, R. J., Grigorenko, E. L., Ferrari, M., & Clinkenbeard, P. (1999). A triarchic analysis of an aptitude–treatment interaction. *European Journal of Psychological Assessment, 15*(1), 1–11.

Sternberg, R. J., & Lubart, T. I. (1995). *Defying the crowd: Cultivating creativity in a culture of conformity.* New York: Free Press.

Sternberg, R. J., & Lubart, T. I. (1996). Investing in creativity. *American Psychologist, 51*(7), 677–688.

Sternberg, R. J., & the Rainbow Project Collaborators. (2004). Augmenting the SAT through assessments of analytical, practical, and creative skills. In W. Camara & E. Kimmel (Eds.). *New tools for admission to higher education.* Mahwah, NJ: Erlbaum.

Sternberg, R. J., Torff, B., & Grigorenko, E. L. (1998). Teaching triarchically improves school achievement. *Journal of Educational Psychology, 90,* 374–384.

Sternberg, R. J., & Williams, W. M. (2001). *Educational psychology.* Boston: Allyn & Bacon.

Wigdor, A. K., & Garner, W. R. (Eds.). (1982). *Ability testing: Uses, consequences, and controversies.* Washington, D.C.: National Academy Press.

Zenderland, L. (1998). *Measuring minds: Henry Goddard and the origins of American intelligence testing.* New York: Cambridge University Press.

CHAPTER 3

A MOTIVATIONAL APPROACH TO REASONING, RESILIENCE, AND RESPONSIBILITY

Catherine Good and Carol S. Dweck

Intellect, personality, and character are usually seen as distinct and unrelated. For example, you can imagine a person who is smart with a charming personality, but lacks character, or someone who has a winning personality and strong character, but lacks intelligence. As we show in this chapter, however, intellect, personality, and character share an underlying influence that can shape all three attributes, especially as they relate to student success. We will see that students' motivational beliefs and goals foster the reasoning skills that make up intellect, the resilience that can shape personality, and the sense of responsibility that defines character. In this sense, motivational processes are central to far more aspects of school success than many have realized.

SELF-THEORIES OF INTELLIGENCE: AN OVERVIEW

In our work, we have looked extensively at students' beliefs about the nature of their intelligence. Do they see their intelligence as a fixed trait,

Optimizing Student Success in School With the Other Three Rs:
Reasoning, Resilience, and Responsibility, 39–56

something they can't change? Or do they see it as an expandable quality, something they can develop through effort and learning? Students who hold a fixed view of intelligence—known as entity theorists—are highly concerned with outcomes that convey what their "true" abilities are. Within this belief system, you either have the requisite amount of intelligence or you don't, and your academic performance indicates which side of the ability scale you fall on.

On the other hand, students who hold a view of their intelligence as malleable—known as "incremental theorists"—do not interpret outcomes as indicative of underlying ability. Within this belief system, poor academic performance does not label them as lacking in ability; rather, it indicates that their present skill level needs to be improved in order to attain success in the future.

How do these two belief systems affect students' approach to academics? Research has shown that the belief in fixed ability versus the belief in malleable ability orients students toward different goals (Dweck & Leggett, 1988; Robins & Pals, 2002). Because an entity theory defines intelligence as relatively fixed, entity theorists become concerned with demonstrating their intelligence. As a result, they adopt "performance goals"—goals that focus on validating their ability while at the same time avoiding any demonstration that they may lack ability. That is, they want to look smart and avoid looking dumb. Unfortunately, these goals can lead students toward pursuing tasks that have less chance of improving their future abilities—easy, low-effort tasks, as opposed to challenging ones.

In contrast, an incremental theory suggests that people can influence their level of intellectual skill. Incremental theorists focus on "learning goals"—acquiring new knowledge and skills and ultimately increasing their competence (Dweck & Leggett, 1988). These goals lead students toward pursuing challenging tasks that hold the potential for skill development even if there is a high probability of initial failure. As we will see in the studies discussed below, students' goals—together with the self-theories that can give rise to them—affect their reasoning, resilience, responsibility, and ultimately their achievement.

IMPACT OF GOALS AND SELF-THEORIES ON REASONING

Goals

Let's look at the idea of how the goals students pursue affect their ability to reason effectively. In this section, we show that students with learning goals are more able to apply their knowledge to a novel situation and process information at a deeper level, resulting in better performance on difficult reasoning tasks than students with performance goals.

The ability to take knowledge acquired in one domain and transfer it successfully to a different domain involves reasoning abilities. Students must take the newly learned information and figure out how that information applies to the new situation. A study by Farrell and Dweck (1985) shows that students' goal orientation influences their ability to transfer information to novel situations successfully. In this study, junior high school students were taught a challenging new unit in their science class. The unit dealt with a scientific principle that applied to several types of problems (i.e., pulleys, inclined planes, etc.). For the task itself, students were trained on one type of problem (e.g., pulleys), and then were given a "transfer" test to see whether they could apply the same principle to another type of problem (e.g., inclined planes).

Before the unit began, the researchers assessed whether students endorsed performance goals (i.e., to look smart and avoid mistakes) or learning goals (to learn new things, even if they might get confused and make mistakes).

Both the performance-goal and the learning-goal students learned the initial material equally well. Differences emerged, however, when they were asked to transfer their knowledge to a new type of problem. Compared to students with performance goals, students with learning goals showed greater transfer of the principle to the new set of problems. Furthermore, even when they did not transfer the principle correctly, those with learning goals generated more work and more hypotheses and strategies in their attempts to solve the novel problems—that is, they showed more evidence of reasoning. In short, learning goals enabled the students to transfer the knowledge needed to reason their way through the novel problem.

The idea that goals predict reasoning abilities on a specific task may not be surprising. But what may be less intuitive is whether or not goals can also predict more sustained types of reasoning abilities that students apply throughout a difficult course. And as the next study shows (Grant & Dweck, 2003), they do. Grant and Dweck (2003) followed college students during their introductory chemistry course, a difficult entry course for the pre-med curriculum. The researchers found that the more students endorsed learning goals, the more they reported engaging in deep processing of the course material. Students with learning goals were more likely to outline the course materials, to find relations between concepts, and to integrate the course material across units. In this sense, learning goals predicted higher levels of reasoning at a broad level. Whereas the previous study illustrated the effects of learning goals on students' micro-reasoning abilities—that is, on a specific task—this study illustrates the effects of learning goals on students' macro-reasoning abilities—over the course of an entire semester. Not surprisingly, this level of reasoning was predictive of higher course grades, even after controlling for prior ability as measured by the SAT.

Many intelligence tests also require students to apply reasoning abilities in order to be successful. Goals can be important predictors of students' IQ test performance as well. Mueller and Dweck (1998) examined students' goals and their reasoning ability on the Ravens Progressive Matrices Task (Raven, Styles, & Raven, 1998), which is an IQ test that is constructed to assess a person's intellectual and reasoning ability independent of language and formal schooling. In this study, the test was constructed so that the participants succeeded on the first set of moderately difficult problems and were then given praise feedback. The feedback oriented the students toward either a learning goal ("That's a good score, you must have worked hard") or a performance goal ("That's a good score, you must be really smart at these"). We then measured their goals, and had students then work on a new set of problems that was much more difficult than the first set.

How did the difficulty affect their achievement? How did they perform when they next worked on a third set of problems that was similar in difficulty to the first set?

Students who were oriented toward learning goals not only outperformed the students oriented toward performance goals on the difficult reasoning problems, but also performed better on the third set as well. What's more, the different goals that students held predicted either increased or decreased performance. Specifically, after encountering difficulty, those with learning goals performed significantly *better* than they had on the first trial, whereas those with performance goals performed significantly *worse* on the third set than they had on the first.

These studies illustrate the important role that goals play in students' reasoning and intellectual performance. When students encounter difficulty—whether they are engaged in a novel task requiring them to apply prior knowledge, are learning difficult course material, or are tackling a challenging IQ test—those students who hold learning goals are often able to generate higher levels of reasoning than are those with performance goals.

Theories of Intelligence

If students' goals are indeed fostered by their self-theories of intelligence (Bandura & Dweck, 1985; Dweck & Leggett, 1988), then we should find that theories of intelligence affect students' academic achievement, at least in part, through students' goals. We should also find that changing students' theories of intelligence should affect their school achievement, and this change should be related to changes in students' goal orientations. This is precisely what we have found.

Whether students' existing theories are tapped or students are taught a theory, incremental theorists show an advantage on academic tasks, particularly when those tasks are challenging. Consider, for example, students' achievement in junior high school, a time in which many students experience their first real academic challenge and their first academic setbacks. Many students are able to rebound from this setback, but many do not. Do students' theories of intelligence have anything to do with their ability to rebound or not? Two studies looked at the effect of junior high students' self-theories of intelligence on their grades as they made the challenging transition to junior high school (Blackwell, Dweck, & Trzesniewski, 2004; Henderson & Dweck, 1990). In both of these studies, holding an incremental theory conferred benefits for students' achievement.

In the first study, Henderson and Dweck (1990) found that compared to entity theorists, incremental theorists earned significantly higher grades in the first year of junior high school even after controlling for prior achievement.

In the second study, Blackwell, Trzesniewski, and Dweck (2004) looked more deeply into the effects of junior high students' theories of intelligence on their achievement. In this study, the researchers measured students' theories of intelligence at the beginning of the seventh grade and followed the students until the end of the eighth grade. Results showed that students who entered junior high with an incremental theory of intelligence earned steadily increasing math grades over the seventh and eighth grades (Blackwell et al., 2004, Study 1). In contrast, students who entered junior high endorsing an entity theory of intelligence did not show this upward trajectory in grades. In fact, their math grades steadily *decreased* from seventh to eighth grade. What's more, incremental theorists' increase in grades was fostered by their greater emphasis on learning goals and effort. These two studies demonstrate that holding an incremental theory of intelligence results in different trajectories of achievement.

Because students' self-theories of intelligence are consistent predictors of their achievement, it follows that explicitly teaching students about the incremental nature of intelligence could be a fruitful method of ensuring their mastery-oriented approach to problem solving and thereby increasing their achievement. Three studies investigated just this possibility in college and junior high student samples.

In the first study, African American and white college students increased their grade point averages as well as their enjoyment of the educational process (Aronson, Fried, & Good, 2002). How did the researchers ensure such positive gains for the participants? In this study, students were randomly assigned to one of three groups and received one of three experimental manipulations. The first group received training in the incremental theory of intelligence by watching a compelling film depicting the way the brain forms new connections and "grows" every time you learn new things. They also participated in a pen-pal program in which they wrote letters to junior high students. In the letters, they emphasized the incremental nature of intelligence and the usefulness of effort and hard work in learning. The second group also participated in the pen-pal program but received training in a different perspective on intelligence—they were taught that there are many kinds of intelligence, and that people may have abilities in one area but not another. They emphasized this perspective in their pen-pal letters. The third group was the control group and received no training.

At the end of the semester, the researchers assessed participants' enjoyment of academics, their valuing of academics, and their grade point averages. The group receiving the incremental intervention reported greater enjoyment of academics and greater valuing of academics than both of the other groups. What's more, they also earned higher grade point averages. This study is particularly noteworthy because of its effect on the academic outcomes of African American students, a group historically troubled by low academic achievement compared to their white counterparts. Because the incremental training conferred benefits to both the white and the black students, this could represent a method of increasing the achievement of groups with a history of low academic performance.

A second intervention was conducted with junior high school students and with equally encouraging results (Good, Aronson, & Inzlicht, 2003), particularly as they apply to females in math and Hispanic students in reading. In this study, college students mentored seventh-grade students over the course of the school year and, at year's end, the seventh graders took statewide standardized achievement tests in math and reading comprehension. Both the math test and the reading comprehension test required students to apply their reasoning skills in order to identify the correct answer. One group of students was mentored in the malleability of intelligence, and with the mentors' guidance, created Web pages that endorsed this view. A second group was mentored in the idea that difficulties experienced in seventh grade could be attributable to the novelty of the junior high experience and that over time, the difficulties would decline. They also created Web pages advocating this view. A third group was mentored with both perspectives and created Web pages that included both views. A fourth group, the control group, was mentored in the perils of drug use and created antidrug Web pages.

Analysis of the students' standardized test scores showed that the typical gender gap in math achievement existed for students in the control group. Males scored significantly higher than females. However, the three experimental manipulations greatly reduced this achievement gap. In particular, female students who received mentoring that included incremental perspectives on intelligence not only scored significantly higher on the standardized math test than did females in the control group, but also achieved math scores on par with the males. In addition, Hispanic students in the control group scored significantly worse on the standardized reading comprehension test than Hispanic students in the other three experimental conditions.

This study illustrates that teaching an incremental theory to students can lead to increased standardized test scores in two domains that require students to apply their reasoning abilities—math and reading comprehension. And as in the previous intervention (Aronson et al., 2002), some of the groups represented in the study (females and Hispanics) have a history of low performance in the domain tested (math and reading, respectively). Thus, the benefits for these groups provide encouragement that the persistent gaps in achievement between females and males in math and between Hispanics and white students in reading can be reduced.

A third intervention study used similar techniques and, not surprisingly, showed similar results (Blackwell et al., 2004, Study 2). Specifically, junior high students who were taught an incremental theory of intelligence showed more positive academic outcomes compared to a control group who did not receive the incremental training. In this study, two groups of seventh graders participated in a workshop that taught study skills. For one group, however, the workshop included an additional unit on the brain structure and how the brain forms new connections with effortful learning. At the end of the semester, the students' math teachers, who were blind to the study conditions, were asked to indicate whether they noticed any motivational changes in their students. Teachers singled out significantly more of the students in the incremental group, as follows:

> Lately I have noticed that some students have a greater appreciation for improvement in academic performance.... R. was performing below standards.... He has learned to appreciate the improvement from his grades of 52, 46, and 49 to his grades of 67 and 71.... He valued his growth in learning mathematics."

L., who never puts in any extra effort and often doesn't turn in homework on time, actually stayed up late working for hours to finish an assignment early so I could review it and give him a chance to revise it. He earned a B+ on the assignment (he had been getting C's and lower).

M. was [performing] far below grade level. During the past several weeks, she has voluntarily asked for extra help from me during her lunch period in order to improve her test-taking performance. Her grades drastically improved from failing to an 84 on the most recent exam."

Students' motivational changes were not the only positive benefit of the incremental intervention. Students' grades also were affected. For example, despite the fact that students in the experimental and control groups had earned identical math grades prior to the intervention, the incremental group earned significantly higher math grades than their peers in the control group after the intervention.

These studies clearly illustrate that teaching students about the incremental nature of intelligence results in improved motivational outcomes, greater liking and valuing of academics, and increased grades and standardized test scores. Furthermore, the data suggest that the resulting changes in achievement were accompanied by changes in focus on learning, improvement, and effort. What's more, incremental training may be particularly beneficial for students who have a history of low performance in a domain—females in math, Hispanic students in reading, and African American students in academics more generally—perhaps because an incremental theory protects these students from the undermining stereotypes that suggest that their group is inherently limited in their abilities, a predicament known as "stereotype threat" (Steele & Aronson, 1995). We discuss this possibility in more detail in the next section.

IMPACT OF SELF-THEORIES AND GOALS ON RESILIENCE

As we have seen, students who endorse an incremental theory of intelligence and adopt learning goals have an advantage in their reasoning and subsequent achievement over those who endorse an entity theory of intelligence and adopt performance goals. Importantly, the students in these studies do not differ in intellectual ability at the outset of the studies; rather, their beliefs and goals lead to differences in intellectual performance and skill development over time. This is what we mean when we say that self-theories can affect intellect.

Can self-theories of *intelligence* affect something that is often viewed as distinct from intellect, namely, *personality*? As our research shows, students' theories and goals have important consequences for their resilience, which is often considered to be a key element of personality (Block & Kremen, 1996). In all of the studies we have discussed, students confronted challenges or obstacles: they worked on difficult problems (Farrell & Dweck, 1985), navigated school transitions (Blackwell et al., 2004; Good et al., 2003), were presented with challenging coursework (Grant & Dweck, 2003), or were members of stereotyped groups and thus were vulnerable to stereotype-induced performance deficits (Aronson et al., 2002; Good et al., 2003). And in all of these studies, self-theories and goals—not initial ability differences—distinguished between those who succumbed to difficulty and those who thrived.

For example, in the Grant and Dweck (2003) study of students in a difficult pre-med course, many students performed poorly on their initial exam. What distinguished those students who bounced back from this initial failure from those who continued earning low grades? Students' goal orientation was the strongest predictor. Specifically, students with strong learning goals were likely to recover after performing poorly on their initial exam; those with strong performance goals often did not.

Another example of resilience is provided in the Blackwell and colleagues (2004) study of students confronting the transition to junior high school. Although all students experienced an initial decline in math grades (prior to the study's intervention), the students who were taught about the incremental nature of intelligence not only halted the initial decline in math grades but also reversed this trend after the intervention and *increased* their math grades. The students in the control group continued on their downward trajectory. In sum, students who have strong learning goals (Grant & Dweck, 2003) and who believe in the incremental nature of intelligence (Blackwell et al., 2004) appear to be more resilient. They are more likely to recover from poor performance and to reverse the downward trend in school achievement that often accompanies a difficult transition.

Moreover, subscribing to an incremental theory and learning goals create resilience for populations who are vulnerable to stereotype-based underperformance, otherwise known as stereotype threat (see Steele, Spencer, & Aronson, 2002). Much research has demonstrated that the achievement gaps that are so prevalent between black and white students and between males and females in math may be due in part to the stereotypes that these groups face about their abilities in the stereotyped domain.

As Aronson and colleagues (2002) argue, stereotypes that convey limited ability may create motivational mindsets that are similar to those of entity theorists. That is, stereotyped students may be motivated to disprove the stereotype by demonstrating that they have high ability; thus, they may temporarily adopt performance goals when the stereotype is salient. As the intervention studies discussed above demonstrate (Aronson et al., 2002; Good et al., 2003), encouraging stereotyped students to adopt an incremental theory of intelligence can go a long way toward creating resilience in the face of stereotype threat, as shown by the increasing grades (Aronson et al., 2002) and the narrowing of the achievement gap for groups taught an incremental theory (Good et al., 2003). Incremental theories, then, can create resiliency to the stereotype's debilitating message and enable stereotyped individuals to live up to their potential.

The Impact of Fixed-Ability Versus Malleable-Ability Environments on Resilience

In many of the studies we have discussed (Aronson et al., 2002; Blackwell et al., 2004; Good et al., 2003), the researchers went to great lengths to explicitly teach students that intellectual skills are attainable. Yet, this is probably not the way that fixed and malleable views are typically communicated in the real world. Indeed many educators may espouse the view that skills are expandable and that all students can learn, but they may contradict these views with their day-to-day actions.

For example, entity-oriented teachers may unwittingly convey fixed-ability messages to their students through their classroom discourse and practices. This often may occur through statements or practices that are actually meant to motivate students. For example, teachers may attempt to make a math lesson more engaging and human by discussing the life of famous mathematicians, like Pythagoras, in a way that stresses their mathematical genius, and implies that great discoveries came to these mathematicians naturally and without great effort.

However, extolling the genius or talent of great mathematicians may convey an entity theory to students, which in turn can make them vulnerable when they later encounter difficulty. Indeed, the day-to-day entity (or incremental) messages embedded in the environment may be just as powerful as explicit messages in conveying the idea that intellectual skills are relatively fixed (or acquirable).

What's more, academic contexts that convey the idea that intelligence is a fixed trait may create a special problem for students belonging to stereotyped groups. By telling them that abilities are fixed, it may make them more likely to feel that stereotypes are true. In contrast, academic contexts that portray skills as acquirable may create resiliency to the negative implications of stereotypes. Although the stereotype may be present—and thus convey that a person may be limited because of his or her group membership—an acquirable-ability environment may counter the stereotype's message by promoting the view that all students can increase their ability, regardless of their stereotyped status.

We recently tested the effect of students' learning environments on their resilience in a study of female calculus students (Good, Dweck, & Rattan, 2004). In this study, we also investigated a new variable that we thought would be an important predictor of students' resilience—how much they felt that they fit in or belonged to the academic domain in which they are negatively stereotyped. We refer to this new variable as "sense of belonging."

In this study (Good et al., 2004) we measured a sense of belonging by asking students how much they felt accepted by their math peers, felt like valued members of the math community, and felt at ease in their math classes. Students also reported their perceptions about whether their math classes conveyed (1) messages that math ability is fixed and (2) gender stereotyping about math ability.

We found that students' perceptions of their environment affected their sense of belonging and their resilience to negative stereotypes. Specifically, female students who perceived fixed-ability environments *and* high gender stereotyping were most susceptible to lowered sense of belonging. What's more, those who did not feel a sense of belonging were less likely to say that they intended to pursue math in the future, even when they earned A's in their math course. This could well be the way that many of our highly able female students are lost to math.

In contrast, females who perceived malleable-ability environments maintained a sense of belonging to math *even when they perceived their environments as highly gender-stereotypical*. In this sense, perceiving an incremental learning environment created resilience to the stereotype's debilitating message.

ATTENTIONAL MECHANISMS UNDERLYING DIFFERENCES IN REASONING AND RESILIENCE

We've seen that an incremental theory can lead to better reasoning and to resilience, but we have not seen *how* this happens. Could self-theories affect the kind of information students pay attention to? Could entity theorists be tuning out the very kind of information that could help them learn best? To shed light on this question, Dweck, Mangels, and Good (2004) used neurophysiological methods to provide an understanding of how students with different self-theories about intelligence attend to and process feedback, and how this differential processing can affect their learning.

In this study, we monitored students' brain activity during a challenging general knowledge task. On the task (see Butterfield & Mangels, in press), entity and incremental theorists answered general information questions and then received ability-relevant feedback (whether or not their answer was correct), followed by learning-relevant feedback (what the correct answer to the question was). Each type of feedback was preceded by a brief "waiting" period, during which students' brain waves were recorded. The pattern of brain waves could tell us whether they were garnering their attention to receive the information—were they preparing to process the ability-relevant or the learning-relevant information?

Later, participants completed a surprise retest that was composed of items that they initially answered incorrectly. This allowed us to assess how their attentional patterns might have affected their learning.

First, we found that students' theories of intelligence predicted differences in performance on the retest. Although there were no differences between entity and incremental theorists in the number of questions they attempted or their overall accuracy during the initial test, incremental theorists corrected more errors in several categories of answers on the retest. Thus, incremental theorists learned more from the feedback than did entity theorists.

How did this performance difference relate to attentional differences? By examining students' brain waves we saw that entity theorists paid attention only to the ability-relevant feedback—that is, whether they were right or wrong. In fact, they were particularly quick to orient toward the feedback when they were wrong! Yet once they had this information, they did not harness their attention for the learning-relevant feedback that followed. This differential attention could reflect entity theorists' lack of interest in learning, or perhaps entity theorists' lack of resilience in the face of errors. Regardless of the underlying causes, entity theorists paid attention to the feedback about how they were doing, but not the feedback that they could actually learn from. These results suggest that entity theorists are vulnerable to maladaptive attentional processes, especially when faced with negative feedback about their performance.

Incremental theorists, in contrast, were not undone by their errors. Compared to entity theorists, incremental theorists were deeply invested in the learning-relevant feedback—they not only paid attention to the learning-relevant feedback, but they also engaged in deeper processing of that feedback, perhaps because they were mentally elaborating the feedback in the hopes of learning something from their mistake. And as the performance on the retest indicates, this greater attention and processing paid off. In short, incremental theorists are more likely to pay attention to and learn from their mistakes. This study begins to reveal the brain-based attentional patterns that may lie at the heart of our differences in reasoning and resilience.

IMPACT OF SELF-THEORIES AND
GOALS ON RESPONSIBILITY

Students with an incremental theory and learning goals often have the edge in terms of intellectual performance (reasoning) and in terms of certain aspects of personality (resilience). What about character? They also take more responsibility for their own motivation and learning, as well as the learning of others.

Self-theories and goals predict students' willingness to take responsibility not only for their current performance, but more importantly, for their motivation and future performance. For example, in the study by Grant and Dweck (2003), chemistry students with strong learning goals took charge of their learning process by using active and deep strategies to study and learn the material. They were more likely to outline the chapter and to search for and find connections across units, strategies that had clear links to subsequent performance.

They also took charge of their motivational processes by finding ways of keeping themselves interested and motivated. For example, regardless of how poor the instructor was, or how boring they found the material, incremental theorists were more likely to say that they actively worked to maintain interest in the material, stay positive about taking chemistry, and keep themselves motivated to study. These strategies not only led to greater learning, but also are examples of the different ways in which incremental theorists took responsibility for their own learning and motivation.

Blackwell and her colleagues (2004) illustrate another example of incremental theorists taking responsibility for their achievement and future learning. In this study, students read a short paragraph that asked them to imagine that they received a poor grade on a test. Students were then asked to rate what they would think and what they would do in response to the hypothetical failure. Following this failure scenario, entity theorists were more likely than incremental theorists to say they would study *less* on the next test. They also were more likely to say that they would seriously consider cheating on the next test. These behaviors certainly do not demonstrate taking responsibility for their outcomes.

In contrast, incremental theorists clearly indicated steps they would take to ensure their success in the future. For example, they reported that they would try harder and study more the next time around. As in the study of pre-med students by Grant and Dweck (2003), they took a more active role in, and more responsibility for, advancing their learning. Certainly, this is part of what we mean when we refer to "character."

Of course, there are many components that make up a person's character. Willingness to help others is another example. And as the following research shows, incremental theorists are more likely than entity theorists to take an active role in advancing others' learning. That is, they care more about helping others and are better at giving helpful advice.

In a study by Heyman and Dweck (1998), second graders were asked what kind of advice they would give to a failing student. Entity theorists provided little useful information for the student, perhaps because they believe that if others do not have ability, there is nothing that can be done about it—not even increasing their effort on a task. Therefore, entity theorists are literally at a loss for anything to say to another student who may be struggling. Incremental theorists, in contrast, provided a wealth of sage advice (Heyman & Dweck, 1998, Study 1):

> I'll help you a little—come to my house and what you are bad at, we will do.

> Listen better and ask your parents to practice addition cards with you.

> Do you quit a lot? Do you think for a minute and then stop? If you do, then you should think for a long time—two minutes maybe—and if you can't get it, you should read the problem again. If you can't get it then, you should raise your hand and ask the teacher.

Another example of entity theorists' less helpful approach toward others emerges when we consider the competitive behavior exhibited by entity theorists. Because entity theorists use normative information to assess their own abilities (Butler, 2000), another student's success calls their own ability into question. In contrast, a peer's success does not undermine incremental theorists' sense of their own abilities. For example, in several studies (see, e.g., Dweck, 1999), students were presented with the following question: "Sometimes students feel smart in school and sometimes they don't. When do you feel smart?" Those with an entity theory often indicated that they feel smart when they do well and others do poorly.

In contrast, students with an incremental theory do not base their assessment of their abilities on others' failures (Dweck, 1999). Rather, they say they feel smart when they work on hard things and when they help other students understand and learn new material. In short, entity theorists compete with their peers precisely because their assessment of their abilities depends on others' failures; incremental theorists, in contrast, have a more helping stance toward their fellow students. They not only feel smarter when they put their knowledge to use to help others, they are better equipped and are more able to give assistance to a fellow student. In this sense, self-theories shape character.

CONCLUSION

We've seen that different self-theories and goals lead to different levels of reasoning, resilience, and responsibility. An entity theory and performance goals can undermine reasoning, resilience, and responsibility, while an incremental theory and learning goals can promote "the other three R's." Because self-theories and goals are clear predictors of students' academic success, we believe that this presents an opportunity for educators to intervene in order to optimize achievement for all students. Fostering an incremental theory of intelligence not only can help them overcome difficult moments in their educational lives—such as the transition to junior high school or a challenging college course—but also can help stereotyped students become more resilient in the face of negative stereotypes about their abilities.

How can teachers foster an incremental theory of intelligence? Directly teaching an incremental theory is certainly one method that teachers could use. However, the day-to-day entity or incremental messages that are embedded in teachers' pedagogical practices may also be powerful conveyers of either an entity or an incremental theory. For example, when math teachers refer to the "genius" of prominent mathematicians, they are sending the message that mathematicians are born, not made—that is, that math intelligence is a fixed trait.

Yet researchers who study outstanding creative achievement agree that great contributions result from years of dedication and effort (Sternberg, 1999). Thus teachers can refrain from suggestions that famous scientists, artists, or authors achieved their glory exclusively because of an inborn trait, and instead could emphasize the hard work and dedication that most often preceded scientific discoveries or great works of art or literature.

The way teachers praise students—either praising the trait or the process—can encourage them to adopt either an entity or an incremental view of intelligence (Mueller & Dweck, 1998). After children experience a success, many teachers, in an effort to boost their students' confidence and self-esteem, lavish praise upon them by telling them how smart they are. This well-meaning approach sends the unintended message that intelligence, per se, is the important and valued thing and that it can be measured by performance. This type of "trait praise" encourages a fixed-ability mindset, leads children to pursue easier tasks even if it means sacrificing learning, and results in low persistence in the face of difficulty.

Alternatively, students who are given "process praise"—that is, those who receive praise for their effort or strategies—are more likely to adopt an incremental view of intelligence, to prefer tasks that enable them to learn new things even if the task is difficult, and they are resilient in the face of setbacks.

Process praise means not praising low-challenge, low-effort, no-mistake successes, for this sends the message to children that they are praiseworthy only when they do things quickly and easily. Thus, when praising a success, teachers can emphasize the strategies and choices that led to the success, not just the outcome and what it means about the child's intelligence.

Even failures present opportunities to give process praise. But the praise should include more than a simple encouragement to try harder. Rather, teachers should use the failure as an opportunity to explore with their students new strategies and approaches that could lead to a better outcome in the future. Within this approach, failures should be a cue to search for new and better problem-solving processes.

Although process rather than trait praise is beneficial for all students, it may be particularly beneficial to children who face stereotypes about their abilities. Because the stereotype focuses on a trait that the child supposedly possesses (e.g., low intelligence or low math ability), orienting these children away from trait-based explanations for success and toward a process explanation may make the stigmatized trait less viable as an explanation for failure when it occurs.

Finally, with an incremental theory and learning goals as objectives, assessment takes on a new focus. Rather than assessing students' skills in order to distinguish the haves from the have-nots or to label students, assessment should be about identifying areas in which students can increase their skills, and then about finding ways to promote learning.

To summarize, we've seen that motivation-related variables, like self-theories and goals, affect critical aspects of students' school behavior and performance. A self-theory that orients students toward measuring themselves can, in the face of obstacles, lead to impaired reasoning, lessened resilience, and lowered levels of responsibility. In contrast, a self-theory that orients students toward learning can lead to more active attention, strategizing, and reasoning, to heightened resilience, and to a greater sense of responsibility both for their own achievement and for their peers'. We have thus seen that intelligence, personality, and character may not be as distinct as we thought!

REFERENCES

Aronson, J., Fried, C., & Good, C. (2002). Reducing the effects of stereotype threat on African American college students by shaping theories of intelligence. *Journal of Experimental Social Psychology, 38*, 113–125.

Bandura, M., & Dweck, C. S. (1985). *The relationship of conceptions of intelligence and achievement goals to achievement-related cognition, affect, and behavior.* Unpublished manuscript, Harvard University.

Blackwell, L. S., Dweck, C. S., & Trzesniewski, K. (2004). *Implicit theories of intelligence predict achievement across an adolescent transition: A longitudinal study and an intervention.* Unpublished manuscript, Columbia University.

Block, J., & Kremen, A. M. (1996). IQ and ego-resiliency: Conceptual and empirical connections and separateness. *Journal of Personality and Social Psychology, 70*, 349–361.

Butler, R. (2000). Making judgments about ability: The role of implicit theories of ability in moderating inferences from temporal and social comparison information. *Journal of Personality and Social Psychology, 78*, 965–978.

Butterfield, B., & J. A. Mangels (in press). Neural correlates of error detection and correction in a semantic retrieval task. *Cognitive Brain Research.*

Dweck, C. (1999). *Self-theories: their role in motivation, personality, and development.* Philadelphia: Psychology Press.

Dweck, C. S., & Leggett, E. L. (1988). A social-cognitive approach to motivation and personality, *Psychological Review, 95*, 256–273.

Dweck, C. S., Mangels, J., & Good, C. (2004). Motivational effects on attention, cognition, and performance. In D. Y. Dai & R. J. Sternberg (Eds.), *Motivation, emotion, and cognition: Integrated perspectives on intellectual functioning.* Manhwah, NJ: Erlbaum.

Farrell, E., & Dweck, C.S. (1985). *The role of motivational processes in transfer of learning.* Unpublished manuscript, Harvard University.

Good, C., Aronson, J., & Inzlicht, M. (2003). Improving adolescents' standardized test performance: An intervention to reduce the effects of stereotype threat. *Journal of Applied Developmental Psychology, 24*, 645–662.

Good, C., Dweck, C. S., & Rattan A. (2004). *Perceiving a malleable-ability versus a fixed-ability environment: The effect on women's sense of belonging to math.* Unpublished manuscript, Columbia University.

Grant, H., & Dweck, C. S. (2003). Clarifying achievement goals and their impact. *Journal of Personality and Social Psychology, 85*, 541–553.

Henderson, V., & Dweck, C.S. (1990). Achievement and motivation in adolescence: A new model and data. In S. Feldman & G. Elliott (Eds.), *At the threshold: The developing adolescent* (pp. 308-329). Cambridge, MA: Harvard University Press.

Heyman, G. D., & Dweck, C. S. (1998). Children's thinking about traits: Implications for judgments of the self and others. *Child Development, 69*, 391–403.

Mueller, C. M., & Dweck, C. S. (1998). Intelligence praise can undermine motivation and performance. *Journal of Personality and Social Psychology, 75*, 33–52.

Raven, J. C., Styles, I., & Raven, M. A. (1998). *Raven's Progressive Matrices: SPM plus test booklet.* Oxford, UK: Oxford Psychologists Press.

Robins, R. W., & Pals, J. (2002). Implicit self-theories in the academic domain: Implications for goal orientation, attributions, affect, and self-esteem change. *Self and Identity, 1,* 313–336.

Steele, C. M., & Aronson, J. (1995). Stereotype threat and the intellectual test performance of African-Americans. *Journal of Personality and Social Psychology, 69,* 797–811.

Steele, C. M., Spencer, S. J., & Aronson, J. (2002). Contending with group image: The psychology of stereotype and social identity threat. In M. P. Zanna (Ed.), *Advances in experimental social psychology* (Vol. 34, pp. 379–440). San Diego, CA: Academic Press.

Sternberg. R. J. (1999). *Handbook of creativity.* New York: Cambridge University Press.

PART I

SPECIAL FOCUS ON REASONING

CHAPTER 4

THE ROLE OF KNOWLEDGE IN THE DEVELOPMENT OF MATHEMATICAL REASONING

Richard E. Mayer

What does a student need to know in order to solve mathematical problems? Blending the findings of the National Research Council's recent book, *Adding It Up: Helping Children Learn Mathematics* (Kilpatrick, Swafford, & Findell, 2001), and a recent revision of Bloom's taxonomy, *A Taxonomy for Teaching, Learning, and Assessing* (Anderson et al., 2001), I focus on five strands of knowledge that support mathematical reasoning—factual knowledge, conceptual knowledge, strategic knowledge, procedural knowledge, and attitudinal knowledge. As you can see, I am using "knowledge" in the broadest sense of the word to include basic cognitive knowledge (e.g., facts, concepts, and procedures), metacognitive knowledge (e.g., strategies), and attitudinal knowledge (e.g., beliefs and feelings).

According to a knowledge-based approach, the major obstacle to optimizing mathematical achievement for all students is a failure to ensure that all students develop the specifically relevant knowledge needed for success in mathematics. The solution to this problem is to use cognitive analysis techniques to determine the specifically relevant knowledge

Optimizing Student Success in School With the Other Three Rs:
Reasoning, Resilience, and Responsibility, 59–74
Copyright © 2006 by Information Age Publishing

needed for various mathematical tasks and to create and evaluate instructional methods that help all students develop this knowledge. There is ample evidence in the cognitive science literature—including research on the development of expertise—that problem-solving proficiency depends on learnable knowledge (Mayer, 1999; Sternberg & Grigorenko, 2003). Instruction and assessment should be focused on determining the knowledge that students possess, and providing instruction aimed at helping students build needed knowledge. Overall, the knowledge-based approach to optimizing student success is based on the premise that all students can become proficient in mathematical reasoning.

Poor performance in secondary school algebra courses can preclude admission to high-quality colleges and universities. The ability to solve word problems is an essential—and perhaps, the quintessential—skill in algebra. Therefore, I focus on obstacles that students may face in becoming proficient in solving word problems.

Consider the task of solving the following problem (Hegarty, Mayer, & Monk, 1995):

At Lucky, butter costs 65 cents per stick.
This is 2 cents less per stick than butter at Vons.
If you need to buy 4 sticks of butter,
how much will you pay at Vons?

What are some obstacles preventing all students from academic success on solving word problems like this butter problem? From the vantage point of a cognitive scientist, I see that a major obstacle to mathematical reasoning is a lack of learnable knowledge (Mayer, 2003).

First, suppose a student does not know that there are 100 cents in a dollar or that Vons and Lucky are the names of supermarkets or that butter is sometimes sold by the stick. Without this kind of knowledge—which I refer to as *factual knowledge*—a student will not be able to solve mathematical problems effectively. A variant of factual knowledge is *linguistic knowledge*, that is, knowledge of the English language.

Second, suppose a student does not know that a common type of word problem is a total cost problem in which (total cost) = (unit cost) × (number of units). In this case, the student cannot recognize that the butter problem belongs in the category of total cost problems. Lack of knowledge of problem types—which I refer to as a form of *conceptual knowledge*—represents another kind of obstacle to successful mathematical reasoning.

Third, suppose a student does not know how to develop a solution plan for solving the butter problem. For example, a useful strategy is breaking the problem into two parts, namely, computing the unit price at Vons by adding .02 to .65, and then computing the total cost at Vons by multiplying 4 times the unit price. Lack of what can be called *strategic knowledge* (including *metacognitive knowledge*) represents a third kind of obstacle to successful mathematical reasoning.

Fourth, suppose a student does not know how to add .02 to .65 or how to multiply .67 × 4? Knowledge of how to carry out arithmetic operations such as addition, subtraction, multiplication, and division represents a fourth kind of knowledge required for success on solving word problems—which I refer to as *procedural knowledge*.

Finally, suppose a student harbors unproductive beliefs about solving word problems, such as "I am not good at algebra" or "If I don't know the answer right away, I will never be able to figure it out." When confronted with a difficult problem, the student is disposed to give up. Unproductive beliefs—which can be called *attitudinal knowledge*—represent a fifth kind of obstacle to successful mathematical reasoning.

The five knowledge-based obstacles to academic success in mathematical problem solving are described in Table 4.1. As you can see, the first two types of knowledge concern what a student knows about the world—factual knowledge consists of simple facts whereas conceptual knowledge is more organized and broader. Similarly, the next two types of knowledge concern how to do things—procedural knowledge consists of simple procedures that always yield an answer whereas strategic knowledge consists of more general methods that may not always work. The fifth kind of knowledge reflects the student's beliefs, including epistemological beliefs about how learning works. Difficulties arise when a student lacks appropriate facts, concepts, strategies, procedures, and/or beliefs.

Table 4.1. Five Kinds of Knowledge Required for Mathematical Problem Solving

Type	Definition	Example
Factual	Facts	65 cents is .65 dollars
Conceptual	Concepts and categories	This is a total cost problem type: (total cost) = (unit cost) × (number of units)
Strategic	Strategies	Break problem into two parts: unit cost = .65 + .02 total cost = unit cost × 4
Procedural	Procedures	.65 + .02 = .67 .67 × 4 = 2.56
Attitudinal	Beliefs	"I am good at this."

OVERCOMING OBSTACLES TO FACTUAL KNOWLEDGE

The first step in solving the butter problem is to be able to comprehend each sentence, a process that I call *problem translation*, and which is supported by appropriate factual (and linguistic) knowledge. This step can become an obstacle if students lack appropriate factual and linguistic knowledge to represent sentences mentally. For example, students have a particularly hard time comprehending relational statements such as "This is 2 cents less per stick than butter at Vons." In a relational statement, two variables are compared, such as the cost of a stick of butter at Lucky and the cost of a stick of butter at Vons. In contrast, students have little difficulty with assignment statements, such as "At Lucky, butter costs 65 cents per stick." In an assignment statement a value is assigned to a variable, such as the cost of a stick of butter at Lucky is 65 cents.

For example, Riley, Greeno, and Heller (1982) asked elementary school students to listen to a word problem, such as "Joe has three marbles. Tom has five more marbles than Joe. How many marbles does Tom have?" When they were asked to repeat the problem, a common error involved eliminating the relational statement, such as: "Joe has three marbles. Tom has five marbles. How many marbles does Tom have?" Apparently, students had difficulty in mentally representing the relational statement. In a similar study (Mayer, 1982), college students were asked to read and then recall a set of eight algebra story problems. They made three times more errors in recalling relational statements than in recalling assignment statements. Again, students seem to have difficulty in mentally representing a relational statement. Finally, in a straightforward study (Soloway, Lochhead, & Clement, 1982), college students were asked to write equations for relational statements such as "There are six times as many students as professors at this university." A common incorrect answer was "6S = P," again indicating that students have difficulty understanding relational statements.

Difficulties in this seemingly simple task of mentally representing a sentence may distinguish successful from unsuccessful problem solvers. In one study, students were asked to solve 12 word problems, including ones like the butter problem, and afterwards took a multiple-choice recognition test in which they were given four versions of the problem and asked to choose the one they had seen (Hegarty et al., 1995). Students who scored low on solving the 12 word problems were more likely to make a memory error by choosing a version in which the relational statement was factually incorrect but retained the wording of "less," such as "At Lucky, butter costs 65 cents per stick. Butter at Vons is 2 cents less per stick than butter at Lucky. If you need to buy 4 sticks of butter, how much will you pay at Vons?" Students who scored high on solving the 12 word problems were more likely to make a memory error by choosing a version in which the relational statement was factually correct by changed the wording of "less," such as "At Lucky, butter costs 65 cents per stick. Butter at Vons is 2 cents more per stick than butter at Lucky. If you need to buy 4 sticks of butter, how much will you pay at Vons?" Thus, successful problem solvers were more likely to represent the information correctly in the relational statement than were the unsuccessful problem solvers.

How can we remove this obstacle to academic success in solving word problems? Lewis (1989) developed a two-session program in which students received practice in how to translate relational statements into a diagram on a number line. Students who received translation training showed a much larger pretest-to-posttest decline in errors on solving word problems than did a control group. Thus, there is encouraging evidence for the effectiveness of focused instruction on a specific kind of knowledge that is needed for success on an academic task.

OVERCOMING OBSTACLES TO CONCEPTUAL KNOWLEDGE

The next step in solving the butter problem is to use all the relevant information in the problem to build a coherent mental representation of the problem situation, which can be called a *problem model* (or situation model). This process can be called *problem integration* and it depends on conceptual knowledge, including knowledge of problem types (or problem schemas). For example, in the butter problem, the problem solver needs to organize the problem as a "total cost problem" based on the structure, (total cost) = (unit cost) × (number of units).

Hinsley, Hayes, and Simon (1977) identified 18 problem types familiar to high school students, such as work problems, time–rate–distance problems, area problems, mixture problems, and so on. In an analysis of mathematics textbooks, Mayer (1981) identified approximately 100 problem types, including statistics on how frequently each type appeared in math textbooks.

An obstacle to successful reasoning occurs when a student categorizes a problem incorrectly. For example, Quilici and Mayer (1996) asked college students to sort statistics word problems into categories based on similarity, that is, grouping together problems that could be solved in the same way. Students who had little experience with statistics sorted the problems based on surface features—that is, they put problems about rainfall rates in one category, problems about typing rates in another category, and problems about reading rates into a third category—whereas students who had taken several statistics classes sorted the problems based on structural features—that is, they put t-test problems in one category, correlation problems in another category, and chi-square problems in another. Similarly, in a study involving seventh graders, Silver (1981) found that successful problem solvers were more likely to sort arithmetic word problems based on structure whereas unsuccessful problem solvers were more likely to sort them based on surface features.

As another example, consider a version of the butter problem in which the keyword (e.g., "less") is consistent with the required arithmetic operation (e.g., subtraction): "At Lucky, butter costs 65 cents per stick. Butter at Vons costs 2 cents less per stick than butter at Lucky. If you need to buy 4 sticks of butter, how much will you pay at Vons?" This version can be solved by a "number grabbing" approach in which the problem solver simply extracts the numbers and uses keywords to determine what to do with them (e.g., the first two numbers are 65 and 2, and the keyword "less" primes subtraction). Although this approach leads to correct answers for consistent versions of problems, it leads to incorrect answers for inconsistent versions such as, "At Lucky, butter costs 65 cents per stick. This is 2 cents less per stick than butter at Vons. If you need to buy 4 sticks of butter, how much will you pay at Vons?" In an eye movement study, Hegarty and colleagues (1995) found that unsuccessful problem solvers treated consistent and inconsistent problems the same way—focusing mainly on numbers and keywords. In contrast, successful problem solvers spent more time with inconsistent problems, and tended to focus on variable names (e.g., Vons and Lucky) before focusing on numbers. These results are consistent with the idea that successful problem solvers try to build problem models whereas unsuccessful problem solvers sometimes use a more superficial approach.

Even mathematics teachers have trouble building problem models for word problems. For example, Ma (1999) asked U.S. math teachers to create a word problem that corresponded to 1¾ divided by ½. Ninety-six percent of the teachers either gave an incorrect model or none at all. For example, a typical incorrect model involved confusing division by ½ with division by 2: "If you have one pie and ¾ of another pie to be divided equally between two people, how much pie will each person get?" Another incorrect model is to confuse division by ½ with multiplication by ½: "If you have one pie and ¾ of another pie, what is half of the total?" These findings demonstrate that problem solvers have difficulty in building a problem model.

How can teachers help students overcome this obstacle to academic success on solving word problems? Again, the solution involves helping students develop a specific kind of knowledge—in this case, knowledge of problem types. If students have a schema for a problem, they should be able to tell which information is relevant and which is not. Low and Over (1990; Low, 1989) found success on solving word problems was strongly correlated with ability to identify whether a problem had sufficient, irrelevant, or missing information. Low (1989) developed an 80-minute training program in which students received a series of problems and had to determine if the problem needed more information, had irrelevant information, or had sufficient information. Students received specific feedback for each problem. Schema training had a strong positive effect on the subsequent problem-solving performance of the experimental group, as compared to a control group. Thus, it appears that focused practice on a specific kind of knowledge can remove obstacles to academic success.

OVERCOMING OBSTACLES TO STRATEGIC KNOWLEDGE

Once you have mentally represented the problem, the next step is to develop (and monitor) a solution plan. This process can be called *solution planning and monitoring*, and it requires strategic knowledge. For example, Schoenfeld (1979, 1985) taught students how to apply five problem-solving strategies to mathematics problems, such as breaking a problem into subgoals. Students who received the strategy training showed large pretest-to-posttest improvements in solving word problems, but students who simply practiced solving problems did not show much improvement.

A common method of teaching of solution strategies is to provide students with worked-out examples that show the solution steps and explain each step (Mayer, Sims, & Tajika, 1995; Reed, 1999). Several researchers have shown that students who study well-explained worked-out examples perform better on solving new problems than do control students who simply practice solving problems (Catrambone, 1995; Reed, 1987; Sweller & Cooper, 1985). Thus, teaching by worked-out example is a promising way to remove some obstacles to academic success.

OVERCOMING OBSTACLES TO PROCEDURAL KNOWLEDGE

The most obvious obstacle to academic success in mathematics concerns procedural knowledge—students may not know arithmetic and algebraic procedures, for example. Perhaps because of this, a focus on computational skill is foremost in many U.S. classrooms (Stigler & Hiebert, 1999). Although much effort goes into teaching basic computational procedures in the United States (Stevenson & Hiebert, 1999), national and international assessments indicate that computational efficiency is not the major obstacle facing U.S. students (Mayer, 1999). The primary technique for teaching computational skill is drill and practice, in which students solve arithmetic problems and are given feedback (Mayer, 1999). This approach, which has been part of educational practice for more than 100 years (Thorndike, 1922), is a tried and true way to build procedural skill. Although mastery of procedural skill is necessary, it is not sufficient for academic success. A major challenge for students is the need to link their procedural knowledge with other forms of knowledge, including conceptual knowledge.

OVERCOMING OBSTACLES TO ATTITUDINAL KNOWLEDGE

Another set of obstacles to mathematical reasoning is unproductive beliefs that leave the learner unwilling to exert the effort needed for academic success. Instead, students need what can be called a productive disposition, which is the "habitual inclination to see mathematics as sensible, useful, and worthwhile, coupled with a belief in diligence and one's own self efficacy" (Kilpatrick et al., 2001, p. 5).

Schoenfeld (1992) found many students agreed with the idea that ordinary students cannot expect to understand mathematics or that one should give up on any assigned problem that cannot be solved in 5 minutes or less. Lester, Garofalo, and Kroll (1989. p. 84) found that many of the third graders they tested thought "all story problems could be solved by applying the operations in the key words present in the story (e.g., in all suggests addition, left suggests subtraction)." Many students believe that word problems do not need to make sense, but rather require blindly applying procedures (Vershaffel, Greer, & De Corte, 2000). Schoenfeld (1991, p. 316) describes how school children engage "in what can be called suspension of sense-making—suspending the requirement that the way in which the problems are stated makes sense." These beliefs "develop in school, as a result of schooling" (Schoenfeld, 1991, p. 316).

Unproductive beliefs can lead to unsuccessful performance on academic tasks. For example, consider the problem: "An army bus holds 36 soldiers. If 1,128 soldiers are being bused to their training site, how many buses are needed?" Although the overwhelming majority of students correctly divided 36 into 1,128 to get 31 remainder 12, most students concluded that the answer was "31 remainder 19" or simply "31" (Carpenter, Lindquist, Matthews, & Silver, 1983). In short, students treated the problem as an exercise in symbol manipulation rather than as a meaningful task. Thus, unproductive beliefs can be an obstacle to academic success.

A related obstacle concerns students' beliefs about the sources of their successes and failures on mathematical tasks. Stevenson and Lee (1990) propose that one reason that U.S. students perform lower on mathematical achievement tests than do Japanese students is that U.S. students are more likely to attribute their successes and failures to ability whereas Japanese students are more likely to attribute their successes and failures to effort. Ability attributions encourage students to give up on hard problems whereas effort attributions encourage students to work harder.

Self-efficacy refers to beliefs about one's personal expectations concerning accomplishing some task. Such beliefs are related to academic success: Students who have low self-efficacy for solving arithmetic problems tend to score lower on mathematics achievement tests than do students who score high on self-efficacy for solving arithmetic problems (Schunk, 1989).

Can productive beliefs be taught? Schunk and Hansen (1985) developed an instructional lesson that improved students' self-efficacy for solving arithmetic problems, that is, their beliefs about their competence to solve arithmetic problems. Some third graders viewed a model—another child—solving arithmetic problems while making positive statements such as "I can do this one" or "I like doing these." Others viewed an adult demonstrating how to solve the same problems but without making positive statements about efficacy. The student model group showed a larger pretest-to-posttest gain in self-efficacy and in mathematics achievement as compared to the teacher model group. These results are encouraging because they suggest that belief-based obstacles to academic achievement can be changed.

IMPLICATIONS FOR OPTIMIZING STUDENT SUCCESS

The thesis of this chapter is that academic success in mathematical reasoning depends on the student's knowledge. In short, from my vantage point as a cognitive scientist, I see that a focus on "what the student knows" is the key to optimizing student success in mathematical reasoning in schools. For any academic task—such as solving word problems—it is necessary to determine the specific facts, concepts, procedures, strategies, and beliefs needed to successfully accomplish the task. The most straightforward implication for improving students' reasoning is that students need learning experiences that foster the development of these specific facts, concepts, procedures, strategies, and beliefs. In this section, I examine how my view can help answer questions about how to optimize student success in schools.

What are the major obstacles to optimizing achievement for all students? According to the knowledge-based view, the major obstacles to optimizing achievement for all students—including the ability to reason—is that some students have not acquired the knowledge necessary for success in academic tasks. National and international assessments indicate that the major obstacles are not necessarily lack of procedural knowledge, but rather lack of factual, conceptual, strategic, and attitudinal knowledge (Anderson et al., 2001; Pellegrino, Chudowsky, & Glaser, 2001).

Why are these obstacles in place? Learning depends on students having productive opportunities to learn. There is some evidence that mathematics instruction in the United States focuses on the acquisition of procedures in spite of the fact that student difficulties are mainly with concepts, strategies, and beliefs. For example, an analysis of U.S. mathematics texts reveals that most space is devoted to drill and practice on computation problems, that is, on procedural knowledge (Mayer et al., 1995) and analyses of classroom activities yields similar conclusions (Stevenson & Stigler, 1992; Stigler & Hiebert, 1999). Thus, those in charge of determining the curriculum seem to have opted for a lack of instructional focus on concepts, strategies, and beliefs needed for academic success.

What can be done to remove obstacles so that all students can achieve to their level of potential? The solution involves four steps: (1) curricular decision— decide what students need to be able to do (such as comprehend text, write essays, and solve word problems); (2) cognitive step—conduct a cognitive task analysis to determine the knowledge required for success on these fundamental academic tasks; (3) instructional step—determine how to help students build the knowledge for these tasks in a way that allows transfer to a variety of versions of the tasks; (4) assessment step—develop assessments that are sensitive to what students know and use the results of assessments to tune the instructional process.

What evidence is there to support my views? During the past 20 years, researchers in cognitive science and educational psychology have made great progress in building a research base for the knowledge-based approach. In particular, I point to progress in three major literatures: psychologies of subject matter pinpoint the specific knowledge needed in academic tasks in content areas such as reading, writing, mathematics, science, history, and second language learning (Bruer, 1993; Mayer, 1999); cognitive process instruction pinpoints methods for teaching of specific cognitive strategies such as how to summarize a passage or how to plan a solution to a math problem (Pressley & Woloshyn, 1995); and teaching for transfer pinpoints instructional methods for integrating learning of knowledge within the context of specific tasks (McKeough, Lupart, & Marini, 1995).

How do my views relate to those of others? A distinguishing feature of the knowledge-based approach to educational reform is that it is based on scientific research. In my opinion, the major contribution of psychology to the improvement of education is the development of research-based theories of how people learn in academic settings (Bransford, Brown, & Cocking, 1999) and the development of research methods that enable testing of educational theories (Shavelson & Towne, 2002). Three popular alternatives to a scientific approach are a slogan approach, an ideological approach, and a political approach.

First, consider the slogan approach. A school district I know has adopted the motto: "All Students Can Learn." The motto is printed on school letterhead and on a large sign in the school district's boardroom. Although I agree wholeheartedly with the motto, I fear it is a bit too general to be of much guidance for teachers. Good intentions do not necessarily translate into successful schools without a lot of consideration of specific details. My view offers a much more specific and detailed approach to implementing the well-intentioned slogans of educational enterprises.

Second, consider the ideological approach. The most prominent alternative approach to educational reform among academics is ideological. Educational researchers have exerted a great deal of energy in their search for the optimal version of constructivism (Phillips & Burbules, 2000), including the radical constructivist view that all knowledge is constructed only in social context and exists only in social context. An interesting variant is the expert-says approach, in which recommendations for educational practice are attributed to well-known experts (such as "Vygotsky says..."). The problem with an ideological approach (and its variants) is that it lacks the self-correcting mechanism of science, and thereby can perpetuate unproductive approaches to education.

Third, consider the political approach. A common version of the political approach involves a vision of class struggle in which certain classes of students are seen as being impeded from academic success by institutional barriers. The political approach focuses on factors that contribute to differences in academic achievement based on economic, racial, ethnic, gender, and other factors. The task of educational reform becomes one of eliminating differences in performance among groups. A limitation of a purely political approach is that in order to help all students learn, it is still necessary to have a clear and effective vision of how people learn (Slavin & Madden, 2001). In short, a great equalizer among students is knowledge, so it makes sense to focus on how to help all students develop the knowledge they need for academic success.

What are the implications of my views for instruction and assessment? Common complaints about assessments are that (a) assessments are not useful in improving instruction, (b) assessments are not aligned with what was taught, and (c) assessments focus mainly low level knowledge such as rote facts and procedures (Anderson et al., 2001; Pellegrino et al., 2001). A knowledge-based approach to assessment can address each of these problems by ensuring that assessments focus on a broad survey of the specific pieces of knowledge that are required for success on targeted academic tasks—including the needed facts, procedures, concepts, strategies, and beliefs.

For example, consider the assessment of a simple procedure such as three-column subtraction. A typical assessment might consist of 15 subtraction problems, such as $564 - 472 =$ ____ , and the outcome measure might consist of the percent correct, such as saying that Gail got 80% correct. This information is useful but it could be even more tightly connected to instruction implications if the teacher knew exactly which part of the subtraction procedure was causing the problem. Brown and Burton (1978) developed an assessment, which identified the specific "bugs" in each student's subtraction procedure. For example, a student might give answers such as $564 - 472 = 112$ and $493 - 125 = 372$. This student may have the "smaller-from-larger" bug in which the student subtracts the smaller number from the larger number in each column regardless of which one is on top. If an assessment can give specific information about what needs to be repaired in a student's knowledge, instruction can become more focused and efficient.

Next, consider the assessment of word problem solving. A typical assessment might consist of some word problems for the student to solve, with a score based on the percent of correct answers. Suppose Paul gets a score of 20%. This information is useful but it could be more closely tied to instruction if the teacher knew exactly which aspects of problem solving that Paul was having trouble with—such as whether he had trouble with carrying out arithmetic operations (i.e., procedural knowledge), knowing how to convert ounces to pounds (i.e., factual knowledge), recognizing which numbers were relevant to the problem (i.e., conceptual knowledge), building a mental model of the problem (i.e., conceptual knowledge), developing a solution plan (i.e., strategic knowledge), and/or persisting on the problem in the face of an impasse (attitudinal knowledge). For example, to assess conceptual knowledge, we could present a word problem and ask the student to determine which numbers in the problem were needed to solve the problem, or to assess strategic knowledge, we could give a problem and ask the student to tell what computations were needed (Mayer, Tajika, & Stanley, 1991).

How might teacher training be modified to reflect my views? In some cases, current practice in teacher training involves an activity-based focus on clever things to do with students or a doctrine-based focus on making sure that teachers adhere to an educational philosophy such as constructivism. In contrast to a focus solely on practical issues or philosophical issues, teacher training should be modified to include a focus on what the student needs to learn. According to the knowledge-based view, teacher training should include a knowledge-based focus on the specific knowledge that students at each level need to know.

For example, research on reading demonstrates that success in early reading depends on students possessing a specific kind of knowledge called *phonological awareness*—that is, knowledge of the more than 40 sound units in English (Bradley & Bryant, 1983; Goswami & Bryant, 1990). Similarly, research on mathematics learning demonstrates that learning arithmetic depends on students possessing a specific kind of knowledge called *number sense*—knowledge of a mental number line (Griffin & Case, 1996; Griffin, Case, & Siegler, 1994). Research on reading comprehension demonstrates that students need to possess specific schemas for *rhetorical structures*—knowledge of the ways that information can be organized such as a compare-and-contrast structure that is like a matrix, a hierarchy structure that is like an outline, a process structure that is like a flow chart, and an enumeration structure that is like a list (Cook & Mayer, 1988). Research on writing demonstrates that students need specific kinds of knowledge such as *planning strategies*—that is, strategies for how to generate material, organize material, and express ideas in ways that are appropriate for the intended audience (Kellogg, 1994).

Teacher education should focus on identifying the specific knowledge that students need to know and explore how to help students learn that knowledge. In addition to facts and procedures, students need to learn concepts, strategies, and beliefs. For fundamental academic tasks, teachers need to learn how to conduct cognitive task analyses—that is, to break down an academic task into the component knowledge needed to perform the task. In short, training should become much more focused on the knowledge that students need for successful reasoning on fundamental academic tasks.

Overall, an important goal of education is to help students become effective reasoners in the domain of mathematics. When confronted with a mathematical problem, students should be able to reason effectively. The development of mathematical reasoning depends on students learning appropriate facts, concepts, procedures, strategies, and beliefs.

REFERENCES

Anderson, L. W., Krathwohl, D. R., Airasian, P. W., Cruikshank, K. A., Mayer, R. E., Pintrich, P. R., et al. (2001). *A taxonomy for learning, teaching. and assessing: A revision of Bloom's taxonomy of educational objectives.* New York: Longman.

Bradley, L., & Bryant, P. (1983). Categorizing sounds and learning to read—a causal connection. *Nature, 301,* 419–421.

Bransford, J. D., Brown, A. L., & Cocking, R. (Eds.). (1999). *How people learn.* Washington, DC: National Academy Press.

Brown, J. S., & Burton, R. R. (1978). Diagnostic models for procedural bugs in basic mathematical skills. *Cognitive Science, 2,* 155–192.

Bruer, J. T. (1993). *Schools for thought: A science of learning in the classroom.* Cambridge, MA: MIT Press.

Carpenter, T. P., Lindquist, M. M., Matthews, W., & Silver, E. A. (1983). Results of the third NAEP mathematics assessment: Secondary school. *Mathematics Teacher, 76,* 652–659.

Catrambone, R. (1995). Aiding subgoal learning: Effects on transfer. *Journal of Educational Psychology, 87,* 5–17.

Cook, L. K., & Mayer, R. E. (1988). Teaching readers about the structure of scientific text. *Journal of Educational Psychology, 80,* 448–456.

Goswami, U., & Bryant, P. (1990). *Phonological skills and learning to read.* Hillsdale, NJ: Erlbaum.

Griffin, S., & Case, R. (1996). Evaluating the breadth and depth of training effects when central conceptual structures are taught. In R. Case & Y. Okamoto (Eds.), The role of central conceptual structures in the development of children's thought (pp. 83–102). *Monographs of the Society for Research in Child Development, 61*(Serial No. 246), Nos. 1–2.

Griffin, S. A., Case, R., & Siegler, R. S. (1994). Rightstart: Providing the central conceptual structure prerequisites for first formal learning of arithmetic to students at risk for school failure. In K. McGilly (Ed.), *Classroom lessons: Integrating cognitive theory and classroom practice* (pp. 25-49). Cambridge, MA: MIT Press.

Hegarty, M., Mayer, R. E., & Monk, C. A. (1995). Comprehension of arithmetic word problems: A comparison of successful and unsuccessful problem solvers. *Journal of Educational Psychology, 87,* 18–32.

Hinsley, D., Hayes, J. R., & Simon, H. A. (1977). From words to equations. In M. D. Just & P. Carpenter (Eds.), *Cognitive processes in comprehension* (pp. 89-106). Hillsdale, NJ: Erlbaum.

Kellogg, R. T. (1994). *The psychology of writing.* New York: Oxford University Press.

Kilpatrick, J., Swafford, J., & Findell, B. (Eds.). (2001). *Adding it up: Helping children learn mathematics.* Washington, DC: National Academy Press.

Lester, F. K., Garofalo, J., & Kroll, D. L. (1989). Self-confidence, interest, beliefs, and metacognition: Key influences on problem-solving behavior. In D. B. McLeod & V. M. Adams (Eds.), *Affect and mathematical problem solving* (pp. 75-88). New York: Springer-Verlag.

Lewis, A. B. (1989). Training students to represent arithmetic word problems. *Journal of Educational Psychology, 81,* 521–531.

Low, R. (1989). Detection of missing and irrelevant information within algebraic story problems. *British Journal of Educational Psychology, 59,* 296–305.

Low, R., & Over, R. (1990). Text editing of algebraic word problems. *Australian Journal of Psychology, 42,* 63–73.

Ma, L. (1999). *Knowing and teaching elementary mathematics.* Mahwah, NJ: Erlbaum.

Mayer, R. E. (1981). Frequency norms and structural analysis of algebra story problems into families, categories, and templates. *Instructional Science, 10,* 135–175.

Mayer, R. E. (1982). Memory for algebra story problems. *Journal of Educational Psychology, 74,* 199–216.

Mayer, R. E. (1999). *The promise of educational psychology: Learning in the context areas*. Upper Saddle River, NJ: Prentice Hall.

Mayer, R. E. (2003). Mathematical problem solving. In J. M. Royer (Ed.), *Mathematical cognition* (pp. 69–92). Greenwich, CT: Information Age.

Mayer, R. E., Sims, V., & Tajika, H. (1995). A comparison of how textbooks teach mathematical problem solving in Japan and the United States. *American Educational Research Journal, 32*, 443–460.

Mayer. R. E., Tajika, H., & Stanley, C. (1991). Mathematical problem solving in Japan and the United States: A controlled comparison. *Journal of Educational Psychology, 82*, 69–72.

McKeough, A., Lupart, J., & Marini, A. (Eds.). (1995). *Teaching for transfer.* Mahwah, NJ: Erlbaum.

Quilici, J. H., & Mayer, R. E. (1996). Role of examples in how students learn to categorize statistics word problems. *Journal of Educational Psychology, 88*, 144–161.

Pellegrino, J. W., Chudowsky, N., & Glaser, R. (Eds.). (2001). *Knowing what students know: The science of design of educational assessment*. Washington, DC: National Academy Press.

Phillips, D. S., & Burbules, N. C. (2000). *Postpositivism and educational reform*. Lanham, MD: Rowman & Littlefield.

Pressley, M., & Woloshyn, V. (1995). *Cognitive strategy instruction* (2nd ed). Cambridge, MA: Brookline Books.

Reed, S. K. (1987). A structure-mapping model for word problems. *Journal of Experimental Psychology: Learning, Memory, and Cognition, 13*, 124–139.

Reed, S. K. (1999). *Word problems*. Mahwah, NJ: Erlbaum.

Riley, M., Greeno, J. G., & Heller, J. (1982). The development of children's problem solving ability in arithmetic. In H. Ginsburg (Ed.), *The development of mathematical thinking* (pp. 153-196). New York: Academic Press.

Schoenfeld, A. H. (1979). Explicit heuristic training as a variable in problem-solving performance. *Journal for Research in Mathematics Education, 10*, 173–187.

Schoenfeld, A. H. (1985). *Mathematical problem solving*. Orlando, FL: Academic Press.

Schoenfeld, A. H. (1991). On mathematics and sense-making: An informal attack on the unfortunate divorce of formal and informal mathematics. In J. F. Voss, D. N. Perkins, & J. W. Segal (Eds.), *Informal reasoning and education* (pp. 311–343). Hillsdale, NJ: Erlbaum.

Schoenfeld, A. H. (1992). Learning to think mathematically: Problem solving, metacognition, and sense making in mathematics. In D. A. Grouws (Ed.), *Handbook of research on mathematics teaching and learning* (pp. 334–370). New York: Macmillan.

Schunk, D. (1989). Self-efficacy and achievement behaviors. *Educational Psychology Review, 1*, 173–208.

Schunk, D., & Hanson, A. R. (1985). Peer models: Influences on children's self-efficacy and achievement. *Journal of Educational Psychology, 77*, 313–322.

Shavelson, R. J., & Towne, L. (2002). *Scientific research in education*. Washington, DC: National Academy Press.

Silver, E. A. (1981). Recall of mathematical problem information: Solving related problems. *Journal for Research in Mathematics Education, 12,* 54–64.

Slavin, R. E., & Madden, N. A. (2001). *Success for all: Research and reform in elementary education.* Mahwah, NJ: Erlbaum.

Soloway, E., Lochhead, J., & Clement, J. (1982). Does computer programming enhance problem solving ability? Some positive evidence on algebra word problems. In R. J. Seidel, R. E. Anderson, & B. Hunter (Eds.), *Computer literacy* (pp. 171-186). New York: Academic Press.

Sternberg, R. J., & Grigorenko, E. L. (Eds). (2003). *The psychology of abilities, competencies and expertise.* New York: Cambridge University Press.

Stevenson, H. W., & Lee, S. Y. (1990). Context of achievement. *Monograph of the Society of Research in Child Development, 55*(1-2, Serial No. 221).

Stevenson, H. W., & Stigler, J. W. (1992). *The learning gap.* New York: Simon & Schuster.

Stigler, J. W., & Hiebert, J. (1999). *The teaching gap.* New York: Free Press.

Sweller, J., & Cooper, G. A. (1985). The use of worked examples as a substitute for problem solving in learning algebra. *Cognition and Instruction, 2,* 59–89.

Thorndike, E. L. (1922). *The psychology of arithmetic.* New York: Macmillan.

Verschaffel, L., Greer, B., & De Corte, E. (2000). *Making sense of word problems.* Lisse, The Netherlands: Swets & Zeitlinger.

CHAPTER 5

PROMOTING DEAF CHILDREN'S MATHEMATICAL REASONING BY USING THEIR VISUAL-SPATIAL STRENGTHS

Terezinha Nunes

The educational achievement of deaf pupils has been analyzed in different countries over the last 60 years. A very large number of studies focused on deaf children's language and literacy learning. There are obvious reasons for this. Most deaf children grow up surrounded by hearing people—approximately 90% of children born deaf have hearing parents. The oral language spoken around them provides them with inputs for language learning that they cannot access easily. In order to learn oral language, deaf children (even those with hearing aids and cochlear implants) have to receive systematic help, not required by hearing children. Their parents, teachers, and speech therapists approach their language instruction through carefully designed means. Deaf children of deaf parents, who can learn sign language as naturally as hearing children learn oral language, still require special attention to their communication needs in school. Much of their schooling can be carried out through sign

Optimizing Student Success in School With the Other Three Rs:
Reasoning, Resilience, and Responsibility, 75–94
Copyright © 2006 by Information Age Publishing
All rights of reproduction in any form reserved.

language but if they are going to learn to read, they will learn to read in a second language—for example, they will learn to read in English. Written language represents words from an oral language. So it comes as no surprise that literacy learning is difficult for deaf children, regardless of whether they were educated orally or using sign. Educators have realized for a long time that literacy acquisition is a serious challenge for deaf youngsters and have focused most of their attention on literacy teaching.

This focus on language and literacy seems to have absorbed so much of parents' and teachers' attention that deaf children's mathematics learning has received comparatively little consideration. Yet, at school, most deaf children find mathematics difficult. The level of difficulty displayed by deaf students in mathematics is quite serious: in a recent study using the Stanford Achievement Test, 80% of the deaf students at age 14 showed a level of performance considered basic or below basic in knowledge of mathematics problem solving (Traxler, 2000). Deaf students leave school with significantly less mathematical competence than hearing pupils; this critically interferes with their educational and employment prospects. Does it have to be so?

In this chapter it is suggested that deaf people have information-processing preferences that differ from those of hearing people. Thus, when they are presented in reasoning tasks with information in a form that is difficult for them to process and retain, they are at a disadvantage. However, they can be at considerable advantage in the same reasoning tasks if they are presented with information in a manner that is in line with their strengths. Thus these strengths and difficulties work as resilience and risk factors related to their mathematics learning, depending on whether the teaching environment is designed to match their strengths or not. The first section of this chapter analyzes the interaction between deaf children's information-processing preferences and task demands. This interaction produces different levels of performance by deaf children in tasks that require the same reasoning abilities. The second section describes a program that was designed to match deaf children's strengths and its effectiveness in raising their mathematical achievement.

DEAF CHILDREN'S INFORMATION-PROCESSING PREFERENCES AND TASK DEMANDS

Even those deaf people who have some residual hearing grow up in a world where vision is a much more reliable source of information than hearing. When you grow up in such a world, you end up developing information-processing abilities that may have remained undeveloped if you could use your hearing. Think, for example, of what happens when you are working in the kitchen and someone comes in. If you are a hearing person, you will know someone is coming in if you hear footsteps. If you are deaf, you are likely to see the person from the corner of your eye rather than hear footsteps. Peripheral vision has an important function—one could even say a survival function—in a deaf person's life. Accordingly, deaf people react much more reliably than hearing people to movement in the peripheral vision, irrespective of whether they were educated in sign language or orally (Neville & Lawson, 1987a, 1987b, 1987c).

This strength in visual processing is not restricted to reacting to stimuli: from an early age, deaf children are superior to hearing children in their ability to represent and reproduce visual information.

An experiment by Todman and Seedhouse (1994) provided clear evidence regarding the use of spatial information in rule learning among deaf and hearing children. Todman and Seedhouse compared deaf and hearing elementary school children on a rule-learning task originally designed by Pascual-Leone (1970). In this task, the children are asked to learn an action as a response to an arbitrarily paired visual cue: for example, if a square with a purple background is presented, the child has to open his or her mouth. The task is quite complicated and there are a number of pairings between the figures and responses to be learned. Their rule knowledge is later tested either using a spatial or a sequential presentation. In the spatial presentation, they are shown a matrix with four figures, one at each corner of the display; the figures are then covered and the children are asked to perform the four actions that were paired with the figures. In the sequential presentation, the children are shown the figures one at a time; after the series is completed they are required to perform the actions. In the sequential presentation, recall may be required in the same order as the figures appeared (*serial recall*) or in any order (*free recall*).

Todman and Seedhouse (1994) observed that the deaf children performed *better* than the hearing children in the task where the figures had been presented spatially, in the matrix format. Thus they were better able to encode the spatially presented information and follow the related rules. The sequential presentation produced different results for the serial and the free recall. The hearing children performed better than the deaf children in the serial recall condition but there was no difference between the deaf and the hearing children in the free recall condition. Thus, the way in which the items were presented—spatially or in a temporal sequence—and the way in which they had to be recalled—serial or free recall—affected the children's performance. The deaf children had an advantage when the presentation was spatial and were at a disadvantage when the presentation was sequential and recall was serial. Thus deaf children are at risk in learning environments that require serial recall but can show superior performance in environments where information presentation and recall conditions are appropriate to their strengths.

The study by Todman and Seedhouse (1994) reveals deaf children's information-processing preferences but the task can be considered somewhat artificial and may not be indicative of what happens in tasks that are more ecologically valid and reflect everyday information-processing demands. We (Zarfaty, Nunes, & Bryant, 2004) examined whether this strength in deaf children's learning could be demonstrated on a numerical representation task. We know that deaf children fall behind hearing children in mathematics in school. So we thought it would be important to know whether they are disadvantaged before school on a number task suited for preschool children. Similarly to the experiment by Todman and Seedhouse, we used a task where the response was produced in action, so that the deaf children would not be disadvantaged by linguistic demands. Thus we used a number representation task, where the children saw displays involving specific numbers of blocks and had to reproduce the display after it was no longer visible. Number representation tasks are used to assess preschool children's informal mathematical knowledge (see Ginsburg, Klein, & Starkey, 1998, for a review of young children's informal mathematical knowledge) and are considered as indicators of early mathematical reasoning.

Numbers are used to count both spatially and sequentially presented objects or events. For example, a child may want to know how many marbles he or she has, and these may all be available for counting at the same time. It is just as likely that a child is asked to count, for example, how many times he or she threw the ball in a game. So we decided to use both spatial and sequential presentation of items in a number reproduction task. Our predictions, based on deaf children's information-processing preferences, were that the deaf children would perform better than the hearing children on visual–spatial tasks and similarly to the hearing children on the sequential tasks, because number reproduction does not involve serial recall.

Two groups of children ($N = 20$), deaf and hearing, with a mean age of about 39 months participated in this study. Nine of the deaf children were profoundly deaf; one was moderately deaf. Eight of the profoundly deaf children had cochlear implants. The deaf children were being educated orally in mainstream nurseries and attended a nursery school for deaf children at least twice a week. The hearing children also attended nursery school.

We gave the children 24 number reproduction tasks, where the items were presented spatially or sequentially. All trials were presented on a computer screen. In the spatial presentation, the children saw a row of blocks on the screen, and these were then moved until they disappeared into a box. In half of the trials, the blocks simply appeared on the screen simultaneously and then moved into the box; on the other half of the trials, the children saw a puppet making the row and then putting the blocks into a box. In the temporal, sequential presentation, the blocks appeared and then disappeared into the box one at a time. For half of the trials the puppet opened her hand, showing a block on her palm, and then placed the block into the box; for the other half of the trials, the blocks simply appeared on the screen and then disappeared into the box through animation. Next to the computer were 20 blocks and a box identical to the one seen on the screen.

Once the children had observed the display on the computer, they were asked to do the same thing with the blocks. They had no difficulty in understanding this instruction and placed blocks into the box. The use of two types of presentation, with and without the puppet, made the task more interesting for the children but had no effect on their performance. The number of items in the display did not affect the children's performance either: on average, they were just as accurate with two, three, and four blocks.

The task was of moderate difficulty for both groups of children. The deaf children were correct significantly more often than the hearing children when the displays were presented spatially. There was no difference between the deaf and hearing children when the blocks were presented sequentially. Thus these results support the hypothesis that, when a task matches deaf children's information-processing preferences, they are not at a disadvantage in comparison to hearing cohorts.

To summarize, deaf children's strengths and difficulties interact with task demands, and their level of performance can be higher or lower than that of hearing children in tasks that require the same type of reasoning. We conclude that risk and resilience factors in deaf children's reasoning result from an interaction between their information-processing abilities and the design of learning environments. Deaf children are at a disadvantage if serial recall is involved but do very well when information is presented spatially.

The results of the studies described here are very positive because they show that it is possible to design learning environments that suit deaf children's information-processing preferences and change their chances of success. However, it can still be argued that deaf children are at risk when it comes to the informal learning that takes place in everyday life. Furth (1971) and Rapin (1986) suggested that one of the risks for deaf children is that they do not receive as much information as hearing children do in the course of everyday life because they miss out on the use of one information channel, hearing. Thus they miss out on incidental learning: They do not overhear other people's conversations, they cannot listen to the radio as their parents drive around town, they cannot pick up on their hearing parents' self-instruction behavior. For example, we may be taking the children to a park and have to check whether we have enough money for the entrance tickers. We might say to ourselves, "Do I have to stop at the ATM on the way?" and then take out our money and count it, most likely mumbling, and then decide whether there is a need to get more money on the way to the park. A hearing child would be able to learn something about counting, and particularly counting money, from observing the parent's self-instructions. Gregory (1998) made this point specifically with respect to the informal learning of mathematics: "Hearing children hear mathematical talk almost from birth, 'Wait a minute,' 'That's too small for you now,' 'It's miles away.' Most hearing children are also involved in mathematical talk themselves from early on, of which counting is a prime example" (p. 123). Gregory suggested that, because deaf children miss out on everyday mathematical conversation, this might result in a delay in informal mathematics reasoning.

There is some evidence in the literature to support the idea of an information gap in deaf children's learning and reasoning about numbers. Two significant gaps in deaf children's numerical information in the first years of primary school have been identified: they are behind in learning the counting string and they are also behind in their knowledge of the additive composition of numbers—that is, the knowledge that any number can be formed by the sum of two other numbers. Each of these is discussed briefly in turn.

Knowledge of the Counting String

Many hearing children start primary school with some knowledge of the counting string. This knowledge may be acquired at home or in preschool. Parents enjoy counting with their young children as they perform actions—for example, place apples into a supermarket basket or climb steps—and sing songs and read books that involve numbers. Preschool teachers also invest a considerable effort in teaching hearing children how to count. However, research has shown that children may differ significantly in their counting ability by the time they start school and that these differences are related to cultural practices (Ginsburg, 1982; Ginsburg, Choy, Lopez, Netley, & Chao-Yuan, 1997). Because parents and teachers of young deaf children are so absorbed with teaching them about language, it would not be surprising if they did not provide them with sufficient input for learning to count.

Comparisons between hearing and deaf children have in fact shown that deaf children lag behind the hearing counterparts in their knowledge of the counting string, regardless of whether they are being educated orally (Nunes & Moreno, 1998) or in sign (Leybaert, & Van Cutsem, 2002; Secada, 1984). Because knowledge of the counting string is essential for solving computational problems, this lack of information places deaf children at risk for solving arithmetic problems in school.

Additive Composition of Numbers

A second domain in which deaf children lag behind hearing children is knowledge of money (Austin, 1975). Learning to count money, which is often the result of informal experiences outside school, provides children with experiences that are more cognitively advanced than learning to count objects. When counting, for example, the total composed by one dime and three pennies, children have the opportunity to reason about the additive composition of a number—that is, about the fact that a number can be formed by two other numbers—so that 13 can be formed by 10 plus 3. When counting a dime and three pennies, children practice a way of counting referred in the literature as "counting on": they learn to point to the dime and say 10 and then count on from 10, saying 11, 12, 13. Nunes and Moreno (1998) have shown that deaf children are significantly behind hearing children in counting money. About two-thirds of the hearing children succeed on this task by age 6 whereas the task might prove challenging for some deaf children even at the age of 9 or 10. Both hearing and deaf children who do not succeed in money-counting tasks tend to keep the values of the different coins separate—so they say that a dime and three cents make "10 and 3 cents altogether"—or to count all the coins as ones—thus counting a dime and three cents as "4 cents," even though they recall that the dime is worth 10 cents. This performance indicates that they do not conceive of the number 13 as made of 10 plus 3, but only as a point in the counting string.

Nunes and Bryant (1996) and Moreno (2000) have shown that performance on a money-counting task (designed by Nunes Carraher & Schliemann, 1990) is predictive of children's mathematical competence. Moreno was able to demonstrate this in a longitudinal study with deaf children, where performance on this money-counting task still made a significant contribution to the prediction of mathematics performance on a standardized test after controlling for age, IQ, and language ability. Thus this apparently unimportant lack of information ends up having significant consequences as a risk factor in deaf children's mathematics difficulties.

Two conclusions arise from this analysis of how deaf children's strengths and difficulties interact with task demands and become risk and resilience factors. The first is that task demands can be significant obstacles to deaf children's success in mathematical tasks if the tasks are not designed to match their information-processing preferences. If the task demands are in line with their strengths, the risks for their development can be minimized. The second conclusion is that missing out on informal mathematics learning outside school is also a risk factor. Thus the design of appropriate learning environments for deaf children has to take this information gap into account and provide the experiences that are relevant to overcome it. On the basis of this analysis, we designed an intervention program for promoting deaf children's mathematical reasoning. This program is described in the section that follows.

A LEARNING ENVIRONMENT DESIGNED TO TURN DEAF CHILDREN'S VISUAL ABILITIES INTO A RESILIENCE FACTOR FOR THE DEVELOPMENT OF MATHEMATICAL REASONING

In order to promote deaf children's mathematical reasoning, we (Nunes, 2004; Nunes & Moreno, 2002) developed a program designed to make the most of deaf children's strengths in reasoning about visually and spatially presented materials. The program also considered the two important gaps in deaf children's informal knowledge identified in previous research and thus considered the need to consolidate deaf children's knowledge of the counting string in school, long after this knowledge is expected to be firmly established in hearing children, and the need to provide them with experiences that would promote their understanding of the additive composition of a number.

The program was designed with the collaboration of eight teachers of the deaf who met with the researchers during the design phase to discuss the materials, test them out in their classroom, and provide feedback after these had been tested. It was implemented during the subsequent year by six teachers of the deaf with their 24 pupils during their mathematics lessons. The pupils were aged 7–11. Their performance was assessed before and after the intervention using the NFER-Nelson age-appropriate mathematics achievement test. In order to assess the effectiveness of the intervention, the pre- and post-test results were compared to a baseline obtained with 68 deaf pupils who were attending the same schools and were in the same age range in the year before the intervention was carried out.

The program was composed of four sections, each focusing on a different aspect of numerical reasoning and knowledge: the number system, measurement, additive reasoning, and multiplicative reasoning. The sections on the number system and measurement were designed to consolidate the children's knowledge of the counting string and develop their additive composition reasoning. The sections on additive and multiplicative reasoning focused on problem solving rather than computation skills. The program contained a total of 150 problems, with approximately 30 problems in the first three sections and 50 problems on multiplicative reasoning.

The problems were always presented with the support of drawings and diagrams so that problem presentation relied on visual and spatial resources. The children worked on booklets that contained these drawings and almost no writing. Problem instructions were complemented by the teachers using the language appropriate for the pupils in their own classroom—English, Signed English, or British Sign Language. Thus no adaptation was required for the materials to be used in the different linguistic environments.

Drawings and diagrams were used both for problem presentation and for the children to represent their solutions so that they became an integral part of how the children approached problem solving. The sequence of problems was carefully designed so that the children became accustomed to using drawings and diagrams as part of their problem-solving activity. They also used their drawings and diagrams to discuss their solutions. Figures 5.1 and 5.2 show examples of situations used to encourage

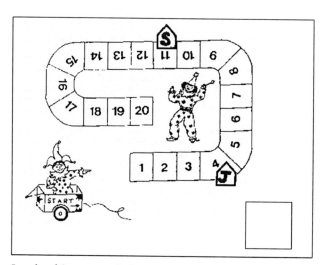

Jamal and Serena are playing a game.
Jamal is at number 4. Serena is at number 11.
Serena is winning. How many squares ahead is Serena?
Put your answer in the box.

Figure 5.1.

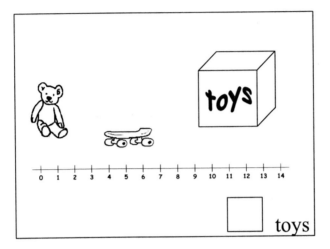

A boy has 12 toys altogether. You can see 2 of his toys.
How many toys are in the box?
Work it out on the number line.
Write your answer in the box.

Figure 5.2.

the children to use visually presented information to reason about the problems. The figures were presented in the children's booklets. The information that appears in writing was provided by the teacher, using the language appropriate for the class. Figure 5.1 shows a problem about a board game, where the presentation of the information is visual and spatial due to the very nature of the problem. Figure 5.2 shows a problem where the children are explicitly instructed to use the number line to work out the solution. Using the number line after solving problems about board games seemed to the children a simple extension of what they had been doing already. Explicit instruction to show the work on the number line, rather than show a computation, encouraged the children to rely on this form of diagram for problem solving.

The children were also encouraged to work with number lines that started anywhere (see Figures 5.3 and 5.4). This resource was introduced with tasks that involved smaller numbers and later suggested for use with tasks that involved larger numbers. The broken ruler problem (Figure 5.4), originally created by Nunes, Light, and Mason (1995), promotes interesting discussions about additive composition. The children must refrain from reading off the number corresponding to the end of the line as they realize that the line is not in correspondence to the length of the ruler up to that number. This visual display helps them analyze the num-

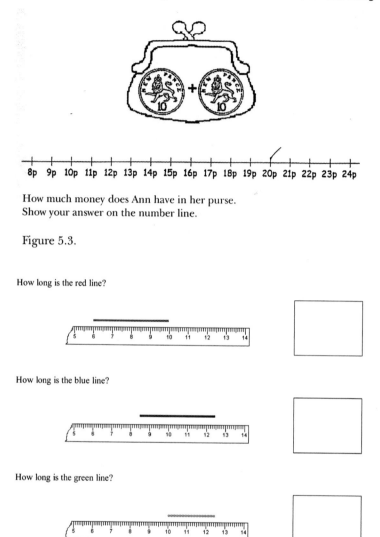

How much money does Ann have in her purse.
Show your answer on the number line.

Figure 5.3.

How long is the red line?

How long is the blue line?

How long is the green line?

Figure 5.4.

bers on the ruler as composed by two parts, one that is not in correspondence with the line being measured, and a second part, which is in
correspondence with the line. Only the second part gives information
about the length of the lines.

The children were given many opportunities to use counting in order
to reinforce their knowledge of the counting string. Situations that

involved counting on, such as solving sums where one of the addends was hidden (Figure 5.2) and counting money (Figure 5.3), were included in the initial stages of the program in order to give them opportunities to work with the concept of additive composition.

Story problems, which typically pose difficulties for deaf children perhaps due to the sequential nature of the information, were also presented with the support of drawings. Figures 5.5 and 5.6 illustrate different types of additive reasoning stories. The possibility of discussing what the story meant and the solutions with the support of drawings and the number line allowed the children to make connections between a spatial and a temporal sequence. Temporal sequences are important for the solution of story problems, as can be seen in Figure 5.6. If the child responded only to the description "her Granny gave her 2 sweets" and concluded that this problem should be solved through addition, the solution would be incorrect. It was reasoned that if the deaf children can become used to representing temporal sequences spatially, this would have a positive impact on their problem-solving ability.

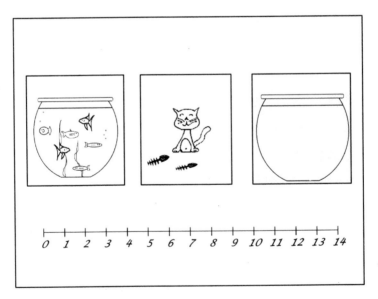

There were 6 fish in the bowl.
The cat ate 2 fish.
How many fish are in the bowl now?
Draw them in the empty bowl.
Show what happened in the story on the number line.

Figure 5.5.

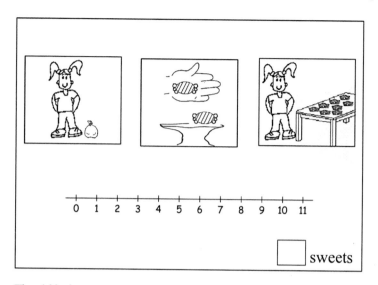

The girl had some sweets.
Her mom gave her 2 sweets.
Now she has 8 sweets.
How many sweets did she have in the bag?
Show what happened in the story on the number line.

Figure 5.6.

Multiplicative reasoning problems were also introduced with the support of drawings and diagrams, which were used by the children to work out solutions. The drawings used in the beginning of the program either contained or prompted the children to use a representation of all the items (see Figures 5.7 and 5.8). At later stages, the information was presented by means of tables and graphs. Tables were used to help the children grasp the idea that there is a fixed ratio between the variables in a multiplication situation (see Figures 5.9 and 5.10). Graphs provide a visual, linear representation of the relation between the variables (see Figure 5.11).

The program was assessed by comparing the project children's scale scores in the pre- and post-test to the performance of the children in the baseline group. Scale scores were used because they allow for controlling for age differences within the same age level; because the number of children was small, this was considered a necessary control. Table 5.1 presents a summary of the results; data for 21 children only are presented because three of the children had become age 11 by the time of post-test so their results could not be compared to those in the baseline, which did not

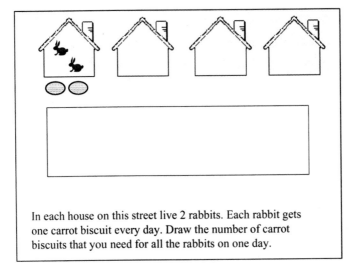

In each house on this street live 2 rabbits. Each rabbit gets one carrot biscuit every day. Draw the number of carrot biscuits that you need for all the rabbits on one day.

Figure 5.7.

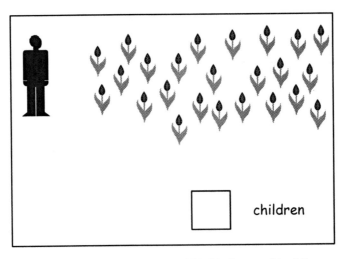

It's the teacher's birthday and each child in his class gave him 2 flowers.
Now the teacher has 24 flowers.
How many children are there in the class?

Figure 5.8.

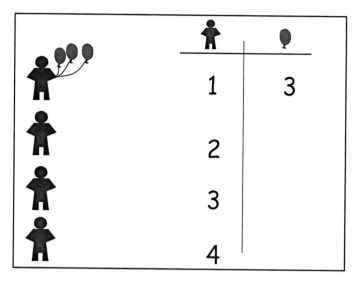

There are 4 children. Each child has 3 ballons.
Can you draw the rest of the balloons?
Can you finish the table?

Figure 5.9.

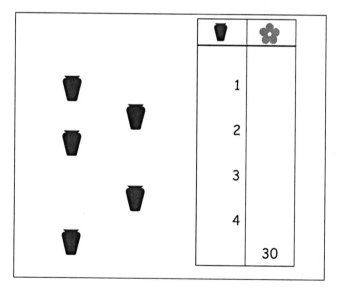

Can you fill in the rest of the table?

Figure 5.10.

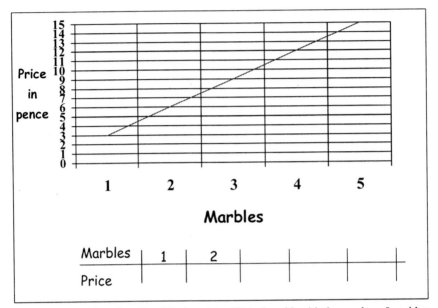

The graph shows the price of marbles in a shop. Fill in the table with the number of marbles and the prices.

Figure 5.11.

include 11-year-olds. The Mann-Whitney test, which is based on the ranks obtained by the pupils in each group, was used to analyze the significance of these differences. This was necessary because the scores were not distributed normally at each age level. In the pre-test, the mean rank for the baseline group was 44.8 and the mean rank for the project pupils was 47.6. This difference was not statistically significant ($p = .66$). In the post-test, the mean rank for the baseline group was 40.4 and the mean rank for the project pupils was 60.35. This difference was statistically significant ($p = 0.002$). So it can be concluded that the project pupils improved significantly in their mathematics achievement during the time that they were engaged in the program. They performed similarly to the baseline group at pre-test and outperformed the baseline group at post-test.

A second analysis was carried out to assess the program, based on the comparison between the progress the children showed from the beginning to the end of the project and the progress that they would be expected to make without any intervention. The NFER norms for the age-appropriate mathematics tests include a prediction of performance on tests administered at a subsequent age taking into account performance at the previous age level. This comparison is informative but must be con-

**Table 5.1.   Mean Scaled Scores in the NFER-Nelson for the
Baseline Group and the Project Group in the
Pre- and Post-Tests by Age-Appropriate Test Taken**

	Age Level			
	7 Years	8 Years	9 Years	10 Years
Baseline pupils	9.9	15.4	27.1	38.3
	n = 22	n = 19	n = 19	n = 8
Project pupils at pre-test	11.4	17.0	27.0	33.0
Project pupils at post-test	22.3	29.3	32.8	43.5
	n = 3	n = 8	n = 3	n = 7

sidered with caution because the norms are produced for hearing, rather than deaf children. Pupils whose observed performance is at a lower level than the predicted score are said to have made less progress than expected. Those pupils whose observed and predicted performances coincide are said to have made average progress. Finally, pupils whose observed score is superior to the predicted score are said to have made more progress than expected.

We observed that 31.8% of the pupils made less progress than predicted and 68.2% had higher observed scores than predicted scores. A statistical test (Wilcoxon Signed Ranks Test for dependent samples) showed that the difference between the predicted and observed scores was significant ($p = .02$). The pupils' performance at post-test was thus significantly better than it would have been if their progress had been equivalent to the average amount of progress expected for hearing pupils during one school year (for further details, see Nunes, 2004; Nunes & Moreno, 2002).

These analyses suggest that the program was effective in promoting the development of deaf children's mathematical reasoning. Therefore, creating a learning environment that matches deaf pupils' information processing preferences and deals with the gaps in their informal mathematical knowledge is a good way to transform risk into resilience factors.

CONCLUSION

Risk factors that forecast learning difficulties in school are often conceived in a static manner, and are identified either in children or in their history. This chapter used a different view in analyzing the cause of deaf children's problems with mathematical reasoning: risk and resilience factors were treated as the result of an interaction between the children's characteristics and the learning environment. The analysis of the literature showed that deaf children's information-processing preferences differ from those of hearing children. Deaf children do not perform as well as hearing children on tasks where information is presented sequentially and responses must preserve the order of presentation. When information is presented visually and spatially, deaf children actually perform better than hearing children on numerical and rule-learning tasks.

Deaf children's strengths in processing visual–spatial information had not been explored previously in the mathematics classroom. We (Nunes & Moreno, 2002) designed a program where not only the information required to solve problems was presented visually and spatially but also the children were encouraged to use visual and spatial representation during problem solving.

The program also considered that deaf children are likely to start school at a disadvantage with respect to their informally learned numerical knowledge. Their knowledge of the counting string and of money lags behind that of their hearing counterparts. This is true of deaf children educated orally or using a sign language and places deaf children at a disadvantage in school. They need to be able to use the counting string to solve numerical problems; so, being behind in this knowledge leads to worse performance in solving problems where counting is required. Counting money is one of the ways in which children develop insight into the additive nature of numbers, and their lack of exposure to money places them at risk for not learning about this important aspect of number. So the program we designed had to provide the children with many opportunities to use the counting string and reflect about the additive composition of numbers.

The program was implemented by teachers during the periods normally used for mathematics lessons. Both children and teachers enjoyed working with the booklets that contained the different types of problems. The children found it easier to explain their own reasoning using the drawings and diagrams provided and, according to the teachers' reports, started to adopt these problem-solving strategies at other times in the mathematics lessons. The children who participated in the project performed similarly to those in a baseline group comprised of deaf children from the same schools at pre-test. At post-test, they outperformed the pupils in the same age level in the baseline group. The project children also made more progress than predicted from their pre-test scores.

This chapter started with a grim finding: deaf adolescents are severely behind their hearing counterparts in mathematical problem solving and this severely thwarts their educational and occupational prospects. But we end the chapter on a positive note. We now know that it is possible to significantly improve deaf children's mathematical achievement if we learn to design teaching that draws on their strong visual and spatial reasoning skills.

AUTHOR'S NOTES

1. The empirical research described in this chapter was supported by two grants from The Nuffield Foundation. The British Academy supported me through a Research Readership during the time this chapter was written. Their support made this work possible and I am very grateful to both institutions.
2. I am extremely indebted to the schools, teachers, and children who participated in this investigation.

REFERENCES

Austin, G. F. (1975). Knowledge of selected concepts obtained by an adolescent deaf population. *American Annals of the Deaf, 120,* 360–370.

Furth, H. (1971). Linguistic deficiency and thinking: Research with deaf subjects 1964–1969. *Psychological Review, 76,* 58–72.

Ginsburg, H. P. (1982). The development of addition in contexts of culture, social class, and race. In T. P. Carpenter, J. M. Moser, & T. A. Romberg (Eds.), *Addition and subtraction: A cognitive perspective* (pp. 191–210). Hillsdale, NJ: Erlbaum.

Ginsburg, H. P., Choy, Y. E., Lopez, L. S., Netley, R., & Chao-Yuan, C. (1997). Happy birthday to you: Early mathematical thinking of Asian, South American, and US children. In T. Nunes & P. Bryant (Eds.), *Learning and teaching mathematics. An international perspective* (pp. 163–209). Hove, UK: Psychology Press.

Ginsburg, H. P., Klein, A., & Starkey, P. (1998). The development of children's mathematical thinking: Connecting research with practice. In W. Damon, I. E. Siegel, & A. A. Renninger (Eds.), *Handbook of child psychology: Child psychology in practice* (Vol. 4, pp. 401–476). New York: Wiley.

Gregory, S. (1998). Mathematics and deaf children. In S. Gregory, P. Knight, W. McCracken, S. Powers, & L. Watson (Eds.), *Issues in deaf education* (pp. 119–126). London: David Fulton.

Leybaert, J., & Van Cutsem, M.-N. (2002). Counting in sign language. *Journal of Experimental Child Psychology, 81,* 482–501.

Moreno, C. (2000). *Predictors of mathematics attainment in hearing impaired children.* Unpublished doctoral thesis, Institute of Education, University of London.

Neville, H., & Lawson, D. (1987a). Attention to central and peripheral visual space in a movement detection task: An event-related potential and behavioral study: I. Normal hearing adults. *Brain Research, 405,* 253–267.

Neville, H., & Lawson, D. (1987b). Attention to central and peripheral visual space in a movement detection task: An event-related potential and behavioral study: II. Congenitally deaf adults. *Brain Research, 405,* 268–283.

Neville, H., & Lawson, D. (1987c). Attention to central and peripheral visual space in a movement detection task: An event-related potential and behavioral study: III. Separate effects of auditory deprivation and acquisition of a visual language. *Brain Research, 405,* 284–294.

Nunes, T. (2004). *Teaching mathematics to deaf children.* London: Whurr.

Nunes, T., & Bryant, P. (1996). *Children doing mathematics.* Oxford, UK: Blackwell.

Nunes, T., Light, P., & Mason, J. (1995). Measurement as a social process. *Cognition and Instruction, 13,* 585-587.

Nunes, T., & Moreno, C. (1998). Is hearing impairment a cause of difficulties in learning mathematics? In C. Donlan (Ed.), *The development of mathematical skills* (pp. 227–254). Hove, UK: Psychology Press.

Nunes, T., & Moreno, C. (2002). An intervention program to promote deaf pupils' achievement in numeracy. *Journal of Deaf Studies and Deaf Education, 7,* 120–133.

Nunes Carraher, T., & Schliemann, A. D. (1990) Knowledge of the numeration system among pre-schoolers. In L. Steffe & T. Wood (Eds.), *Transforming early childhood education: International perspectives* (pp.135–141). Hillsdale, NJ: Erlbaum.

Pascual-Leone, J. (1970). A mathematical model for the transition rule in Piaget's developmental stages. *Acta Psychologica, 32,* 301–345.

Rapin, I. (1986). Helping deaf children acquire language: Lessons from the past. *International Journal of Paediatric Otorhinolaryngology, 11,* 213–223.

Secada, W. (1984). *Counting in sign: The number string, accuracy and use.* Unpublished doctoral thesis, Northwestern University.

Todman, J., & Seedhouse, E. (1994). Visual-action code processing by deaf and hearing children. *Language and Cognitive Processes, 4,* 129–141.

Traxler, C. B. (2000). The Stanford Achievement Test, 9th Edition: National norming and performance standards for deaf and hard-of-hearing students. *Journal of Deaf Studies and Deaf Education, 5,* 337–348.

Zarfaty, Y., Nunes, T., & Bryant, P. (2004). The performance of young deaf children in spatial and temporal number tasks. *Journal of Deaf Studies and Deaf Education, 9,* 315–326.

CHAPTER 6

PERFORMANCE DATA AND PROVEN PRACTICES

Empowering Tools to Spur High Levels of Student Reasoning and Achievement

Tom Luce and Lee Thompson

One key to spurring student achievement is knowing to what level students can perform. A second key is knowing how to bring about such achievement. These two statements appear self-evident. They would seemingly be the first questions one would ask when striving to improve student performance. Unfortunately, this has often not been the case. Poor performance—particularly on the part of minority students and those in poverty—is too often explained but not determined by socioeconomic circumstances or lack of ability. But even those educators who do not accept these fictions and believe that all students can be competent learners battle a second hurdle: how to enable all students to master curricula. Enabling all students to perform at high levels is more complex than simply instructing them in the material; it calls for recognizing students' particular needs and strengths and facilitating students' use of

Optimizing Student Success in School With the Other Three Rs:
Reasoning, Resilience, and Responsibility, 95–109
Copyright © 2006 by Information Age Publishing

higher levels of reasoning, so that they truly learn the material—and are prepared to advance in their education.

The good news is that two proven, replicable tools can build the capacity of educators and others to spur such high levels of student achievement. First, student-linked, privacy-protected longitudinal performance data empower us to determine how students are performing. Such data also enable us to determine students' potential for improvement in the near term by comparing their performance against other students who performed better and yet have similar socioeconomic characteristics. Second, educators can employ practices proven to encourage high levels of student achievement—practices that high-performing schools with disadvantaged socioeconomic circumstances use with success, such as employing districtwide teams of pre-kindergarten through 12th-grade teachers who ensure that there is a continuum of curriculum between grades. Effective use of these tools—using the approach described in this chapter—clearly establishes that in every sort of student population, every subject, and every grade, there are schools achieving outstanding results and that the methods that high performers are using are accessible and replicable. Thus, no matter what the circumstances are of a particular school—no matter how challenging they are—there are examples of similarly situated schools that are delivering an excellent education to their students. Effective use of data and best practices, then, is proven to enable students to overcome what have traditionally been obstacles and to use high-level academic skills and reasoning to attain exceptional achievement levels.

Proposals concerning the use of data and how best to educate students clutter the educational research field, leading to confusion as to what approach works best, reticence to change from current practices, and frustration after well-meaning reforms do not improve student knowledge levels and academic performance. This chapter addresses how those responsible for our children's education can most effectively structure and use data and educational best practices to bring about academic achievement by all students. First we explain the appreciable role data and best practices play in promoting high student achievement. Second, we describe how to employ data and study high-performing schools to determine what educational practices really work.

THE KEY ROLE OF DATA AND BEST PRACTICES: SHOW ME THE EVIDENCE

Researchers and educators have debated for decades how to promote high student achievement. Influential reports produced in the 1960s and 1970s claimed that a student's socioeconomic circumstances largely determined academic achievement, and that school experiences had little effect (Coleman et al.,1966; Jencks et al., 1972). Numerous scholars since have refuted this position. The Effective Schools Movement led by Lawrence Lezotte, Ron Edmonds, and Wilbur Brookover established that each child is able to learn. They also determined that schools control the factors that enable each child to master a core curriculum. In addition, studies associated with the Effective School Movement found that schools that educated all students successfully had various common characteristics, including their use of data and proven practices to enhance student achievement (Lezotte, 2001).

Yet, educators have needed more clarity and specificity than had been provided by the Effective School Movement and other literature as to exactly what to do to improve the performance of all students. They have tried an array of approaches to improve students' learning experiences—from various curricula, to smaller class sizes, to increased monetary investment in schools. Some have succeeded, others have not. Educators and policymakers have often acted without a map; frequently, decisions have been made based on current sentiment that, for example, favors a certain teaching method, and not on solid research that establishes a program's effectiveness (Chall, 2000; Hacsi, 2002; Slavin & Fashola, 1998).

Two primary factors have hampered evidence-based reform: First, the status of the field of educational research has historically been weak and, second, there has largely been a disconnect between education research and the practices that educators employ (Chall, 2000; Hacsi, 2002; Shavelson & Towne, 2003). The reputation of educational research has traditionally been poor, suffering from low quality, lack of objectivity, and contested findings, particularly when compared with research in fields such as medicine and the physical sciences. Consequently, policymakers and educators have felt free to ignore research results (Shavelson & Towne, 2003). The result has often been a disconcerting shift from one promising reform to another—each lacking substantiating evidence that they work—without attaining the ultimate goal: gains in student achievement (Hacsi, 2002). Furthermore, educators and other reform implementers often fail to recognize that the provision of an excellent education is systemic: no single strategy, movement, or reform results in high student performance. As educators in high-performing school systems know, effective instruction results from interdependent, evidence-based strategies tailored by local influences.

Fortunately, we may be heralding a new era in education reform; increasingly those in the field call for programs that are well researched and backed by data of their effectiveness (Corcoran, Fuhrman, & Belcher, 2001; Slavin, 2003). In the federal government, the shift has been clear. Two major pieces of recent education legislation—the No Child Left

Behind Act of 2001 and the Education Sciences Reform Act of 2002—stress the requirement that federally sponsored research be scientifically based, meaning it must be rigorous, objective, and systematic. Indeed, the No Child Left Behind Act mentions scientifically based research 111 times. Likewise, many in the education field are promoting the value of evidence-driven decisions (Chall, 2000; Feldman, Lucey, Goodrich, & Frazee, 2003; Marzano, 2003; Schmoker, 2001, 1996; Slavin & Fashola, 1998).

One particularly hopeful finding that flows from this research is that some perennially low-performing schools with student populations in challenging circumstances (e.g., a high percentage of students in poverty) have attained substantial improvement in student achievement. Two crucial keys to these gains are administrators' and teachers' use of student achievement data to drive decisions and their employment of proven, replicable practices to encourage student achievement (Marzano, 2003; Schmoker, 2002). The following sections explore why these elements are fundamental to attaining high student achievement and the precise process for successfully employing these tools.

USING THE DATA

A core element of effective educational research is basing evaluation and decision making on data. Data provide quantifiable evidence of how students are performing, where improvements are needed, and what circumstances are resulting in high achievement. Furthermore, it is clear from the overwhelming bipartisan approval of the federal No Child Left Behind Act that academic assessment is here to stay. How we collect the data created by our testing systems will be the key to using assessment as a tool to actually improve academic performance school by school. With hard facts in hand, educators, parents, and policymakers can have productive discussions concerning student achievement and set clear goals for improved academic performance. Without such data, incomplete information dictates dialogue and decisions; all concerned are left to guess as to how students are performing and on how best to educate them (American Association of School Administrators [AASA], n.d.).

Research establishes that high-performing school systems employ student performance data to make targeted, effective educational decisions. The Education Trust identified 366 schools in high-poverty circumstances—circumstances that traditionally have resulted in low student performance—in 21 states. One key to their success: "monitoring systems ... for providing ongoing analysis of student achievement data" (Barth et al., 1999, p. 9). As discussed below, studies by the National Center for

Educational Accountability have likewise determined that one practice that differentiates high-performing school systems from average-performing school systems is high performers' effective monitoring of student and school performance through student assessments.

Sadly, in no field is data more fragmented and disparate than in education. Fifty different systems of state standards and state assessment regimes result in a labyrinth that can frustrate anyone trying to determine how schools and students are performing. Add to this mix the dissimilar state methods of collecting data, with some states recording comprehensive performance information and others just cursory data, and the result is an incongruent and often frustratingly incomplete dataset. Yet making sense of this data is crucial to ensuring that all students learn and identifying exemplars of excellence for others to emulate.

To meet the requirements mandated by the No Child Left Behind Act, states are disaggregating their test results by student gender, race, disability status, ethnicity, migrant status, economically disadvantaged status, and English proficiency. As various states press to comply, states should look upon the mandates of the No Child Left Behind Act as an opportunity to retool and optimize their data systems in order to maximize student learning (Dougherty, 2002; Rudner & Boston, 2003).

EMPLOYING STUDENT PERFORMANCE DATA TO MAXIMIZE STUDENT ACHIEVEMENT

The National Center for Educational Accountability has worked for years on how to employ privacy-protected, student-linked longitudinal performance data to promote student achievement gains. Others, too, have recognized the value of analyzing data to trace student performance over time and make targeted reforms (Campanile, 2003; Hunt, 2003; Moore, 2003). The National Center, operating under its trade name, Just for the Kids (JFTK), has developed a unique data analysis approach in terms of its accessibility and easily comprehendible format.

The Just for the Kids approach views data as the beginning—not the end—of the reform process. It employs data to indicate how students are performing in each school, points the way to high-performing schools in similar circumstances as your school, and presents the practices that those high performers in like circumstances to your school are using to attain results, all with the goal of enabling your school to get better results. Central to the Just for the Kids approach is the principle that if a school is performing at a higher level than yours with student demographics (e.g., the percentage of students in poverty or who are English language learners) that are equally or more challenging than your school's student demographics, your students can reach that level of performance as well.

States across the nation employ the JFTK approach—from Washington to Texas to New Jersey. In addition, the National Center in partnership with Standard & Poor's School Evaluation Services produced a website, www.schoolresults.org, that provided online data tools to aid all 50 states in fulfilling the data reporting and analysis requirements of the No Child Left Behind Act at no cost to states; the project was funded by the Broad Foundation and the U.S. Department of Education.

Research conducted by JFTK confirms the effectiveness of the approach: in a random sample of 168 Texas elementary schools, researchers found that schools that employed the JFTK data and best practice information to set goals, study high-performing schools, or make program or staff changes attained from 3–8% greater gains in proficiency scores on Texas state assessments in reading, math, and writing between 1999 and 2001 than comparable schools that did not employ JFTK data and best practice info (Dougherty & Collins, 2002).

As Columbia Law School Professors James S. Liebman and Charles F. Sabel have noted, JFTK acts as an intermediary between the state education agencies that generate data (which these agencies often present in an incomprehensible format to nonstatisticians) and educators, parents, and the public by presenting student performance data and the best practices of high-performing schools in an easily accessible and usable format. JFTK thus "provides parents with the most useful data for building a constituency for reform" while it also "most effectively culls best practices from the successes of the leading schools and districts for use by less successful institutions" (Liebman & Sabel, 2003, p. 1738).

We first discuss the first component of the JFTK approach—that is, the organization and use of student performance data. Next we turn to the second and equally integral component of the JFTK tools: the best practices of high-performing schools.

JFTK data analysis involves six core concepts; each is crucial to the effectiveness of the approach. The resulting JFTK data analysis method is both replicable across the country and easily accessible to educators, parents, policymakers, and the general public.

Step 1: Work with States to Improve the Accuracy and Completeness of Student Performance Data. As noted above, the rigor and comprehensiveness of data systems vary dramatically from state to state. As states—and the districts and schools in those states—augment their data collection and reporting to meet the requirements of the No Child Left Behind Act, it is crucial that they include certain components not specifically required by the federal statute. These elements will enable states, districts, schools, and others to use data as a tool to pinpoint how students are performing at each grade level in each school, where improvement is needed, and which schools are successfully eliciting and supporting high achievement. Thus, National Center research concludes that effective data collection must incorporate nine essential elements:

1. **A unique statewide personal identification number for each student,** which enables us to see how that student performed over time;

2. **Enrollment data for each student,** including information on each student's school of enrollment, ethnicity, gender, grade level, economic disadvantaged status, and participation in programs such as bilingual education and special education;

3. **State test data for each student,** with the capability to disaggregate the data by individual test questions and academic skill;

4. **Data on untested students** to ensure accuracy in the performance profile of a certain school;

5. **Course completion information for each student,** including advanced courses to indicate each student's preparation level for college;

6. **SAT, ACT, and Advanced Placement results for each student,** which also indicate each student's readiness for college;

7. **Graduation and dropout data for all students;**

8. **Audit process to ensure the accuracy of state data,** involving statistical checks of information school districts submit, criteria for identifying when district data may be erroneous, investigation of the flagged data, spot checking of data that is not flagged, and imposition of penalties on school districts that submit incorrect or incomplete information; and

9. **Capacity to link K–12 and higher education data at the student level** to show how high school students perform in college.

Only through these essential elements of data collection can we ensure that all students are accounted for and that uses of the data in the following steps reflect a true picture of student performance (Dougherty, 2003).

Step 2: Track Performance of Students Over Time. Assessing how students perform over time holds vast advantages over taking a one-time look at how students performed in a certain year. It also enables us to ascertain which students have attended a school for some time, and which have recently transferred into a school. This information allows us to focus on the performance of students who have attended a school over a number of years as evidence of achievement levels at the school. Just for the Kids analysis, for example, considers students who have been enrolled in a school for three years or more as being "continuously enrolled" at the school; it is the performance of these continuously enrolled students that JFTK analysis concentrates on.

Step 3: Compare School Performance on an Apples-to-Apples Basis and Identify High-Performing Schools with Equally or More Disadvantaged Student Populations. Using the data made available through Steps 1 and 2, we can ascertain student performance at each school in each grade and each subject matter. We can then compare student performance at each school with schools across the state whose students performed at a higher level and that have equally or more disadvantaged student populations based on the percentage of economically disadvantaged students and English language learners. This enables us to pinpoint who the top comparable schools are for each grade and subject.

Step 4: Identify the Opportunity Gap for Each School. Through this apples-to-apples comparison of schools, we can learn the potential achievement level of each school in the near term based on evidence of how others in like or more difficult circumstances are performing. This potential for improvement—termed the "opportunity gap"—indicates the difference between the performance of continuously enrolled students in a certain subject and grade and the performance of continuously enrolled students in that grade and subject at top comparable schools. If an opportunity gap exists in that grade and subject, educators and parents can easily see that higher levels of student achievement are possible, and that justifying lower performance on the basis of challenging circumstances is not appropriate. Thus, using student performance information to recognize who the top comparable schools are can help inspire lower-performing schools to reach similar high levels.

Step 5: Track School Performance Over Time. Accurate and complete data collection not only enables us to see how a school performed during a certain year, but also how that school performed over time. Through data that track school performance over time, educators and parents can clearly see whether student achievement in that grade and subject is increasing or decreasing. Such results would indicate, for example, whether a curriculum that was instituted in 2000 has had a positive effect on student performance; whether teachers are having success in teaching their students or whether they may need additional instructional support; and whether students have improved or are in need of extra help in a certain subject.

Step 6: Identify Consistently High-Performing Schools Across Grades, Subjects, and Years for Best-Practice Studies. Complete and accurate data collection also makes possible the identification of schools that have been consistently high performing across multiple grades, years, and subjects. (This is distinct from pinpointing the top performing schools for a single grade, subject, and year in Steps 2 through 5.) Identifying consistently high-performing schools forms the foundation for the vital study of educational best practices. Discussed below, such best-practice research focuses on schools that are identified as high performing over a number of years, subjects, and grades and compares these perennial high performers to consistently average-performing schools in order to pinpoint what the high-performing schools are doing to enable their students to excel.

For such best-practice research to accurately reflect the practices of high performers, the identification of which schools have demonstrated consistent high performance must come through a rigorous and reliable approach. These consistent high performers must meet far more stringent criteria than the top comparable schools, which are highlighted because of their comparatively high performance in a single grade, subject, and year. Factors considered in the identification of consistent high performers are (1) the school's performance on the state's assessment test, (2) the demographic characteristics of the student body, including the percent of economically disadvantaged students, and (3) the students' preparation for the school (e.g., when analyzing tenth graders, considering the average eighth-grade scores of students the year before entering high school).

The analysis compares the performance of each school in each tested grade and subject to the average performance of demographically similar schools in those same grades and subjects. The school's distance from this average is ranked among schools with similar schoolwide percentages of economically disadvantaged students, and all of the ranks for that school for a single subject—across 3 years and multiple grades—are averaged to give an overall performance ranking of the campus for a particular subject. Those campuses whose overall ranks are considered among the best are identified as high performing in the subject. If they are subsequently identified as high performing across multiple subjects, they may be selected for best-practice research.

The effective use of data enables one to see how a school's students are performing and to recognize the level they can attain. Educators, policymakers, and parents are thus empowered by information and can be assured that when they make decisions concerning children's education, their actions can be specific and structured to spur academic achievement by all students.

ACTING ON THE DATA: DETERMINING AND PRACTICING WHAT IS WORKING IN SCHOOLS

By analyzing data that result from the techniques described above, educators, parents, and others can see which schools with similar student characteristics are performing at a higher level than theirs. Most importantly, educators and policymakers can then contact these high-performing schools to learn what they are doing to attain this achievement (AASA, n.d).

Furthermore, more extensive best-practice studies provide educators with specific educational practices to emulate in order to attain results. A broad number of researchers now concentrate on "proven practices" and on the foundational components of those practices, including:

- clear and rigorous academic standards that specify what students should know at each level,
- methods for assessing the effectiveness of those standards,
- the alignment of instructional methods and materials with the standards, and
- adjusting those standards, methods, and materials based on feedback from student performance (Lezotte, 2001; Marzano, 2003; University of Pittsburgh Institute for Learning, n.d.; What Works Clearinghouse, n.d.).

Through a 4-year best practice study of hundreds of school systems located across the country, Just for the Kids has developed a rigorous, encompassing process to determine what differentiates the practices employed by high-performing versus average-performing schools and districts in states across the country (see www.just4kids.org/bestpractice/). Central to the integrity of the process is the strong link it makes between best practices and data concerning student performance. (No other study, to our knowledge, uses student performance data as such an integral element to determine exactly who the high-performing schools and districts are and how specifically their performance differs from average performers.)

The findings from this process are specific, immediately applicable, and fall into five major themes:

- curriculum and academic goals;
- staff selection, leadership, and capacity building;
- instructional programs, practices, and arrangements;
- monitoring, compilation, analysis, and use of data; and
- recognition of high performance and intervention and adjustment in areas of performance weaknesses.

Three elements undergird effective practices. First, although the core elements of best practice remain constant among high-performing school systems, the specific methods that high performers use to carry out these practices vary depending on local circumstances. For example, one school district might schedule a shared meeting period for teachers to discuss curriculum while another may establish an electronic discussion board to serve the same purpose. Second, educators at the district, school, and classroom levels must each employ distinct yet complimentary best practices. Third, there must be a distribution of responsibility among district, school, and classroom educators to accomplish educational goals to avoid overburdening classroom teachers with too much responsibility for student performance. For instance, successful staff selection and capacity building occurs (1) through district selection of instructional leaders who further the academic goals of district schools; (2) when these instructional specialists and master teachers ensure that each teacher in each district school is using effective teaching strategies; and (3) when classroom teachers meet with others who teach the same grade or subject matter to coordinate curriculum and instructional strategies. This three-tiered approach ensures that district and school administration foster excellent instruction and that teachers deliver high-quality teaching.

The rigorous process that the National Center developed to pinpoint these determinative practices includes four steps. The process is highly replicable: Any study that is trying to determine what spurs high academic performance can effectively employ this four-step approach.

Step 1: Compare High-Performing Schools and Districts to Average Performers: The Importance of a Control Group. Rather than comparing high-performing schools and districts to low performers, the better approach is to compare those schools and districts that are excelling with those that are average performing. This allows for the identification of specific factors that high-performing school systems incorporate at the district, school, and classroom levels that allow students to excel. In addition, the inclusion of average-performing school systems as a control group is crucial for the study to be valid and useful. In the absence of control groups, researchers simply cannot ascertain whether a given practice or program influences performance levels, and thus whether it is a factor that is driving high performance (Bainbridge, 2003; Slavin, 2003; Slavin & Fashola, 1998).

Step 2: Apply Strict Criteria Regarding Which Schools and Districts to Include in the Study. The study should base school and district selection as a high performer or average performer on student achievement data to a significant degree. Criteria should be demanding and include, for example, how students continuously enrolled in the school or district for at least 3 years performed vis-à-vis continuously enrolled students at other schools or districts; how the school or district compares to similar schools or districts in the number of students who score at a proficient level on state assessments; and whether there was a certain minimum number of continuously enrolled students in each tested subject, grade, and year. Researchers should then further cull the pool of average- and high-performing schools and districts in order for those studied to represent the geographic and demographic spectrum of the state or area under study. This culling takes into account the poverty, language proficiency, and ethnicity of students at each school and district as well as the location of the school and district. It also includes further examination of student performance.

Step 3: Conduct Rigorous, Thorough Site Visits to Both High- and Average-Performing Schools and Districts and Perform Document Collection. Researchers should visit high-performing and average-performing schools and districts to conduct interviews and focus groups with district, school, and classroom educators. At times, these conversations also include school board members, community members, parents, and students. It is also crucial for researchers to gather documents in order to pinpoint effective practices. By analyzing in detail what schools and districts with high student achievement are doing that those with average student achievement are not, researchers can make specific, targeted conclusions for others to emulate.

Step 4: Study and Specify Best Practices at the Classroom, School, and District Levels. Researchers increasingly stress how important a systemic approach to education reform is. Because the quality of education that a student receives is influenced by educators at the district, school, and classroom levels, we must ensure that educators at all three levels are using effective practices in order for students to receive a high-quality education (Lezotte, 2001, p. 3; Snipes, Doolittle, & Herlihy, 2002, p. 8). Without effective action at the district and school level, classroom teachers bear an unsustainable burden to improve student achievement on their own. In addition, only at the district level can administrators ensure that students experience an aligned, quality curriculum from kindergarten through 12th grade. The study, then, should focus on practices that district-, school-, and classroom-level educators employ to ensure sustained student performance (National Center for Educational Accountability, 2003).

Much best-practice information gives educators general principles to follow, but the process outlined here allows us to determine specific practices to employ and helps us to understand the relationships between those practices. Through a rigorous process that includes demanding school selection procedures, a control group of average-performing schools, and the study of practices at the district, school, and classroom levels, we can determine precisely what high-performing schools and districts are doing to reap results.

For too long, educators and policymakers have adopted fruitless reforms—reforms that were promising at face value but that had no research-based track record. The result has been a disappointment for many educators and policymakers and a tragedy for students who then received a poor-quality education. Only when we make decisions based on rigorous evaluation of data and proven best practices will we be able to fulfill a crucial responsibility: to provide an excellent education to every student that enables them to attain high levels of knowledge, reasoning, and achievement and, thus, to thrive academically.

REFERENCES

American Association of School Administrators (AASA). (n.d.). *Using data to improve schools: What's working.* Arlington, VA: Author.

Bainbridge, W. L. (2003). Education research should be nothing to laugh at. *EducationNews.org.* Retrieved January 2, 2004, from http://www.educationnews. org/Educational-Research-Should-Be-Nothing-to-Laugh-At.htm

Barth, P., Haycock, K., Jackson, H., Mora, K., Ruiz, P., Robinson, S., & Wilkins, S. (Eds.). (1999). *Dispelling the myth: High poverty schools exceeding expectations.* Washington, DC: Education Trust.

Campanile, C. (2003, July 7). Firm will create city online-up of schools. *New York Post,* p. 2.

Chall, J. S. (2000). *The academic achievement challenge: What really works in the classroom?* New York: Guilford Press.

Corcoran, T., Fuhrman, S.H., & Belcher, C.L. (2001). The district role in instructional improvement. *Phi Delta Kappan, 83*(1), 78–84.

Coleman, J. S., Campbell, E. Q., Hobson, C. J., McPartland, J., Mood, A. M., Weinfield, F. D., & York, R. L. (1966). *Equality of educational opportunity.* Washington, DC: United States Department of Health, Education, and Welfare, Office of Education.

Dougherty, C. (2002). States must improve data for adequate yearly progress. *Education Assessment Insider, 1*(5), 6–7.

Dougherty, C. (2003). *Nine essential elements of statewide data-collection systems.* Austin, TX: National Center for Educational Accountability.

Dougherty, C., & Collins, S. (2002). Use of the Just for the Kids data by Texas elementary schools (National Center for Educational Accountability Research Report #1). Austin, TX: National Center for Educational Accountability. Retrieved January 2, 2004, from http://www.nc4ea.org/files/implementation%20study%201-30-02.pdf

Feldman, J., Lucey, G., Goodrich, S., & Frazee, D. (2003). Developing an inquiry-minded district. *Educational Leadership, 60*(5). Retrieved January 2, 2004, from http://www.ascd.org/publications/ed_lead/200302/feldman.html

Hacsi, T. A. (2002). *Children as pawns: The politics of educational reform.* Cambridge, MA: Harvard University Press.

Hunt, J. B. (2003, Spring). Unrecognized progress. *Education Next*, pp. 24–27.

Jencks, C., Smith, M., Acland, H., Bane, M. J., Cohen, D., Gintis, H., et al. (1972). *Inequality: A reassessment of the effect of family and schooling in America.* New York: Basic Books.

Lezotte, L. W. (2001). *Revolutionary and evolutionary: The Effective Schools Movement.* Retrieved January 2, 2004, from http://schools.tdsb.on.ca/albertcampbell/spri/docs/Revolutionary.pdf

Liebman, J. S., & Sabel, C. F. (2003). The Federal No Child Left Behind Act and the post-desegregation civil rights agenda. *North Carolina Law Review, 81*(4), 1703–1749.

Marzano, R. J. (2003). *What works in schools: Translating research into action.* Alexandria, VA: Association for Supervision and Curriculum Development.

Moore, M. (2003, July 9). NCPA's value-added report card on Texas schools: A model for meaningful assessments. *NCPA Brief Analysis, 446.*

National Center for Educational Accountability. (2003). *Texas best practice study background and significance.* Unpublished manuscript.

Rudner, L. M., & Boston, C. (2003). Data warehousing: Beyond disaggregation. *Educational Leadership, 60*(5), 62–65.

Schmoker, M. (1996). *Results: The key to continuous school improvement.* Alexandria, VA: Assocation for Supervision and Curriculum Development.

Schmoker, M. (2001). *The results fieldbook: practical strategies from dramatically improved schools.* Alexandria, VA: Association for Supervision and Curriculum Development.

Schmoker, M. (2002). Up and away. *Journal of Staff Development, 23*(2). Retrieved August 19, 2003, from http://www.nsdc.org/library/jsd/schmoker232.html

Shavelson, R. J., & Towne, L. (Eds.). (2003). *Scientific research in education.* Washington, DC: National Academy Press.

Slavin, R. E. (2003). A reader's guide to scientifically based research. *Educational Leadership, 40*(3), 12–16.

Slavin, R. E., & Fashola, O. S. (1998). *Show me the evidence! Proven and promising programs for America's schools.* Thousand Oaks, CA: Corwin Press.

Snipes, J., Doolittle, F., & Herlihy, C. (2002). *Foundations for success: Case studies of how urban school systems improve student achievement,* Executive Summary. New York: MDRC of the Council of the Great City Schools. Retrieved July 29, 2004, from http://www.mdrc.org/publications/47/execsum.html

University of Pittsburgh Institute for Learning (n.d.). *Principles of learning.* Retrieved January 2, 2004, from http://www.lrdc.pitt.edu/netlearn/POL/polframepage.htm

What Works Clearinghouse (n.d.). *Evidence report topics.* Retrieved January 2, 2004, from http://www.w-w-c.org/b4.html

PART II

RESILIENCE

CHAPTER 7

RESILIENCE AND RISK IN LEARNING

Complex Interactions and Comprehensive Interventions

Mary E. Walsh and Mary M. Brabeck

The pendulum of education reform swings widely, and sometimes wildly depending on prevailing views about factors that affect the achievements of school-age children. As early as the mid-19th century, Francis Galton argued that hereditary factors determine one's biologically ordained intelligence quotient (IQ) (Robinson, 1976). This argument has a long history and was advanced most recently in the controversial book *The Bell Curve* (Herrnstein & Murray, 1994). The book has been challenged on methodological, theoretical, and philosophical bases, and the nature–nurture debate, particularly when it centers on race and gender, is likely to continue into the future.

In the 1960s, following the research reported by James Coleman and colleagues (1966), socioeconomic variables and factors associated with families were identified as the most influential in affecting school achieve-

Optimizing Student Success in School With the Other Three Rs:
Reasoning, Resilience, and Responsibility, 113–142
Copyright © 2006 by Information Age Publishing
All rights of reproduction in any form reserved.

ment. Coleman's report deemphasized the effects of classroom factors (e.g., teachers, curriculum, class size) on achievement, and one can surmise that this report was influential in moving psychological research away from classrooms. In the words of Coleman and his colleagues, "When the socioeconomic background of the students is taken into account...it appears that differences between schools account for only a small fraction of differences in pupil achievement" (pp. 21–22).

However, in the 1990s the focus of education reform switched to the classroom. Following his influential 1998 study, William Sanders reported, "The single biggest factor affecting academic growth of any population of youngsters is the effectiveness of the individual classroom teacher. The answer to why children learn well or not isn't race, it isn't poverty, it isn't even per-pupil expenditure at the elementary level. It's teachers, teachers, teachers" (Sanders, 1999). As a nation, we are now rushing to develop standardized tests to measure "adequate yearly progress" in learning. When classrooms, teachers, and schools do not meet the challenge, children are offered the opportunity to be removed to what is perceived as a more promising environment.

These three arguments are similar in that they are all single-factor models. However, developmental research over the past two decades clearly indicates that a host of behavioral outcomes, including academic achievement, are the result of the complex interaction of many variables over the course of development (Lerner, Walsh, & Howard, 1998).

As an example of the complex interactions that impact developmental outcomes, Turkheimer, Haley, Waldron, D'Onofrio, and Gottesman (2003) report that the influence of genes on intelligence varies by class. Turkheimer and colleagues' study draws from the National Collaborative Perinatal Project, which started in the late 1960s and was funded by the National Institutes of Health. The sample consisted of almost 50,000 pregnant women, and more than half of these women were African American and living in poverty. The women's median incomes were $22,000 or less in 1997 dollars, one out of every four women in the sample were not educated past the ninth grade, and most of the employed women were "service workers." Turkheimer and colleagues found that the impact of environmental factors on their children's IQ was four times stronger for the poorest families than the wealthiest families. Furthermore, the lower a child's socioeconomic status, the less impact genetic inheritance had on IQ.

In a similar vein, M. Beth Casey (1996; Casey & Brabeck, 1989) has been studying the subgroup of women (Casey & Brabeck, 1990) who excel in mental rotation skill, the spatial skill with the most robust and universal findings of gender differences. They have found that women who excel in the ability to mentally rotate objects have *both* a biological predisposition as marked by handedness as well as the experiences associated with male behaviors (e.g., tomboyism, involvement in sports). Once again, multiple factors are implicated in the development of complex human behaviors such as spatial ability.

Resilient children and youth are both academically successful and psychologically healthy. Understanding the factors that lead to such positive outcomes is critical. It makes intuitive sense that good teaching, good genetics, and a good family will result in high academic achievement and well-being (Kagan, 1990; Kagan, Moore, & Bredekamp, 1995). However, it is difficult to know precisely which factors contribute to such outcomes and at what developmental points. The specific teaching variables that produce high achievement remain unknown (Wilson, Floden, & Ferrini-Mundy, 2001). It has been equally challenging to identify the psychosocial factors that affect well-being (Becker & Luthar, 2002). One factor that repeatedly emerges in the literature as contributing to both decreased achievement and poor psychological well-being is poverty.

POVERTY AND ITS EFFECTS

It is clear from the research that poverty affects students' learning and that the number of children living in poverty is high (McLoyd, 1998; McLoyd & Wilson, 1990). The Annie E. Casey Foundation (1999) reports that the percentage of children and youth living in poor neighborhoods where there are large numbers of welfare recipients, unemployed individuals, and single-parent families increased from 3% in 1970 to 17% in 1990. More than 4 million of these children are under the age of 6 (McLoyd & Wilson, 1990; National Center for Children in Poverty, 2002). Poverty also interacts with race. Poverty rates are highest among Native American, African American, and Hispanic children; among children living in single-parent, female-headed households; and among urban residents (National Center for Children in Poverty, 2002). On average, poor children and children living near the poverty level perform significantly less well than non-poor and middle-class children on many indicators of academic achievement, including achievement test scores, mathematics grades, grade retentions, course failures, placement in special education, high school graduation rate, high school dropout rate, and completed years of schooling (Conger, Conger, & Elder, 1997; Entwisle & Alexander, 1990; Haveman & Wolfe, 1995; Hill & Duncan, 1987; Patterson, Kupersmidt, & Vaden, 1990; White, 1982). Among traditional indicators of socioeconomic status (SES), family income is the highest single correlate of academic achievement (White, 1982). Despite the growing support for state and federally funded programs designed to boost early childhood literacy and learning, children's socioeconomic status has remained a robust predictor of their academic achievement (Barton, 2001).

Research has demonstrated that students are less likely to succeed when they live in communities that are economically deprived, disorganized, and lacking in opportunities for employment or youth involvement (Hawkins, Catalano, & Miller, 1992). The negative aspects of such neighborhoods have effects on childhood IQ and school-leaving, even after the differences in the socioeconomic characteristics of families are taken into account. For example, the socioeconomic mix of children's neighborhoods is related to the number of completed years of schooling. Research has demonstrated that youth who grow up in affluent communities or communities with a higher percentage of affluent families complete more years of school and have lower school dropout rates than youth from similar families who grow up in poor neighborhoods or neighborhoods with fewer affluent families (Brooks-Gunn, Duncan, Klebov, & Sealand, 1993). Recently, researchers have begun to acknowledge that witnessing community violence has a negative impact on students' learning capability as well (Overstreet & Braun, 1999; Shavers, 2000; Skurulsky, 2001).

While challenges are greatest for children living in poverty, the stakes are high for *all* of today's youth. The 2001 Youth Behavior Survey (Centers for Disease Control and Prevention, 2002) indicated that the following percentages of 14- to 17-year-olds in the United States engaged in diverse problem behaviors:

- Sexual activity: 33.4% had engaged in sexual intercourse during the prior 3 months, and 14.2% had four or more sexual partners in their lifetime.
- Substance abuse: 29.9% had five or more drinks on one or more occasion during the prior 30 days, 28.5% had smoked cigarettes at least once during the prior 30 days, and 42.4% had smoked marijuana at least once in their lifetime.
- Suicide: during the prior 12 months, 8.8% reported attempting suicide, and 19.0% had seriously considered suicide.
- Violence: during the preceding 12 months, 33.2% had been involved in a physical fight, and during the prior 30 days, 5.7% had carried a gun.

While research has shown that poverty negatively impacts learning, the real challenge is identifying the ways in which poverty can limit academic achievement (Bronfenbrenner, 1979; Murray & Weissbourd, 2003; Schorr, 1988). A number of factors that appear to be associated with poverty are also known to impact achievement. They include biological factors (e.g., nutrition, health status) (Barton, 2003; Center on Hunger, Poverty, and

Nutrition Policy, 1993; Murphy et al., 1998; Needleman, Schell, Bellinger, Leviton, & Allred, 1990; Taylor, Klein, & Hack, 2000), psychological factors (e.g., school engagement, school readiness, social-emotional functioning, family engagement) (Books, 1998), and social factors (e.g., community stability, violence levels, environmental health conditions are related to achievement) (Books, 1998).

RESILIENCY

Although children and youth are confronted with many risks and challenges, there is a substantial body of research that points to the ability of children to "spring back, rebound, successfully adapt in the face of adversity and develop social, academic, and vocational competence despite exposure to severe stress or simply to the stress inherent in today's world" (Henderson & Milstein, 1996, p. 7). In fact, studies indicate that upwards of 50% of children who have faced significant adversity (e.g., extreme poverty, abuse, death of a parent) nevertheless develop into competent adults who are able to maintain healthy relationships, are gainfully employed, and are hopeful about the future (Werner & Smith, 1992).

Historically, psychological research has tended to focus on the deficits that children bring with them into the classroom (e.g., learning disabilities, behavioral problems, low-income families). However, researchers are increasingly realizing the importance of paying attention not only to children's deficits, but also to their strengths. Research by Milbrey McLaughlin (1994) has indicated that some urban youth have "beat the odds," far exceeding the bleak expectations for children who have encountered severe adversity. These inner-city youth have participated in effective neighborhood programs that offer community support, guidance from older mentors, enriching activities, and a safe haven, all of which seem to have mediated the potentially harmful effects of their adverse circumstances. Rather than focusing solely on the risks that inner-city youth face, these neighborhood-based programs have chosen to focus on the strengths that these children possess and their potential for resiliency. Similarly, Peter Benson, the president of Search Institute, has focused his research on the assets of youth that can be utilized to foster positive development in the face of adversity (Benson, 1993; Benson, Scales, & Roehlkepartain, 1998).

This capacity of children for resiliency has recently prompted some researchers to investigate what factors play a role in protecting children from long-term negative consequences. Studies on resiliency have found that a number of characteristics are associated with children who manifest normal development and achievement despite the significant challenges that they face (Masten & Coatsworth, 1998). Some of these protective factors are internal to or can be developed by the child (e.g., intelligence, pleasant disposition, self-confidence, faith, personal talents), others are related to the child's family (healthy child–parent relationship, discipline in the home), and still others are related to factors external to the child and family (supportive community, attending effective schools, good relationships with other adults). Of these factors, it seems that the two most important characteristics of resilient children are a healthy relationship with a caring parent or mentor and good intellectual capability (Masten & Coatsworth, 1998). In short, psychologists and educators are realizing that while it is crucial to assess the risks that children face in order to address their needs, it is equally important to consider children's assets and strengths and to utilize these positive factors in prevention and intervention programs.

In the remaining pages of this chapter we examine the impact of some of the psychological variables associated with academic resilience, learning, and achievement. We show that these factors, in turn, are related to family, community, and school conditions. We then discuss a complex community intervention that includes diverse professionals and is designed to address a wide range of mediating variables, and we present some preliminary analyses of the outcomes from our work that are directed at promoting resiliency in children and youth.

SCHOOL ENGAGEMENT

School engagement, sometimes referred to as school attachment, has been defined as "student interest in school, perceived support from teachers, and feelings of belonging to and valuing school" (Somers & Gizzi, 2001, p. 3). School attachment serves as either a risk or protective (resiliency) factor for adolescents and school-age children. Lack of attachment is typically referred to as school disengagement and characterizes students who are lonely, isolated, and alienated from the school community. DeWitt (1996) identified three components of attachment: academic aspects of the school; relationships with friends, teachers, and other school personnel; and extracurricular activities.

Children living in poverty tend to experience lower levels of school engagement. Tout, Scarpa, and Zaslow (2002) have shown that children in low-income families (e.g., families currently receiving welfare, families that recently left welfare, and families with poverty-level incomes but no recent history of welfare) fare worse on measures of school engagement than children in more affluent families (Tout et al., 2002; Vandivere, Moore, & Brown, 2000)

Numerous studies have demonstrated the impact of school engagement on academic achievement (Stipek, 1997). From their early school years, students who are not given opportunities to become engaged in school are at risk for school failure, alienation, and dropping out (Rossi & Montgomery, 1994). While the impact of school attachment on academic achievement is important for all teens, the effect is stronger for teens in step- or single-divorced families (Boyce Rodgers & Rose, 2001). Battistich, Solomon, Kim, Watson, and Schaps (1995) have demonstrated that a sense of school community is positively associated with a number of measures of academic attitudes and motives, particularly among the students who are most disadvantaged.

School engagement also promotes resiliency by reducing behaviors that limit academic success. When a sample of youth (more than 90,000 students in grades 7–12) felt engaged with or connected to their schools, they were less likely to use alcohol and illegal drugs, less likely to become pregnant, and less likely to experience emotional distress (Blum, McNeely, & Rinehart, 2002). The amount of support that students perceive from their teachers contributes to these kinds of outcomes.

Unengaged students perceive a low level of support and encouragement from the school personnel as well as from their peers (Mouton, Hawkins, McPherson, & Copley, 1996). Numerous studies have linked students' perceptions of teacher support to their academic achievement (Goodenow, 1993; Wentzel & Asher, 1995). Students who feel that their teachers provide encouragement show increased motivation for learning and have more positive academic outcomes (Harachi, Abbott, Catalano, & Haggerty, 1996). In Murdock, Anderman, and Hodge's 2000 study, students' perceptions of their teachers' support were the most consistent and significant predictors of student achievement outcomes. The research on teacher expectations shows a similar pattern. Students' perceptions of teacher expectations are significant predictors of academic outcomes.

In disadvantaged populations, students are more likely to perceive their teachers as having low expectations for their educational potential. There is substantial evidence that teachers' expectations of students are often influenced by student characteristics such as socioeconomic class and ethnicity (Eccles & Harold, 1993). Teachers tend to perceive poor and low-SES students less positively and have lower achievement expectations for them than for non-poor children. These perceptions rest largely on the basis of noncognitive considerations (e.g., speech patterns and dress) (White, 1982). Students of color are also more likely to encounter lower teacher expectations (Murdock et al., 2000). When students perceive that their teachers have low expectations of their academic ability, they are at a clear disadvantage for academic achievement.

SCHOOL READINESS

School readiness is a major protective factor and contributor to successful academic outcomes. School readiness not only describes the child's preparedness to learn when he or she enters kindergarten or first grade, but also describes the child's readiness to engage in school tasks at every level of schooling. While there is less research on school readiness in later elementary, middle, and high school students, it is an important variable in learning across age groups. United States students did well in a recent international comparison of reading achievement of fourth graders, the Progress in International Reading and Literacy Study (PIRLS) (Mullis, Martin, Gonzalez, & Kennedy, 2003). The study also found that home and school early literacy activities were associated with the attainment of reading skills.

The National Center for Education Statistics (NCES) examined PIRLS results within the U.S. sample (Ogle et al., 2003), finding that both race and poverty levels affect reading scores. Using the number of children eligible for free lunches in school as a measure of poverty, researchers found that the higher the poverty level, the lower the scores on PIRLS. In the highest poverty schools, only about 3% of fourth graders reach the top 10% benchmark and only 14% of students in the highest poverty schools reach the upper quartile benchmark. In general, white and Asian students in the United States outperform African American and Latino students. Although the NCES researchers did not analyze the interaction between race and poverty, this interaction would constitute a plausible hypothesis for further study.

Poverty appears to be complicit in PIRLS scores across the 35 countries studied. Boston College researchers reported that in every country, students who live in homes that have large numbers of books perform better. Although there is not a perfect correlation between poverty and the number of books in a household, they are highly correlated. When families are involved in early literacy activities (e.g., singing, playing word games, telling stories), children's scores on PIRLS are higher. Similarly, children whose parents read to them before they enter school score better as fourth graders. Students with the highest scores on PIRLS had parents who enjoyed reading and spent more than an average of 6 hours reading to their children.

The PIRLS results are supported by other data indicating that socioeconomic status (SES) affects school readiness to read (Coley, 2002). While 61% of children in families at or above the poverty line are read to daily, only 48% of children below the poverty line are read to daily (Barton, 2003). Some racial–ethnic differences have also emerged in the research. Using data from the Early Childhood Longitudinal Study kindergarten class of 1998–99, Coley (2002) found that Asian and white students outperformed other racial groups in reading and math proficiency. In a review of the literature, Barton (2003) reports that while 64% of white children are read to daily, only 48% of black and 42% of Hispanic children are read to daily. However, "Nearly all racial/ethnic differences in reading and mathematics disappeared when children were grouped into similar SES" (Coley, 2002, p. 3). Holding SES constant reduced the level of differences between the races, although it did not disappear completely. While white and Asian parents were more likely to read to their children, racial/ethnic differences in at-home reading disappeared when children were grouped by SES, indicating the powerful influence of poverty on student resiliency and academic achievement. As Drew Gitomer, Senior Vice President of Educational Testing Service (ETS), wrote, "Without intervention the future is already being scripted, and it looks to be very consistent with the present" (Coley, 2002, p. 2).

FAMILY ENGAGEMENT

Other family attributes associated with school attendance and achievement among students include monitoring of television viewing, reading to young children on a daily basis, expressing high expectations for academic success, and helping with homework (Barton, 2003; Wang, Haertel, & Walberg, 1997). A recent report from ETS concludes, "Families, of course, are America's smallest schools" (Barton, 2003, p. 36). Active engagement of families (e.g., participating in school management teams, being involved in parent-developed workshops, providing tutoring, assisting teachers in classroom or after-school activities) is associated with improved student achievement, increased school attendance, and decreased student dropout, delinquency, and pregnancy rates. In short, educational intervention programs designed to involve family members are significantly more effective than those targeted exclusively to students (Epstein, Salinas, & Simon, 1996; Ogbu, 1995; Walberg, 1984). An NCES 2001 report indicates that 57% of teachers believe that low parent involvement was a significant problem, and the rate was much higher in high-poverty schools. Since students with involved parents tend to have fewer behavior problems and higher academic achievement, children from low-income families are at a significant disadvantage.

Students who are not supervised after school or return to an empty home confront additional challenges. Risky behavior such as sexual activity, alcohol and drug use, and juvenile crime increase significantly from 3:00 PM to 6:00 PM (Fox & Newman, 1997). Furthermore, violent juvenile crime triples, and children are at a greater risk of being victims of violent crime in the after-school hours (National Institute on Out-of-School Time, 2001). These risk factors contribute significantly to children's academic difficulties (Posner & Vandell, 1999). For example, even when the family's social class and the child's prior adjustment are taken into account, both first and third graders who spent more time unsupervised were less socially competent and received lower academic grades in sixth grade than children who spent less time on their own (Pettit, Laird, Dodge, & Bates, 1997). The Boston After-School Time Study found that children from low-income households displayed more behavior problems such as aggression, defiance, and hyperactivity when they were unsupervised for longer periods of time (Marshall et al., 1997). Despite the obvious need for after-school programming, the U.S. General Accounting Office estimated that in the year 2002, the current number of out-of-school time programs for school-age children would meet as little as 25% of the demand in urban areas (National Institute on Out-of-School Time, 2001). In short, it is evident that family engagement in the lives of children and youth plays a crucial protective role in preventing risky behavior and academic failure.

SOCIOEMOTIONAL FUNCTIONING

As noted earlier, poverty has a profound effect on the socioemotional and academic functioning of children and adolescents. Research has demonstrated that compared to their middle-class peers, children who come from conditions of poverty are more at risk for emotional and behavior problems (Brooks-Gunn et al., 1993; McLoyd, 1998). While poverty has an impact on both externalizing disorders (e.g., conduct problems, fighting, oppositional behaviors) and internalizing disorders (e.g., depression, anxiety), the effects have been found to have a greater influence on externalizing disorders. The risk factors associated with both externalizing disorders and poverty are considerable. Children from impoverished neighborhoods are at greater risk for chronic delinquent behavior, risk-taking behaviors, and persistent antisocial attitudes (McLoyd, 1998). These factors have a reciprocal effect on the family system and the community. In other words, family discord and community violence both influence and in turn are influenced by delinquent and violent behavior.

The effects of poverty on socioemotional functioning are not limited to the family and neighborhoods. Poor socioemotional functioning has also been linked to poor academic performance and school failure. "An important and often-neglected precursor to early adolescent achievement performance and motivation in urban school reform efforts is the state of children's mental health" (Becker & Luthar, 2002, p. 203). Both internalizing and externalizing disorders impact academic functioning. For example, children with internalizing disorders often fail to engage in academic tasks (e.g., homework, studying) that will make them successful (Roeser & Eccles, 2000). Symptoms of depression, an internalizing disorder, are associated with lower grades and standardized test scores, lack of persistence in the face of academic difficulties, and a lack of classroom participation among both children and adolescents (Walsh & Murphy, in press).

Externalizing disorders are also associated with lower teacher-rated grades and standardized test scores, and these students also exhibit more behavioral problems both inside and outside of the classroom. Behavior problems often cause the child to miss class time because the child needs to be removed from the group. In addition, aggressive children are more likely to experience social difficulties in school, such as rejection by peers and disfavor on the part of teachers (Parker & Asher, 1987; Wentzel & Asher, 1995).

Academic difficulty and poor socioemotional functioning can be mutually reinforcing over the course of a child's development. Roeser and Eccles (2000) delineate two pathways that explain how academic and socioemotional difficulties influence one another in terms of the development and course of both internalizing and externalizing disorders. In the first pathway, poor school performance exacerbates socioemotional difficulties due to the child attributing poor performance to his or her own personal incompetence. This in turn leads to feelings of shame, self-doubt, low self-esteem, and alienation, all of which are associated with internalizing disorders. Similarly, children who do poorly in school and attribute their poor performance to others often experience the feelings of anger, alienation, and hostility that are associated with externalizing disorders.

In the second pathway, emotional distress influences cognitive processes and learning, which in turn leads to academic difficulties. Students who experience anxiety or depression (internalizing disorders) often experience difficulties with concentration and attention. Likewise, children who are hostile and angry often find it difficult to stay in class and to attend to what they are being taught. Research has begun to focus on the effect of mediating variables such as school engagement and experiences in school to gain a better understanding of the complicated dynamic between academic performance and emotional health (Becker & Luthar, 2002).

One of the major contributors to psychological distress is the physical, emotional, and/or sexual abuse of children. One-fourth of 10- to 16-year-olds report being assaulted or abused in the previous year (Finkelhor & Dziuba-Leatherman, 1994). Physical and sexual abuse and neglect have been demonstrated to be related to below average IQ, learning problems, and many social-emotional problems ranging from aggression and hostility to apathy and withdrawal (Sexton, 1999). Maltreated children demonstrate less academic engagement, more social skills deficits, and lower ego resiliency than nonmaltreated children. Additionally, maltreated children manifest multiple forms of academic risk and show more externalizing and internalizing behavior problems (Shonk & Cicchetti, 2001).

Child maltreatment is related to poor grades, increased absenteeism and worsening elementary school behavior over time, retention in a grade, and involvement in special education programs (Leiter & Johnson, 1997). Exposure to family violence also correlates with a rise in absenteeism, an increase in behavior problems, and an overall detrimental impact on the child's school experience (Brener, 1999).

Sometimes, simply keeping maltreated children in school is a success. Cunningham-Howard (1994) studied 50 students who received in-home family and support services. Many of the children had been physically and/or sexually abused as children or had incarcerated or drug-dependent parents. The children were diagnosed with PTSD, major depression, anxiety disorders, and a number of learning and behavior disorders. The social and psychological supports from the Family Preservation Program resulted in a decreased level of requests for help with academic problems, decreased school failure, and prevention of out-of-home placements (p. 39).

SOLUTIONS

Complex human problems require complex solutions, and no single profession possesses all of the answers. Research by Brabeck, Walsh, and Latta (2003) shows that helping students develop psychosocial resilience and closing the achievement gap cannot be accomplished by schools alone. Indeed, class size has been shown to account for about 8% of the achievement gap. Instructional practices in the classrooms account for another 40–60% (Darling-Hammond, 2000). Consistent with what Maeroff (1998) and others argue, family and community issues account for the remainder.

> Those who desire improvements in classroom learning must realize and acknowledge that school reform, especially when it focuses on disadvantaged students, cannot easily succeed if it ignores the circumstances of their out-of-school lives. (p. 5)

Addressing these latter issues by providing students and families with learning supports (both services and resources) is essential if the achievement gap is to narrow or disappear (Stallings, 1995; Wang, Haertel, & Walberg, 1993). Fortunately, teachers, parents, and researchers are concluding that student learning and well-being are the result of complex interactions between biological, psychological, and social factors (West, Germino-Hausken, & Collins, 1993). Children and youth, especially poor children and youth, have numerous professionals in their lives who are trying to meet their physical needs (nurses, medical doctors), social needs (social workers, counselors), legal needs (lawyers), and mental health needs (psychologists). Too often these services are delivered in a manner that is fractured and fraught with turf battles. Lacking coordination, children and youth are in danger of falling between the cracks that professionals create. To more adequately address all of these needs in a holistic way, professionals need to learn to work together.

Schools are increasingly being recognized as excellent settings for teams of professionals to deliver complex prevention and intervention programs (Kolbe, Collins, & Cortese, 1997). Schools are often the only institutions in the community that have contact with every family that has children between the ages of 5 and 18. They are efficient and cost-effective sites for programs and interventions designed to promote developmental competence. The centrality of schools in the lives of children makes them the ideal center for a comprehensive, community-based system of care.

At the same time that schools are being recognized as critical sites for complex prevention and intervention programs that can enhance development, society is also acknowledging that schools cannot do it alone (Barton, 2003; Riley, 1998). Teachers cannot assume the roles of social workers, nurses, lawyers, or psychologists. The community has a vital role to play in promoting resiliency by offering needed resources to children and families. While schools can provide a limited range of services and resources to students, they need assistance in order to address the wide range of issues that prevent some students from achieving at high levels. Community agencies and institutions offer a wide range of services and resources that will support and enhance the development of children. In addition to supplementing services offered by schools (e.g., mental health, health care, and after-school programs), community agencies are likely to offer services and resources that are typically not available in the school (e.g., legal assistance for youth and families, more intensive medical care, and government-based social services). Collaborative arrangements between schools and community agencies can help to deliver needed support to schoolchildren and their families. Effective partnerships between schools and local community agencies and institutions can create a coordinated and comprehensive web of supports for schoolchildren and their families that can maximally impact learning.

Recently, a number of theoretical models that outline the psychological basis for complex interventions of multiple professionals have begun to emerge (Spencer, 1990; Walsh & Galassi, 2002). Walsh and Galassi (2002) have identified the major principles of a developmental theory of change for complex interventions; the principles can be useful in interventions to promote psychosocial resilience. First, contexts that promote children's health and safety simultaneously provide conditions that support children's academic achievement; conversely, contexts that impede children's physical, emotional, and social development are likely to contribute to academic failure. Second, children's development occurs simultaneously at many levels, including the biological, psychological, and social levels. These various levels of development are continually interacting with and changing one another. Children's learning, then, is not independent of their physical and mental health status or of their social well-being. Third, human development occurs over the entire lifespan. Adults, who are developmentally mature, are more likely to be positive influences on the children for whom they care (Lykken, 2001) and this care affects achievement. Teachers who experience good health, positive personal and work relationships, and job satisfaction are more likely to engender academic success in their students (Henson & Eller, 1999). Fourth, risk and resilience occur at any stage of development. Children who are developing in healthy ways can encounter challenges that lead them in more negative directions. At the same time, children who are initially developing in negative directions can be supported to develop in more positive ways. As noted in the research reviewed above, resilience can be the result of individual factors, such as personality or intelligence (Masten & Coatsworth, 1998), or environmental factors, such as social support or quality of family life (Black & Krishnakumar, 1998; Spencer, 1990; Stack, 1975). Interventions that promote strengths and reduce risks are more likely to lead to academic success.

In order to ground the fundamental principles of a developmental theory of change in a concrete program that can be delivered in schools, a conceptual framework for organizing the various domains in which prevention and intervention can be implemented is required. While the literature has proposed a number of conceptual models for interventions to support the healthy development of school-age children, the most widely used conceptual framework is the "comprehensive, coordinated school health" model articulated by the Centers for Disease Control and Prevention (Allensworth & Kolbe, 1987; Marx, Wooley, & Northrup, 1998). The CDC model identifies nine major components that are considered critical to a coordinated and comprehensive approach to student support: (1)

health education, (2) physical education, (3) health services, (4) nutrition services, (5) counseling, (6) psychological and social services, (7) healthy school environment, (8) health promotion for staff, and (9) parent/community involvement. These nine components can serve as a conceptual framework for school districts that are reorganizing or redesigning student support services. They are consistent with recent national reports on healthy development, including *Education Goals 2000* and *Healthy People 2010* (Goals 2000: Educate America Act, 1994; U.S. Department of Health and Human Services, 2000).

A developmentally based approach to student support that utilizes the components identified by the CDC can be implemented systemically within a single school (e.g., full-service schools), across a number of geographically related schools, or across an entire school district. "Best practice" in implementing these prevention-intervention programs requires that they involve effective cross-institutional partnerships among schools, community agencies, and other community institutions such as universities and businesses (Education Development Center, 2002). These complex arrangements require new infrastructures that facilitate and support collaboration across the various schools and agencies/institutions as well as across the various professions. They must utilize a wide range of prevention and intervention strategies, relying particularly on those for which there is empirical evidence. Similarly, these arrangements must involve multiple professionals (e.g., educators, psychologists, social workers, health care providers, lawyers, housing specialists, youth development specialists). Finally, evaluation must be a central function of program implementation, utilizing multiple methods and multiple outcome measures.

There is some evidence that prevention and intervention efforts involving complex school–community collaborations are effective models of service delivery to children, youth, and families (Greenberg et al., 2003; Hawkins, 2000; Hawkins, Catalano, & Associates, 1992; Hawkins, Catalano, & Miller, 1992; Holtzman, 1997). The work of researchers and practitioners at Boston College and their partnering school collaborators was designed utilizing both a developmental approach and the CDC model of comprehensive coordinated school health. Selected initial results of the research on this complex intervention are presented in the next section.

THE BOSTON CONNECTS PROGRAM

"Boston Connects" is a complex, comprehensive intervention designed to promote psychosocial resilience by addressing the nonacademic barriers to learning across a subset of schools located within the same geographic area in the large urban school district of Boston. This geographic area, comprised of the Allston–Brighton and Mission Hill–Roxbury neighborhoods of Boston, has 10 elementary schools serving approximately 5,500 preK–12 children and youth. Boston Connects is directed and implemented by a school–community–university partnership linking these 10 schools, the Greater Boston YMCA and other community partners, and Boston College. The goals of the partnership are twofold. The first is to offer school students in the Allston–Brighton/Mission Hill communities access to a full range of student services and resources. Professionals and students-in-training assess student needs, coordinate community-based service delivery, provide student and teacher support, design and implement an integrated on-site professional development program, and implement summative and formative longitudinal evaluations of the initiative and its components. The second goal is to build a strong infrastructure to manage and support the partnership and ensure that project objectives are carefully defined, that progress is systematically measured and evaluated, and that professionals are accountable to funders and to the schools and communities they serve.

Based on the premise of a direct cause-and-effect relationship between the effects of poverty and the likelihood of poor academic performance and behavioral problems, the Boston Connects Program posits that addressing children's broader context and their support needs will enhance students' in-school learning. The Boston Connects Program seeks to create systemic change within the schools and specific surrounding neighborhoods by connecting individual student needs with effective in-school and after-school student support services and enrichment opportunities. Community agencies that can provide medical, social, and emotional supports as well as a variety of positive youth development opportunities to children and families are linked in a coordinated and comprehensive system through the school. By providing sustainable, coordinated, and integrated educational supports, the Boston Connects Program creates a school-based "connection" for students to improve their academic performance while linking them with community resources that encourage health, well-being, and social competence.

The program's infrastructure includes a School-Based Instructional Support Team anchored by a School-Site Coordinator at each school, a neighborhood-wide Student and Family Instructional Support Center, and a Resource Coordinating Council. These components provide the infrastructure for the program:

- The *School-Based Instructional Support Team* includes a coordinator, teachers, and other on-site and community-based professionals who work in the schools as nurses, educational psychologists, and mental health clinicians and/or social workers. The team provides instructional and behavioral consultation to classroom teachers and identifies the individual direct service needs of students and their families. The Site-Based Coordinator serves as the school's liaison to the centrally based Student and Family Instructional Support Center.

- The *Student and Family Instructional Support Center* is the base for the coordinators of the center and the health educators, who work across the schools, and the parent–family outreach worker who assists families in addressing issues that interfere with children's progress in school. This centrally located center allows for the most efficient deployment of resources within the community.

- The *Resource Coordinating Council* advises and supports the center coordinator regarding existing and needed programs and services in the neighborhood that address barriers to learning and development. The council also provides leadership and advocacy in the coordination, integration, and strengthening of student support services and in establishing linkages with community, city, state, and federal agencies.

Graduate interns from multiple professions, along with student tutors and mentors, implement a common behavior management program and social skills instruction, enrichment activities through out-of-school time programs, classroom observation, and crisis management. For students requiring more intensive services, the Boston Connects Program provides focused support, including case management, medical and mental health services, middle school transition support, family counseling, teacher consultation, and follow-up.

Expected long-term outcomes include:

- significantly increasing students' academic achievement as measured by classroom performance and standardized tests;
- reducing barriers to learning through the provision of student and family support services, including mental health and social services; and
- expanding learning opportunities and building students' engagement and motivation through academic and cultural enrichment activities.

SELECTED INITIAL RESULTS

Agency Involvement

After 2 years of implementation, early evaluation data across the first six schools in which the project was initially implemented reveals that there has been a substantial increase in the number of agencies working in or with the schools (see Appendix A, Figure A1). In particular, there has been a significant increase in the number of mental health agencies working in or with the schools (see Appendix A, Figure A2).

Typically, students who are identified with learning and/or behavior problems are referred to the Student Support Team (SST) for individualized assessments. Historically, there were few options for these students. If the initial informal assessment led the team to believe that the student potentially had a need for Special Education (SPED) services (e.g., learning disability tutoring), the student was referred for a formal SPED evaluation costing approximately $2,000. Since the inception of the Boston Connects Program, the number of students recommended for SPED has decreased (see Appendix B, Figure B3).

Historically, if the SPED evaluation determined that SPED services were needed, the student would then be classified as "in need of special education" and receive appropriate services. If, however, the evaluator informally concluded that the student would not potentially benefit from SPED services, no alternative services were recommended because they were not available. One of the early tasks of the Boston Connects Program was to develop service alternatives to SPED—alternatives that address risk and promote resilience. These alternatives included after-school programs, tutoring and academic support, mental health evaluations and counseling services, one-on-one mentoring, health-related services, summer school, family services, and classroom-level interventions. Figure B4 (Appendix B) illustrates that of the number of students referred to the SST, the largest proportion of children are now receiving alternate service recommendations.

Academic Achievement

Early indicators suggest that academic performance is improving for those who have been identified with a learning or behavioral problem and who are receiving support services. Initial findings from data gathered at the school that has implemented the program for the longest period of time affirm the potential of the comprehensive, coordinated model for delivering nonacademic support services. Students at the school who were identified with a learning problem or behavioral problem and who received support services improved their academic achievement at the same rate or a faster rate than those who were not identified and who, therefore, did not receive services. This data suggests that effectively addressing nonacademic barriers to learning contributes to reducing the achievement gap of elementary students who have documented learning and/or behavioral problems. See Appendix C for graphs of preliminary achievement trends for students utilizing support resources.

Figure C5 (Appendix C) illustrates fourth-grade reading achievement among students using none, one, two, or three types of service support in 2002–2003. Generally, students who received at least one type of support service demonstrated gains over the course of a year—as measured by the Scholastic Reading Inventory (SRI)—that paralleled students who were not recommended for service support.

Figure C6 (Appendix C) illustrates SRI score gains for fifth-grade students compared on counseling support use. The SRI score gains for students receiving licensed counseling services parallel the gains for students who receive no service.

Figure C7 (Appendix C) highlights SRI score gains for students who receive different levels of tutoring support. Clearly, all students demonstrate some type of gain. However, while students receiving no tutoring posted the highest overall scores, students receiving a combination of student and teacher tutoring made the most gains over the course of the year. This pattern makes sense in the context of the program.

Students who receive services are selected based on demonstrated need. Therefore, students recommended for teacher tutoring or a student/teacher combination probably had serious academic needs. This is reflected in the initial scores. However, from fall to the spring, students receiving the highest levels of support also made the strongest gains.

This sample of achievement outcomes is consistent with the overall program theory for the Boston Connects Program. Students with demonstrated needs are receiving services and youth development opportunities. In preliminary analyses, this support is associated with noticeable achievement gains.

IMPLICATIONS AND CONCLUSIONS

Given the current national priorities and rising budget deficit, poverty is not likely to be reduced in the immediate future. Psychologists need to identify solutions for poor children that will help them achieve at high levels. No single, isolated solution is working. Rather, it appears that multiple interventions are needed to make a difference in students' learning and well-being. This means that university faculty from both education and psychology as well as other professions must collaboratively work to promote psychosocial resilience. Researchers need to employ multifactorial models in studying the development of psychosocial resilience, and service providers need to identify the potential professionals to partner with in meeting the complex needs of poor children and youth. Only then will we be able to eliminate the achievement gap and have *all* children learning at high levels, and *all* children and youth enjoying health and well-being.

APPENDIX A: SELECTED DATA ILLUSTRATING AGENCY
INVOLVEMENT BETWEEN 1999 AND 2003

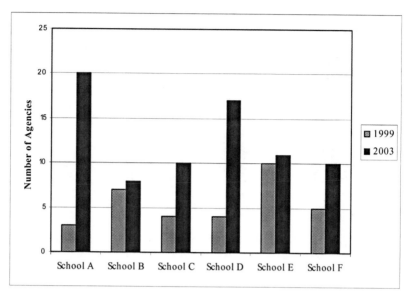

Figure 7.A1.   A comparison of community agency involvement in the first six Boston Connects Program schools between 1999 and 2003.

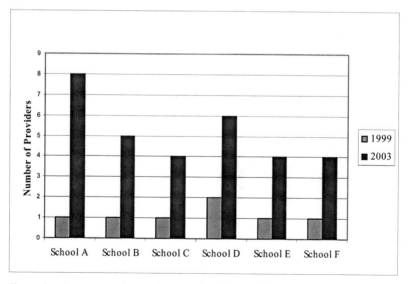

Figure 7.A2. A comparison of mental health providers' involvement in the first six Boston Connects schools between 1999 and 2003.

APPENDIX B: SELECTED DATA ILLUSTRATING SPECIAL
EDUCATION AND ALTERNATIVE SERVICES

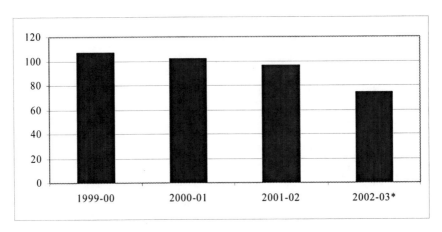

Figure 7.B3. Number of students recommended for Special Education (SPED) evaluation from 1999 to 2003.

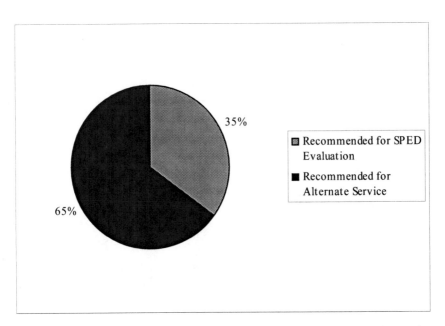

Figure 7.B4.   Percentages of students recommended for Special Education evaluation versus recommended for alternative services.

APPENDIX C: SELECTED DATA ILLUSTRATING RELATIONSHIP BETWEEN SUPPORT SERVICE USE AND ACHIEVEMENT

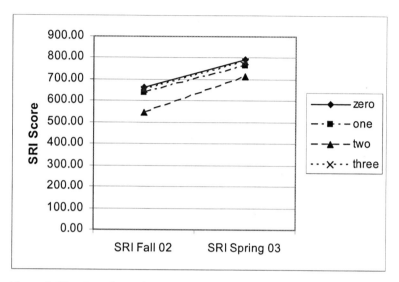

Figure 7.C5.   Fourth-grade SRI achievement by service enrollment, 2002–2003.

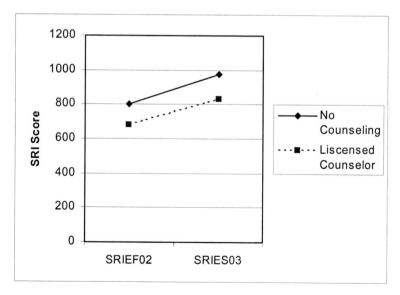

Figure 7.C6.   Fifth-grade achievement by counseling support status.

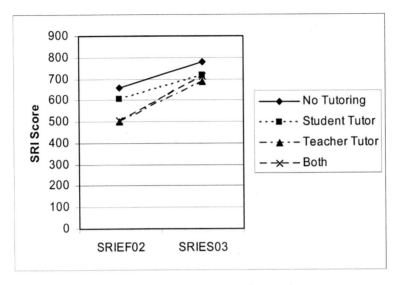

Figure 7.C7.   Fourth-grade SRI achievement by tutoring support status, 2002–2003.

REFERENCES

Allensworth, D., & Kolbe, L. (1987). The comprehensive school health program: Exploring an expanded concept. *Journal of School Health, 57*(10), 409–412.

Annie E. Casey Foundation. (1999). *Kids count data book.* New York: Carnegie Foundation.

Barton, P. E. (2001). *Facing the hard facts in education reform: A policy information perspective.* Princeton, NJ: Educational Testing Service.

Barton, P. E. (2003). *Parsing the achievement gap: Baselines for tracking progress.* Princeton, NJ: Policy Information Center and Educational Testing Service.

Battistich, V., Solomon, D., Kim, D., Watson, M., & Schaps, E. (1995). Schools as communities, poverty levels of student populations, and students' attitudes, motives, and performance: A multilevel analysis. *American Educational Research Journal, 32,* 627–658.

Becker, B. E., & Luthar, S. S. (2002). Social-emotional factors affecting achievement outcomes among disadvantaged students: Closing the achievement gap. *Educational Psychologist, 37*(4), 197–214.

Benson, P. L. (1993). What works in prevention: The search continues. *Journal of Emotional and Behavioral Problems, 2*(3), 36–42.

Benson, P. L., Scales, P. C., & Roehlkepartain, E. C. (1998). *A fragile foundation: The state of developmental assets among American youth.* Minneapolis, MN: Search Institute.

Black, M. M., & Krishnakumar, A. (1998). Children in low-income, urban settings: Interventions to promote mental health and well-being. *American Psychologist, 53*(6), 635–646.

Blum, R. W., McNeely, C. A., & Rinehart, P. M. (2002). *Improving the odds: The untapped power of schools to improve the health of teens.* Minneapolis: University of Minnesota, Center for Adolescent Health and Development.

Books, S. (Ed.). (1998). *Invisible children in the society and its schools: Sociocultural, political, and historical studies in education.* Mahwah, NJ: Erlbaum.

Boyce Rodgers, K., & Rose, H. A. (2001). Personal, family, and school factors related to adolescent academic performance: A comparison by family structure. *Marriage and Family Review, 33*(4), 47–61.

Brabeck, M. M., Walsh, M. E., & Latta, R. (Eds.). (2003). *Meeting at the hyphen: Schools-universities-communities-professions in collaboration for student achievement and well-being. 102nd Yearbook of the National Society for the Study of Education: Part II.* Chicago: University of Chicago Press.

Brener, M. L. (1999). A qualitative examination of the effects of family violence on children's educational experience. *Dissertation Abstracts International, 60*(5), 1509A.

Bronfenbrenner, U. (1979). *The ecology of human development.* Cambridge, MA: Harvard University Press.

Brooks-Gunn, J., Duncan G., Klebov, P., & Sealand, N. (1993). Do neighborhoods influence child and adolescent development? *American Journal of Sociology, 99,* 353–395.

Casey, M. B. (1996). Understanding individual differences in spatial ability within females: A nature/nurture interactions framework. *Developmental Review, 16,* 241–260.

Casey, M. B., & Brabeck, M. M. (1989). Exceptions to the male advantage on a spatial task: Family handedness and college major as factors identifying women who excel. *Neuropsychologia, 27,* 689–696.

Casey, M. B., & Brabeck, M. M. (1990). Women who excel on a spatial task: Proposed genetic and environmental factors. *Brain and Cognition, 12,* 73–84.

Center on Hunger, Poverty, and Nutrition Policy. (1993). *Statement on the link between nutrition and cognitive development in children.* Medford, MA: Tufts University, School of Nutrition.

Centers for Disease Control and Prevention. (2002). Surveillance summaries. *Morbidity and Mortality Weekly Report, 51* (No. SS-4).

Coleman, J., Campbell, E. Q., Hobson, C. J., McPartland, J., Mood, A. M., Weinfeld, F. D., et al. (1966). *Equality of educational opportunity.* Washington, DC: U.S. Government Printing Office.

Coley, R. J. (2002). *An uneven start: Indicators of inequality in school readiness.* Princeton, NJ: Educational Testing Services, Statistics and Research Division, Policy Information Center.

Conger, R. D., Conger, K. J., & Elder, G. (1997). Family economic hardship and adolescent academic performance: Mediating and moderating processes. In G. Duncan & J. Brooks-Gunn (Eds.), *Consequences of growing up poor* (pp. 288–310). New York: Russell Sage Foundation.

Cunningham-Howard, K. (1994). *School-based histories and educational outcomes of children & youth receiving community mental health services through the Texas Children's Mental Health Plan* (Final Report). Austin: University of Texas at Austin.

Darling-Hammond, L. (2000). Teacher quality and student achievement: A review of state policy evidence. *Educational Policy Analysis Archives, 8*(1). Retrieved October 31, 2003, from http://epaa.asu.edu/ epaa/v8nl

DeWitt, J. A. (1996). Exploring school attachment: Interviews with highly attached high school students. *Dissertation Abstracts International. Section A: Humanities & Social Sciences, 56 (8-A)*, 3055.

Eccles, J. S., & Harold, R.D. (1993). Parent-school involvement during the early adolescent years. *Teachers College Record, 94*(3), 568–587.

Education Development Center. (2001). *Districts on the move: Unified student service in Boston public schools: Building a continuum of services through standards-based reform.* (National Institute for Urban School Improvement, Education Development Center Inc., 55 Chapel St., Newton, MA. 02458).

Entwisle, D. R., & Alexander, K. L. (1990). Beginning school math competence: Minority and majority comparisons. *Child Development Special Issue: Minority children, 61*(2), 454–471.

Epstein, J. I., Salinas, K.C., & Simon, B. (1996). *Effects of Teachers Involving Parents in Schoolwork (TIPS)—Interactive homework in the middle grades.* Paper presented at the annual meeting of the American Educational Research Association, New York.

Finkelhor, D., & Dziuba-Leatherman, J. (1994). Children as victims of violence: A national survey. *Pediatrics, 94*, 413–420.

Fox, J. A., & Newman, S. A. (1997). *After-school crime or after-school programs: Tuning in to the prime time for violent juvenile crime and implications for national policy. A report to the United States Attorney General.* Washington, DC: Fight Crime, Invest in Kids.

Goals 2000: Educate America Act, 103rd Cong., 103 (1994).

Goodenow, C. (1993). Classroom belonging among early adolescent students: Relationships to motivation and achievement. *Journal of Early Adolescence, 13*(1), 21–43.

Greenberg, M. T., Weissberg, R. P., O'Brien, M. U., Zins, J. E., Fredericks, L., Resnik, H., et al. (2003). Enhancing school-based prevention and youth development through coordinated social, emotional, and academic learning. *American Psychologist, 58*(6/7), 466–474.

Harachi, T. W., Abbott, R. A., Catalano, R. F., & Haggerty, K. P. (1996, April). *The effects of risk and protective factors on antisocial behavior and academic success in the early primary grades.* Paper presented at the annual meeting of the Life History Research Society, London.

Haveman, R., & Wolfe, B. (1995). The determinants of children's attainments: A review of methods and findings. *Journal of Economic Literature, 33*, 1829–1878.

Hawkins, J. D. (2000, June). *Youth development and public policy.* Paper presented at the Bridging Frameworks for Positive Youth Development Conference, Wilmington, NC.

Hawkins, J. D., Catalano, R. F., & Associates. (1992). *Communities that care: Action for drug abuse prevention.* San Francisco: Jossey-Bass.

Hawkins, J. D., Catalano, R.F., & Miller, J.Y. (1992). Risk and protective factors for alcohol and other drug problems in adolescence and early adulthood: Implications for substance abuse prevention. *Psychological Bulletin 112*(1), 64–105.

Henderson, M., & Milstein, M. M. (1996). *Resiliency in schools: Making it happen for students and educators.* Thousand Oaks, CA: Corwin.

Henson, K. T., & Eller, B. F. (1999). *Educational psychology for effective teaching.* Belmont, CA: Wadsworth.

Herrnstein, R. J., & Murray, C. A. (1994). *The bell curve: Intelligence and class structure in American life.* New York: Free Press.

Hill, M. S., & Duncan, G. (1987). Parental family income and the socioeconomic attainment of children. *Social Science Research, 16*, 39–73.

Holtzman, W. H. (1997). Community psychology and full-service schools in different cultures. *American Psychologist, 52(4)*, 381–389.

Kagan, S. L. (1990). *Excellence in early childhood education: defining characteristics and next-decade strategies.* Washington, DC: Information Services, Office of Educational Research and Improvement, U.S. Dept. of Education.

Kagan, S. L., Moore, E., & Bredekamp, S. (1995). Reconsidering children's early development and learning: Toward common views and vocabulary. Washington, DC: National Education Goals Panel.

Kolbe, L. J., Collins, J., & Cortese, P. (1997). Building the capacity of schools to improve the health of the nation: A call for assistance from psychologists. *American Psychologist, 52*(3), 256–265.

Leiter, J., & Johnson, M.C. (1997). Child maltreatment and school performance declines: An event-history analysis. *American Educational Research Journal, 34*(3), 563–589.

Lerner, R., Walsh, M., & Howard, K. (1998). Developmental-contextual considerations: Person-context relations as the bases for risk and resiliency in child and adolescent development. In A.S. Bellack & M. Hersen (Eds.), *Comprehensive clinical psychology* (Vol. 5, pp. 1–24). Oxford: Persimmon.

Lykken, D. T. (2001). Parental licensure. *American Psychologist, 56*(11), 885–894.

Maeroff, G. I. (1998). *Altered destinies: Making life better for schoolchildren in need.* New York: St. Martin's Press.

Marshall, N. L., Coll, C. G., Marx, F., McCartney, K., Keefe, N., & Ruh, J. (1997). After-school time and children's behavioral adjustment. *Merrill-Palmer Quarterly, 43*(3), 497–514.

Marx, E., Wooley, S. F., & Northrup, D. (Eds.). (1998). *Health is academic: A guide to coordinated school health programs.* New York: Teachers College Press.

Masten, A. S., & Coatsworth, J. D. (1998). The development of competence in favorable and unfavorable environments: Lessons from research on successful children. *American Psychologist, 53*(2), 205–220.

McLaughlin, M. W. (1994). Urban sanctuaries: Neighborhood organizations that keep hope alive. *Phi Delta Kappan, 76*(4), 300–306.

McLoyd, V. C. (1998). Socioeconomic disadvantage and child development. *American Psychologist, 53*(2), 185–204.

McLoyd, V. C., & Wilson, L. (1990). The impact of economic hardship on black families and children: Psychological distress, parenting, and socioemotioinal development. *Child Development, 61*, 311–346.

Mouton, S. G., Hawkins, J., McPherson, R.H., & Copley, J. (1996). School attachment: Perspectives of low-attached high school students. *Educational Psychology, 16*(3), 297–304.

Mullis, I. V. S., Martin, M. O., Gonzalez, & E. J., Kennedy, A. M. (2003). *PIRLS 2001 International Report: IEA's Study of Reading Literacy Achievement in Primary Schools in Thirty-five Countries.* Chestnut Hill, MA: Boston College, International Study Center.

Murdock, T. B., Anderman, L., & Hodge, S. (2000). Middle-grades predictors of student motivation and behavior in high school. *Journal of Adolescent Research, 15*(3), 327–351.

Murphy, J. M., Pagano, M. E., Wehler, C. A., Little, M., Kleinman, R. E., & Jellinek, M. S. (1998). Relationship between hunger and psychosocial functioning in low-income American children. *Journal of the American Academy of Child & Adolescent Psychiatry 37*(2), 163–170.

Murray, J., & Weissbourd, R. (2003). Focusing on core academic outcomes: A key to successful school-community partnerships. In M. M. Brabeck, M. E. Walsh, & R. E. Latta (Eds.), *Meeting at the hyphen: Schools-universities-communities-professions in collaboration for student achievement and well-being. 102nd Yearbook of the National Society for the Study of Education: Part II* (pp. 179–197). Chicago: University of Chicago Press.

National Center for Children in Poverty. (2002). *Children in poverty fact sheet.* New York: National Center for Children in Poverty, Mailman School of Public Health, Columbia University.

National Center for Education Statistics. (2001). *The condition of education* (GPO Reference No. NCES 2001072). U.S. Department of Education, NCES. Washington, DC: U.S. Government Printing Office.

National Institute on Out-of-School Time, Center for Research on Women at Wellesley College. (2001). *Fact sheet on school-age children's out-of-school time.* Wellesley, MA: Author.

Needleman, H. L., Schell, A., Bellinger, D., Leviton, A., & Allred, E. N. (1990). The long-term effects of exposure to low doses of lead in childhood: An eleven-year follow-up report. *New England Journal of Medicine 322*(2), 83–88.

Ogbu, J. U. (1995). Origins of human competence: A cultural-ecological perspective. In N. R. Goldberger & J. B. Veroff (Eds.), *The culture and psychology reader* (pp. 245–275). New York: New York University Press.

Ogle, L., Sen, A., Pahlke, E., Jocelyn, L., Kastberg, D., Roey, S., et al. (2003). *International comparisons in fourth-grade reading literacy: Findings from the Progress in International Reading Literacy Study (PIRLS) of 2001* (NCES 2003–073). U.S. Department of Education, NCES. Washington, DC: U.S. Government Printing Office.

Overstreet, S., & Braun, S. (1999). A preliminary examination of the relationship between exposure to community violence and academic functioning. *School Psychology Quarterly, 14*(4), 380–396.

Parker, J. G., & Asher, S.R. (1987). Peer relations and later personal adjustment: Are low-accepted children at risk? *Psychological Bulletin, 102*(3), 357–389.

Patterson, C. J., Kupersmidt, J. B., & Vaden, N. A. (1990). Income level, gender, ethnicity, and household composition as predictors of children's school-based competence. *Child Development. Special Issue: Minority children, 61*(2), 485–494.

Pettit, G., Laird, R. D., Dodge, K. A, & Bates, J. E. (1997). Patterns of after-school care in middle childhood: Risk factors and developmental outcomes. *Merrill-Palmer Quarterly, 43*(3), 515–538.

Posner, J. K., & Vandell, D.L. (1999). After-school activities and the development of low-income children. *Developmental Psychology, 35*(3), 868–879.

Riley, R. (1998). *School/community/university partnerships.* Paper presented at Connecting community building and education reform: Effective school, community, university partnerships–Joint Forum of the U.S. Department of Education & the U.S. Department of Housing and Urban Development, Washington, DC.

Robinson, D. N. (1976). *An intellectual history of psychology.* New York: Macmillan.

Roeser, R. W., & Eccles, J. S. (2000). Schooling and mental health. In A. J. Sameroff, M. Lewis, & S. M. Miller (Eds.), *Handbook of developmental psychopathology* (2nd ed., pp. 135–156). Dordrecht, Netherlands: Kluwer Academic.

Rossi, R., & Montgomery, A. (1994). *Educational reforms and students at risk: A review of the current state of the art.* Washington, DC: U.S. Department of Labor.

Sanders, W. L. (1998). Value-added assessment. *School Administrator, 55*(11), 24–27.

Sanders, W.L. (1999). Teachers, teachers, teachers [Electronic version]. *Blueprint: Ideas for a New Century, 4.* Retrieved October 30, 2003, from http://www.ndol.org/blueprint/fall/99/solutions4.html

Schorr, L. B. (1988). *Within our reach: Breaking the cycle of disadvantage.* New York: Doubleday.

Sexton, E. T. (1999). The relationship between child maltreatment and delinquent behavior. *Reaching Today's Youth: The Community Circle of Caring Journal, 3*(3), 10–12.

Shavers, C. A. (2000). The interrelationships of exposure to community violence and trauma to the behavioral patterns and academic performance among urban elementary school-aged children. *Dissertation Abstracts International, 61,* 4B.

Shonk, S. M., & Cicchetti, D. (2001). Maltreatment, competency deficits, and risk for academic and behavioral maladjustment. *Developmental Psychology, Special Issue, 37*(1), 3–17.

Skurulsky, R. J. (2001). The impact of intrafamilial and community violence on children's psychological adjustment and academic achievement. *Dissertation Abstracts International, 61,* 10B.

Somers, C. L., & Gizzi, T. (2001). Predicting adolescents' risky behaviors: The influence of future orientation, school involvement, and school attachment. *Adolescent and Family Health, 2*(1), 3–11.

Spencer, M. B. (1990). Development of minority children: An introduction. *Child Development, 61*(2), 267–269.

Stack, L. C. (1975). Ecological factors related to first psychiatric admissions. *Journal of Community Psychology, 3*(3), 215–223.

Stallings, J. A. (1995). Ensuring teaching and learning in the 21st century. *Educational Researcher, 24*(6), 4–8.

Stipek, D. (1997). Success in school—for a head start in life. In S. S. Luthar, J. A. Burack, D. Cicchetti, & J. R. Weisz (Eds.), *Developmental psychopathology: Perspectives on adjustment, risk, and disorder* (pp. 75–92). New York: Cambridge University Press.

Taylor, H. G., Klein, N., & Hack, M. (2000). School-age consequences of birth weight less than 750 g: A review and update. *Developmental Neuropsychology, 17*(3), 289–321.

Tout, K., Scarpa, J., & Zaslow, M.J. (2002). Children of current and former welfare recipients: Similarly at risk. *Child Trends Research Brief.* Washington, DC: Child Trends, Inc.

Turkheimer, E., Haley, A., Waldron, M., D'Onofrio, B., & Gottesman, I. I. (2003). Socioeconomic status modifies heritability of IQ in young children. *Psychological Science, 14*(6), 623–628.

U.S. Department of Health and Human Services. (2000). *Healthy people 2010: Conference edition* (Vols. I & II). Washington, DC: Author.

Vandivere, S., Moore, K. A., & Brown, B. (2000). *Child well-being at the outset of welfare reform: An overview of the nation and 13 states. New Federalism: National survey of America's families. Series B, No. B-23. Assessing the New Federalism: An urban institute program to assess changing social policies.* Washington, DC: Urban Institute.

Walberg, H. J. (1984). Families as partners in educational productivity. *Phi Delta Kappan, 65*(6), 397–400.

Walsh, M. E., & Galassi, J. P. (2002). An introduction: Counseling psychologists and schools. *Counseling Psychologist, 30*(5), 675–681.

Walsh, M. E., & Murphy, J. A. (2003). *Children, health, and learning.* Westport, CT: Greenwood Press.

Wang, M. C., Haertel, G. D., & Walberg, H. J. (1993). Toward a knowledge base for school learning. *Review of Educational Research, 63*(3), 249–294.

Wang, M. C., Haertel, G. D., & Walberg, H. J. (1997). Fostering educational resilience in inner-city schools. In H. J. Walberg, O. Reyes, & R. P. Weissberg (Eds.), *Children and youth: Interdisciplinary perspectives* (pp. 119-140). Thousand Oaks, CA: Sage.

Wentzel, K. R., & Asher, S. R. (1995). The academic lives of neglected, rejected, popular, and controversial children. *Child Development, 66*(3), 754–763.

Werner, E. E., & Smith, R. S. (1992). *Overcoming the odds: High risk children from birth to adulthood.* Ithaca, NY: Cornell University Press.

West, J., Germino-Hausken, E., & Collins, M. (1993). *Readiness for kindergarten: Parent and teacher beliefs* (GPO Reference No. NCES 93-257). Washington, DC: National Center for Education Statistics.

White, K. (1982). The relation between socioeconomic status and academic achievement. *Psychological Bulletin, 91*, 461–481.

Wilson, S. M., Floden, R. E., & Ferrini-Mundy, J. (2001). *Teacher preparation research: Current knowledge, gaps, and recommendations.* Seattle: University of Washington, Center for the Study of Teaching and Policy.

CHAPTER 8

RESILIENCE AS A FACTOR IN OVERCOMING OBSTACLES TO HIGH ACADEMIC ACHIEVEMENT

Edmund W. Gordon and Brenda X. Mejia

A primary mission of public schools is to produce students who are intellectively competent, prepared for postsecondary education, and able to respond to the increasingly competitive demands of citizenship and the workforce. However, differences in educational outcomes of students indicate that the impact of our current public school system is, for many students, limited. For instance, one of the most urgent concerns among education stakeholders today is the underrepresentation of African American, Latino, and Native American students among academically high-achieving students. Twenty years after the release of the report "A Nation at Risk," new efforts continue to emerge promising to eliminate the ubiquitous academic disparity and to ensure that "no child [is] left behind." Stakeholders have been working relentlessly to ameliorate educational disparities and to respond to the unprecedented challenge of educating students who, increasingly, come from multicultural, multilingual, and disadvantaged backgrounds. Although the hard work has resulted in signs

Optimizing Student Success in School With the Other Three Rs:
Reasoning, Resilience, and Responsibility, 143–175
Copyright © 2006 by Information Age Publishing
All rights of reproduction in any form reserved.

of progress, more work is necessary to continue to improve student performance.

In this chapter, we reflect upon the resilience construct as a factor in overcoming obstacles to high academic achievement in minority students. We generally refer to the construct resilience conjointly with defiance to reflect our conviction that the former tends to reference a state of being while the latter references a manifestation of human agency. We address several major obstacles that appear to imperil academic achievement among all students. We review a broad range of research evidence and discuss the reasons why these problems of academic underproductivity exist. The constructs of resilience and defiance are discussed to help guide educational intervention efforts and the cultivation of resilience and defiance in students. Consequently, several recommendations are proposed to help students realize their potential for high academic achievement.

RESILIENCE (DEFIANCE)

A considerable amount of empirical research on the concept of resilience has flourished in recent years. Initial research on the construct centered on overcoming or the absence of psychopathology in the context of disadvantaged conditions and experiential hazards. Growing interest in this complex construct has spurred a proliferation of research examining the factors that result in competence and perseverance despite challenging life situations. Many individuals defy the odds, overcome stressful life situations, and others recover from trauma and develop into healthy and successful individuals.

Broadly defined, resilience refers to the developmental process encompassing positive adaptation by individuals despite significant adversity (Garmezy, 1991; Luthar, Cicchetti, & Becker, 2000; Luthar & Zigler, 1991). Important in the definition of resilience is the exposure to negative and/or threatening circumstances. Yet, despite the voluminous research, the construct of resilience has been ambiguously defined in the literature. Luthar and colleagues (2000) point to variations in the use of the concept as an individual trait (resiliency) versus a developmental process (resilience). Building on the work of Masten (1994, as cited in Luthar et al., 2000), these researchers emphasize Masten's recommendation to use the term "resilience" only for describing "the maintenance of positive adjustment under challenging conditions" (p. 546). Like Masten, they refrain from the use of the term "resiliency' because of the misleading personal trait the term connotes.

In addition, the ambiguities in this work are, in part, attributed to issues such as lack of agreement on the domain covered by the construct, its limitations, the categories of adaptive behaviors, or circumstances to which resilience refers (Gordon & Song, 1994) and instability and limited utility of the phenomenon of resilience (Luthar et al., 2000). While the extant research has investigated the causal agents, important events, or combinations of factors and characteristics that result in maladaptive or adaptive behaviors, there is a dearth of research focusing on the processual analysis of the multiple factors by which such behavior can be explained.

In their work, Gordon and Song (1994) have described developmental processes in which multiple factors (individual, familial, and societal) interact dialectically to result in adaptive and maladaptive behaviors. They have studied the correlates of success and failure in the lives of individuals identified as disadvantaged. They refer to a human phenomenon that they call "defiance" to describe the developmental process in which multiple factors interact dialectically resulting in intentional behavior on the part of the developing person or others on his or her behalf in order to adapt to challenges. Gordon and Song argue that "defiance" is a better formulation for understanding the interactive and processual phenomena of success and failure. Although theoretical models of resilience have attempted to explain some of the manners in which individuals manage experiential challenges, the term itself does not capture the relative amount of strength and determination that individuals use in assessing their circumstances and deploying their energy to control their destinies. According to Gordon and Song, the term "defiance" more accurately captures the intentional behavior enacted to "move away" from negative circumstances and toward more positive situations. Most important in this notion of defiance is that although defiers of negative prediction of success may be disadvantaged, they do not feel handicapped by their condition. For instance, despite many obstacles, some such students manage to excel in school and do not permit obstacles to limit their aspirations and their goal-directed behavior. Gordon (2000) suggests the functioning of an attributional or existential phenomenon whereby attributes projected on the components of the interaction are possibly determinant.

FOUR MAJOR OBSTACLES TO ACADEMIC ACHIEVEMENT

Let us turn to what we consider to be the four major obstacles of academic achievement. There appear to be at least four major obstacles to optimizing academic achievement for all students. The first obstacle is the omnipresent effect of inequality of access to relevant resources. The disjuncture between increasing demands of academic achievement and student behaviors and attitudes toward learning presents the second major obstacle. Our literature review suggests that the third major obstacle is the multifaceted ways in which communities and families support academic learning for some students and fail to support it for others. The final obstacle is the quality of preparation of many teachers and their failure to differentiate instruction in response to students' diverse cultural characteristics.

The First Obstacle: Resource Capital

Decades ago, the notable scholar, W.E.B. Du Bois, cogently argued that race was a valuable construct for understanding issues of inequality. Unfortunately, race continues to be a significant variable in understanding inequity in this country. Inequities in the United States exist on many levels: structural, institutional, and individual (Pincus, 1996). Policies implemented by "dominant" groups have resulted in privileges for them and unequal and sometimes harmful effects on groups that lack power. Various forms of human resource development capital, for example, has been enjoyed by groups that possess most of the power in society and are represented in the higher social strata. Those living under policies created and implemented by the "dominant" group have had less access to various forms of human resource development capital and privileges afforded to the dominant group. The NAACP's *A Call for Action in Education* (2001) states "resource inequities often follow race and class divisions between districts and patterns of neighborhood segregation with diverse school districts" (p. 4). Similarly, Jonathan Kozol (1991), an educator who is intimately familiar with the hardships of inner-city schools, revealed the "savage inequalities" that exist in the schooling experiences of poor and minority children—segregated with poorly paid teachers, substandard buildings and educational materials, and poorly funded preschool programs.

Gordon (1999) points out that the resource capital necessary for the investment of education and for the development of academic ability is not equally distributed to low-status persons. Bourdieu (1986), Coleman and colleagues (1966), Gordon and Meroe (1989), and Miller (1995) have described various forms of resource capital that facilitate academic learning and personal development. These forms of resource capital are listed in Table 7.1.

Gordon (1999) cautions that without access to these essential forms of capital, any school reform will meet with a limited degree of success.

Table 7.1. Kinds of Resource Capital

Kinds of Capital	Definition
Health	Physical and developmental integrity, health, nutritional condition
Financial	Income, wealth, family, community, and societal economic resources available for education
Human	Social competence, tacit knowledge, and other education—derived abilities as personal or family assets
Social	Social network relationships, social norms, cultural styles, and values
Polity	Societal membership, social concern, public commitment, political economy
Personal	Disposition, attitudes, aspirations, efficacy, sense of power
Institutional	Quality of and access to educational and socializing institutions
Pedagogical	Supports for appropriate educational treatment in family, school, and community

Source: Gordon and Mejia (2003).

Schools and other social institutions seem to work best when the individuals served are provided with the varieties of capital that facilitate and support human development. Historian V.P. Franklin (2002) writes that while it is true that some schools receive unequal funding, it is not a recent problem in the history of education in the United States. He has written about the contributions of African Americans (e.g., former slaves) to public education in the United States from the antebellum era to the 1960s. Specifically, Franklin describes how African Americans defied access to schooling and disparities in school funding by using their own "social, human, and collective cultural capital" to ensure that financially depressed schools succeeded. The contributions of African American communities and families to their children's education illustrate how collective efforts can help make a difference in students' education and build effective schooling in the process.

The Second Obstacle: Learner Attitudes and Behaviors

Special attention needs to be given to the disjuncture between the increasing demands of academic achievement and students' learning attitudes and learning behaviors. Gordon and Armour-Thomas (1991) refer to students' attitudes as "dispositions" to describe the tendency to behave, engage, and/or respond to the environment. In their research, Blackwell, Stewart, and Pastor (2002) have described how such attitudes were deliberately nurtured by black parents who were determined to enable their children to defy the failures predicted by an oppressive society. In addition, Gordon (1988) identifies four categories of learner behaviors: (1) time on task; (2) energy deployment; (3) resource utilization; and (4) meta-cognitive and meta-componential strategies. Although these behaviors are learnable, they are not explicitly taught in school. Therefore, it is important to teach these behaviors intentionally and train students to recognize them as part of their own repertoire for pursuing academic-related activities. Such explicit socialization is preparation for resilient/defiant adaptation.

Attitudes and behaviors toward academic achievement have been attributed to "acting white," students' stereotypes about abilities, masculine expressions and behaviors, economic payoffs from schooling, and cultural incongruency between home and school. John Ogbu's (1988) oppositional culture theory highlighted the role of culture in understanding racial and ethnic differences in academic achievement. The history of slavery and racism in the African American experience is thought to influence many African American students to lower their goals for schooling because they think that high academic achievement only benefits white students. In addition, Ogbu (1992) also explained that African American students are reinforced to value aspects of society that are in opposition to the values of whites. This "cultural inversion" continues to exist because African Americans feel oppressed and few incentives exist to encourage the rejection of those oppositional values. Considering the persistence of negative images of African Americans in society (Bryson, 1998; Gibbs, 1988; Gordon, in press), it stands to reason that some young people may consciously present themselves in defiance of mainstream expectations. In many such instances the result is school failure or underproductivity. E.T. Gordon (in press) explains such defiance is an effective adaptation for some black students to what they consider hostile school environments. Obviously, many African Americans are doing very well by following the mainstream expectations.

More recently, Claude Steele has argued that ethnic minority students are likely to be vulnerable to the phenomenon he calls "stereotype threat." According to Steele (1997), stereotype threat "is a situational threat that, in general form, can affect the members of any group about whom a negative stereotype exists. Where bad stereotypes of these groups apply, members of these groups can fear being reduced to that stereotype" (p. 614). Negative stereotypes about women and minorities, for example, can have negative consequences on academic performance. Ethnic minority students tend to perform worse on academic tasks if they are negatively stereotyped or reminded of racist stereotypes just before beginning a task. In his study, Steele monitored the underperformance of African Americans in several academic domains and the underperformance of women on mathematics tests. His findings revealed that when members of these groups were given these tests and were asked to identify their race or gender, they were faced with the pressure of confirming/disconfirming negative stereotypes about their groups' abilities. Thus, underperformance in the tests was explained by the anxiety, additional pressure, and distraction the participants experienced when they were under stereotype threat. Steele also proposes that some students detach their self-esteem from academics in order to reduce anxiety. In this way, students who identify with academics are more likely to succeed because they are more motivated. Conversely, students who do not identify with academics are less motivated to succeed because succeeding is not viewed as rewarding. Steele notes that black students do not begin school "disidentified" with academics. Like most students, they begin school with a positive view about academics but negative stereotypes about their abilities result in this disidentification. However, for many students negative stereotypes about their group can operate as catalytic agents of resistance. Negative stereotypes are viewed as challenges to defy and serve as an impetus to prove others they are wrong. Overall, Steele's findings highlight the importance of school contexts in creating non-stereotype-supportive environments for ethnic minority students, especially for African American males.

In order to cope and survive in oppressive and racist contexts, Majors and Billson (1992) propose that young African American urban males have adopted a "cool pose," or what Jackson Katz (1999) calls the "tough guise." According to Majors and Billson, cool pose is a ritualized style of masculinity that helps black males to cope by acting emotionless, fearless, and detached in order to counter the anger, damaged pride, and the low self-confidence that comes from feeling subjugated and alienated from the white world. In school, this "cool" behavior often results in punishment. To outsiders, this cool pose is an expression of superiority and control. This orientation could be categorized under what Boykin and Toms (1985) have described as a "system disengagement orientation" versus a "passive or a systems change orientation." African American male students often adopt strategies and attitudes for identifying with group membership that are incompatible with achievement and academics (e.g., white students) because they have learned that hard work will not yield them the same rewards that are awarded to whites. It is easy then to see how many talented young black males get involved, instead, with drug dealing as an alternative path to economic upward mobility. These capable young males turn to this form of instant gratification (e.g., financial capital) as a replacement for the delayed gratification that education promises.

In a competitive economy where there are few employment opportunities, some black and Latino students leave school because they foresee the bleak opportunities for finding a job with only a high school diploma. Yet, some understand that without a diploma, working at fast-food restaurants may be the only option waiting for them (Fine, 1986). In her interviews with minority students, Fine (1986) found that students drop out of school because they have to "attend to their families' social and health needs, making schooling irrelevant and/or disruptive. Several leave because they had internalized social ideologies about their inabilities and their uselessness" (p. 397). Similarly, Felice (1981) found that black students drop out of high school because they sensed the "futility to continuing school, since it would only lead to the same low paying jobs their parents and friends had and they themselves were destined to get" (p. 420). Ogbu (1974) has reported similar attitudes on the part of black and Latino youth who by their preadolescent years believe that if they complete high school, they are twice as likely to be unemployed compared to whites. If they are fortunate enough to be employed, they are likely to earn 25% less. Understanding the "myth of the meritocracy" in this country, undoubtedly many students of color respond by becoming disengaged and disillusioned with high school.

Studies have also indicated that minority students frequently feel a strong disconnect between the school and their home culture (Delpit, 1995; Jimenez, 2000). This cultural disconnect is described by Delpit as a "cultural power" and by Young (2000) as a "cultural imperialism." Each concept describes "the universalization of a dominant group's experience and culture and its establishment as norm" (p. 45). In cultural imperialism, only the dominant group's cultural expressions are widely disseminated, thus becoming universal. According to Young, the dominant group strengthens its position by evaluating the other groups against its dominant norms. As a result, differences from the dominant group's norms are labeled inferior, deviant, and negatively stereotyped. For many black youth, the behaviors, attitudes, and styles that are accepted and valued within their communities or in the "hood" or "barrio" are not accepted by the "dominant" culture in the school. This is experienced as culturally oppressing for many minority youth. Being forced to speak in Standard English, for example, is considered "acting white" to many students of color (Carter, 2003). Culturally oppressive experiences causes what W.E.B. Du Bois (1903/1969) referred to as "double consciousness." According to this respected scholar, double consciousness is a "sense of always looking at one's self through the eyes of others, or measuring one's soul by the tape of a world that looks on in amused contempt and pity" (p. 45). This feeling of double consciousness arises when the oppressed person refuses to accept these stereotyped visions of the self. Double consciousness, then, may be thought of as an act of defiance/resilience in the face of negative stereotypes. In contrast, because individuals belonging to the dominant culture are rarely provided with the opportunity to experience the world as others know it, they come to believe there is only one universal reality and truth—the one that they know—and are likely to dismiss all other perspectives (Highwater, 1981).

In order to navigate both the school and community cultures, savvier minority students learn to "switch" by becoming competent in both the mainstream and their own culture's ways of communicating. Switching languages is frequently used by many bilingual individuals and appears to be a strategy used by higher-performing black students as well in order to traverse the school and home cultures. For example, between the home and the school cultures a student may "code switch" by communicating in Standard English at school and the language of the "hood" or "Black English" at home. Cross and Strauss (1998) explicate that in black students, code switching is the turning on and off proclivities of "black behavior" in order to use different verbal styles, attitudes, and behaviors. Code switching has been called "fronting" by blacks because it requires that they talk, act, dress, and think in ways that will make others feel comfortable and ensure that they will receive equal treatment in situations like school and work. In this way, code switching helps blacks and other persons of color not to be treated unfairly by others, but rather as just another student or employee (Cross & Strauss, 1998).

In her in-depth interviews with low-income African American youth, Carter (2003) illustrated how these young people have learned to negotiate school and community by employing "dominant" and "nondominant" cultural capital. For instance, students tended to adhere to the dominant culture (e.g., Standard English) in the school setting to demonstrate their "intelligence." But in the community setting, the nondominant culture supplanted the dominant to demonstrate "black" group affiliation. Thus, in their communities, students of color adopted the "black cultural capital" that their peer group embraced in order to maintain a valued status within their community. By adhering to certain speech codes, dress styles, and music preferences that signify a degree of "blackness," young people ensure group affiliation and recognition. This code of conduct provides exclusive membership with other black young people and excludes school personnel and other individuals who could undermine the black cultural capital (Boykin & Ellison, 1995).

Fordham and Ogbu (1986) have also reported that black students are more likely than white or Asian students to find themselves in situations where they have to choose between being popular among peers and performing well in school. Minority students may avoid achieving due to fear of being ostracized by peers if they are viewed as "nerds." Conversely, Asian American and white students are more likely to belong to a peer group that encourages and supports academic excellence (Steinberg, Dornbusch, & Brown, 1992). In short, peer socialization is powerful, often counteracting school socialization because it gives young people an empowering identity. The balancing of the two socialization forces and the selective privileging of each in various situations can be thought of as resilience/defiance behavior.

Many of these cultural styles that signify "blackness" evolved from the urban inner cities and are popularized by the media and the entertainment and music industry. The media impart socializing messages, often promoting images of athletes and music entertainers who possess power and material resources. Young people observe these images and may try to emulate the expressions and characteristics promoted. This is juxtaposed against the relatively limited representations of minorities in the media. Tate (1999) explains that the reason the cultural expression of hip-hop music, for example, is so attractive to young people is because it provides a political commentary on their perceptions about reality, economic, and social stigmatization. Hip-hop has become a cultural movement for youth that highlights the political, social, and economic injustices that exist in society. Ferguson (in press) argues that while rap and hip-hop music have cultural imagery value (e.g., identity) for black youth, they provide entertainment value for more affluent white youth.

These cultural styles emulated from media socialization often supplant those valued by teachers and influence their evaluations of students of color. In the classroom, for example, teachers may look at how some students of color are dressed—baggy pants and backward hat—and assume that they are unintelligent because they do not conform to the dominant style of dressing or with the demeanor that teachers associate with intelligence (Carter, 2003). This erroneous reasoning on the part of teachers could in part explain why the self-concept of many children of color may be "lessened in school settings" (Campbell-Whatley & Comer, 2000).

Collectively, these studies help to elucidate the problem of underachievement and academic disidentification on the part of minority and poor students. They suggest that if we are to ensure that all students achieve their full potential, especially black males, we need to provide them with the appropriate school, community, and family supports. Furthermore, the research also suggests that the failure to affirm and/or recognize the valued cultural components of the community sometimes produces maladaptive consequences for students. On the other hand, productive adaptation is often a function of defiant/resilient behavior.

The Third Obstacle: Opportunities to Learn

A third major obstacle is the multifaceted ways in which communities and families support academic learning for some students and fail to support it for others. The effects of family environments on academic achievement and the opportunities they provide have gained increased interest from researchers. The family is one of the primary sources of socialization for children. Parents are children's first and continuing teachers and the home environment they provide significantly impacts future academic achievement. According to the literature on family environments, children who are academic achievers have parents who set high standards that are both realistic and challenging, and who encourage and support their children to meet their goals. Such parents are in tune with their children's competencies and believe their children can achieve (Heath, 1995).

In 1966, James Coleman and colleagues indicated that differences in the family backgrounds of students, versus school characteristics, accounted for the greatest quantity of variance in school achievement. This finding was later found to be less relevant for low-income and ethnic minority children than for the general population (Gordon, 1999). However, family background and income continue to be considered strong predictors of achievement in school. In similar works, Mercer (1973) and Wolf (1966, 1995) concluded that this association between family status and student achievement might be explained by the presence of family environmental supports for academic development. They highlighted the importance of books, positive models, and help with homework. Likewise, Heath (1995) maintains that parents who provide access to reading materials, encourage children to solve problems, and minimize exposure to television are likely to have children who succeed academically. In addition, Heath states that family environments associated with school achievement include high degrees of verbal interaction, high expectations for achievement, warm and nurturing relationships, and parental confidence in children's abilities. Parental childrearing style has also been linked to outcomes of cognitive development. The authoritative parenting style (Baumrind, 1978), for example, is preferable to the liberal "permissive" and the controlling "authoritarian" childrearing styles. Authoritative parents, according to Baumrind (1978), are responsive, warm, firm, and have consistent rules and high expectations for their children's behavior. Verbal give-and-take and consistent discipline are associated with cognitive development and stable behavior in children.

In addition, studies examining the relationship between parental educational level and socioeconomic status have also highlighted characteristics of home environments that are conducive to academic attainment.

Parental education has been especially connected to the differences between high- and low-achieving students (Martinez, 2000). Ferguson (2005) found that the mother's years of schooling is associated with the number of books in the household and the percentage of families who read daily to their children. Parental occupation has also been implicated in the outcomes for children's academic achievement. Heath (1995), for instance, explains that because middle-class parents have work positions that require originality, ambition, autonomy, and self-control, these parents also expect their children to be autonomous, motivated, and to have internalized control. Children in these families are permitted to verbalize their opinions and receive more elaborate answers to their questions. In contrast, working-class parents tend to work in jobs that demand obedience to rules, respect for authority, and dependability. Therefore, these parents also expect their children to conform, adhere to rules, and respect authority. Working-class parents may also be more directive and less flexible with their children. Conversely, middle-class home environments tend to be more flexible and less rigid in their interactions.

Peters (1981) contends that some of the attitudes children learn from their working-class parents put them at a disadvantage in schools. The socialization practices in the homes of low-income children do not prepare them to cope with teachers' expectations. According to Peters, since the majority of schools are operated by middle-class white teachers and administrators, the school environment may be more encouraging of children who exhibit similar middle-class behaviors. He explains that socialization practices of parents are a form of social "capital" that puts middle-class children at an advantage because they are being equipped with the same skills that are rewarded in the classroom.

Research has also illustrated the relationship between parental involvement and academic achievement. In general, parental involvement has been described as participation in school activities for their children. Other parental involvement activities include helping with homework, reading with children, monitoring leisure activities, and investing in supplementary education activities. Not surprisingly, studies have indicated a positive relationship between parental involvement and student achievement (Chen & Xitao, 1999; Epstein, 1991; Singh et al., 1995). In addition, studies examining the relationship between parental income and level of education have shown that the higher the income and educational attainment, the more likely parents are to be involved in their child's school (U.S. Department of Education, NCES, 2003).

Lastly, it has been posited that opportunities to learn and purposes of schooling are synchronous with the phases of societal development. More than 40 years ago, anthropologist Anthony Wallace (1961) explained the differential purposes of schooling and how they are closely associated with the differential purposes of societal development. He categorized the purpose of schooling depending on one of three phases (i.e., revolutionary, conservative, and reactionary) that society is passing. In the revolutionary societal phase, the dominant focus of schools is on moral development because this society is interested in human rights. The second priority is the development of intellect. Last of all, "technic," or the development of skills such as how to find the square root of a number, is the third priority. A conservative society, on the contrary, is mainly concerned with technic or skill development because skills are needed to sustain a society. Moral development is the next priority, followed by intellectual development since this type of society is mostly concerned with maintaining the status quo. Finally, in reactionary societies, moral development is again given top priority, emphasizing behavioral control. This society favors skill development in people over intellect in order to make individuals in society technically proficient. Wallace suggested that intellectual development is neglected in both conservative and reactionary societies, reducing the number of persons who are capable of thinking logically on matters of public concern. This is problematic because schools will produce generations of children who have been taught to do everything well except thinking. According to Wallace, we should instead cultivate intellect "in all persons to the limit of their abilities" (p. 52). Like Wallace, Gordon (2001, 2002) has reasserted the need for schools to nurture intellective competence in all students. He has argued that the overall purpose of school is incongruent with the basic needs for the society at large, particularly poor minority children. In his book *Education and Justice*, Gordon (1999) explains that while schools are primarily focused on the concerns of the conservative reactionary society, many individuals living in that system are concerned with radical change. The contradiction between the purposes of schooling may help to account for the lack of success in some students, except in those instances where defiance is productively adaptive.

The Fourth Obstacle: Quality of Teachers and Teaching

The final obstacle is the quality of preparation of many teachers and their inability to differentiate instruction to students' diverse cultural characteristics. Repeatedly, studies have shown that teacher's knowledge and qualifications are connected with student learning and achievement (Darling-Hammond, 1999; Ferguson, 1991; Goldhaber & Brewer, 1997). For instance, Goldhaber and Brewer (1997) found that students learned more mathematics from teachers who majored in mathematics than from those who did not. Similarly, Ferguson (1998) found that teachers who had high verbal scores on the SAT or ACT were more effective in helping students perform well on verbal measures. He also found that teacher education and experience accounted for significant variation in student achievement. Furthermore, on the basis of a comprehensive review of 60 studies, Greenwald, Hedges, and Laine (1996) also concluded that teacher education, experience, and ability, together with small teacher–pupil ratio and school size, account for considerable increases in student achievement.

Unfortunately, the research on teacher quality and service to minority students indicates that public schools located in poor communities have less prepared teachers in the classroom. For instance, in a study of 1,000 school districts, Ferguson (1991) found that every additional dollar spent on more highly qualified teachers yielded greater improvements in student academic achievement. According to the Children's Defense Fund's *Key Facts about Education* (2003), students in poor community schools were more likely than their wealthier counterparts to be taught core subjects by a teacher who had not majored in that subject matter. For example, 70% of 7th- through 12th-grade students were taught physical science by unqualified teachers. Students in middle grades were also more likely to be taught by out-of-field teachers or teachers who lack a major or certification in the subject they teach. In fact, the data from 1999–2000 showed that a large number of students in middle grades were taught by out-of-field English, math, science, and social science teachers (NCES, 2003). Minority students are also more likely to be taught by beginning teachers (3 years or less of teaching experience). For instance, NCES (2003) data show that low-income schools and those with large numbers of minority and limited-English-proficient (LEP) students were more likely to hire beginning teachers compared with more affluent schools and schools with fewer minority and LEP students. Given that teachers make a critical difference in what and how students learn, districts need to implement strategies for hiring only qualified teachers who are assigned to teach in those content areas in which they have been prepared to teach. In tandem, districts may want to consider investing in the ongoing professional development of teachers.

There is an emergent literature on exemplary teachers (e.g., Lipman, 1998; Payne, 1994) and their relationship to student achievement. This literature describes successful or exemplary teachers as having the following characteristics: are committed, are aware of student's needs, are attentive to the class at all times, are involved intellectually and emotionally in the class, have high expectations, and can recognize both their students' strengths and weaknesses. Furthermore, exemplary teachers act as advocates for their students, set high standards, are culturally responsive, and work hard to include students who are marginalized. They have the necessary skills and strategies for teaching multicultural students. Unlike successful teachers, ineffective teachers are unreflective of the teaching process, are inflexible, unmotivated, and discount some students as "unreachable or unteachable" (Payne, 1994). Because teachers are invaluable resources in the schools, we need to commit to recruiting dedicated and efficacious teachers who will be motivated to teach minority students. In light of the teacher shortage crisis (Recruiting New Teaching Inc., 2000), particularly teachers of color, we need to ensure that we are retaining qualified and expert teachers, especially in urban school districts. Unfortunately, more experienced teachers are lured by wealthier districts, which can offer higher salaries and better working conditions. Providing incentives such as tuition reimbursement for coursework, giving special recognition to outstanding teachers, and providing teachers more authority in the school and their classroom can reduce teacher attrition. In addition, the literature on mentoring has shown that beginning teachers are more likely to remain in the teaching profession when they have the support of experienced mentors (Darling-Hammond, 1994).

TEACHERS' ATTITUDES TOWARD AND EXPECTATIONS FOR STUDENTS

In addition to teacher quality, researchers have also studied the relationship between teacher's attitudes and expectations about efficacy and student achievement (e.g. Coleman et al., 1966; Felice, 1981; Payne, 1994; Weinstein, 2002) and how such beliefs result in differential treatment of students. Studies on the impact of teacher expectations have shown that teachers tend to react more favorably to higher SES children, to females, to high achievers, to attractive children and to conforming children, as well as to children who do not belong to minority groups (Baron, Tom, & Cooper, 1985; Good, 1981; Proctor, 1984). Sadly, many teachers believe that some students cannot learn and as a result, they do not expect all students to succeed in school. For example, Kenneth Clark (1965) argued that a major factor leading to the academic underachievement of African American students was the fact that their teachers did not expect them to learn. Yet, there is extant evidence that African American students, including males, value education and would like to perform well in school (Noguera, 2001). Unfortunately, lowered expectations can result from labeling some students as not "smart enough" or "tough enough" or not resilient enough by erroneously assuming that resilience is solely an individualistic characteristic.

Furthermore, negative expectations against low socioeconomic status minority students have an adverse effect on their motivation, performance, and achievement. Teachers who hold negative attitudes/stereo-types can create resistance on the part of the students, suppress their development, and become part of the successive factors that lead to detri-mental self-fulfilling prophecies. This is especially relevant in contexts where the cultural and economic backgrounds of the teachers are differ-ent from those of the students (Payne, 1994). It has been suggested that quite often white teachers confess to having racist attitudes toward indi-viduals in the general population, but claim that those attitudes do not apply to their students in their classroom (Ahlquist, 1991). Nevertheless, it is difficult to believe that racist attitudes and ethnocentric views do not manifest themselves in classroom behaviors or practices. Tettegah (1996) correctly reminds us that classrooms are "microcosms of the larger soci-ety" and we must realize that racist attitudes and stereotypes "do not stop at the schoolhouse door" (p. 154).

Teaching and learning go hand in hand, so if minority students feel alienated from teachers, they may become uninterested in not just the teacher but also in learning what the teacher is teaching. Consequently, this may result in both the students and the teacher completely ignoring each other or students disrespecting and disobeying the teacher or his or her instructions. Therefore, it is simple to deduce that negative percep-tions on both the part of the teacher and the student can interfere with the teaching and learning process. One might argue that it may be help-ful to match students and teachers according to their racial or socioeco-nomic backgrounds, but considering that there is a dearth of teachers of color available (Haberman, 1989), this solution cannot be presently ful-filled. It is also an impractical solution, given the reality that students of color have to learn to navigate among and around white groups outside of the school walls. Another reality is that most teacher candidates today, including minority teachers, are trained by white male professors who may not have firsthand experience working with minority and at-risk stu-dents (Grant, 1989). Considering the significant influence that teachers have on their students, it is important that teacher education programs include cultural training for teachers in order to raise awareness about racist attitudes and views.

CULTURALLY RELEVANT PEDAGOGY

As the population of immigrants has rapidly increased throughout the United States, classrooms have also become increasingly diverse. Nation-wide, teachers are faced with the challenge of educating children from different cultures who speak different languages and are from lower socio-economic status, the largest subgroup of whom are Latino students. While individualizing education for every student from diverse backgrounds may not be a feasible goal, proponents of "multicultural" and "culturally competent" education explain that the Anglo-Eurocentric perspectives that underlie the American school curriculum are culturally unresponsive and ineffective for culturally diverse students. Instead, they recommend that educators use a curriculum that is multicultural and representative of today's pluralistic society and perspectives.

In their report, *One Nation, Many Peoples*, members of the New York State Social Studies Review and Development Committee (Gordon & Roberts, 1991) reviewed the social studies syllabi and made several recommendations to the Education Commissioner designed to heighten students' understanding of the cultures and histories of the different groups that compose American society. The members of the committee concluded that the syllabi paid insufficient attention to the many cultural currents in the nation and social studies should be "taught from a global perspective." They called for immediate revisions of omissions, inaccuracies, and misrepresentations in the syllabi. The committee asserted that "if the United States is to continue to prosper in the 21st century, then all of its citizens, whatever their race or ethnicity, must believe that their ancestors have shared in the building of the country and have a stake in its success" (p. 1). In addition, the co-chairpersons, Gordon and Roberts, and members of the committee identified the following seven concepts as responsive to a multicultural social studies curriculum:

1. Democracy—democratic ideals as the foundation of American society
2. Diversity—understanding and respecting others and oneself
3. Economic and social justice—understanding personal and social responsibility for economic and social systems
4. Globalization—recognizing interdependence and world citizenship
5. Ecological balance—recognizing responsibility for the global neighborhood
6. Ethics and values—the pursuit of fairness and the search for responsibility
7. The individual and society—seeing oneself as a participant in society (p. viii).

Respect for ethnic and racial pluralism is a major principle of multicultural education. For this reason, infusing multiple cultural perspectives into the school curriculum is beneficial to the education of all students (Gordon & Roberts, 1991). If classrooms are a reflection of today's pluralistic society, then students need to acquire the knowledge and understanding of the cultures in this nation in which they must eventually function. However, when educators teach from one perspective (Eurocentric), they lose multicultural students along the way because students sense they are not part of the story. White students, on the other hand, can easily relate to almost all the experiences discussed in the classroom because they are taught from the point of view of white perspective and history. For instance, in her review of popular American history textbooks for 5th, 8th, and 11th grades, Cruz (2002) wanted to determine how Latinos are depicted, to what extent they are included in the history of the United States, and whose values are advanced in the textbooks. The content analysis revealed that Latinos were repeatedly omitted from U.S. history and the few times they were included they were portrayed pejoratively as violent, passive, lazy, and resistant to assimilating into the U.S. mainstream. Cruz's findings corroborate the notion that schools teach from a Eurocentric perspective that often excludes the perspective of ethnic minorities from the history of the United States.

Instead of teaching from a Eurocentric perspective, Asante (1991) recommends teaching from a "centrist" paradigm, in which the students' own culture and history are used as a context for learning and helping them relate to other cultural perspectives. As defined by Asante, "centricity is a concept that can be applied to any culture; even a White person educated in such a system does not assume superiority based upon racist notions" (p. 171). According to this view, centrist pedagogy places the indigenous culture of the learner at the center of the learning experience without excluding or demeaning other cultures or perspectives. Robert Moses (2001), for example, has successfully implemented centrist pedagogy in his mathematics curriculum by consistently posing math problems that have as their context indigenous cultural experiences. Similarly, the centrist model can be introduced in subjects like music by integrating traditional music and dances from many cultures in the curriculum. In this way, music education encompasses the ethnic diversity of the students in today's schools.

Multicultural, culturally competent, or centrist perspectives then are not only important for their contribution to effective pedagogy, issues of inclusion, representation, and social justice. These perspectives have the potential to contribute to the cultivation of students' development of higher-level cognitive abilities by preparing them to understand the world from different viewpoints. In modern multicultural societies, this capacity to accommodate to diverse cultures and perspectives is increasingly associated with resilience.

OVERCOMING THE OBSTACLES

Given these four categories of obstacles, intervention to offset their differential impacts will need to be complex with respect to the kinds of interventions and the levels at which the interventions occur. The problem of access to human resource development capital is an issue associated with the political economy of the society. It is not likely to be responsive to professional intervention. However, since some aspects of the utilization of capital are a matter of human choice, professional service and guidance with respect to the accumulation and use of resources may indeed be effective. We believe that persons can be taught to utilize resources effectively. Yet, even in the presence of access to adequate human resource development capital, we continue to find differentials in the levels of academic achievement (Miller, 1995). For example, the academic achievement gap exists among blacks and whites at all income levels. In fact, as SES and achievement levels increase, the gap between lower-status and higher-status groups increases, resulting in a larger academic achievement gap between middle-class blacks and whites than between lower-class blacks and whites (Miller, 1995). This latter finding suggests the operation of an intergenerational sociocultural phenomenon that may be resistant to changes in the political economy as well as to professional intervention. It is possible that these socioeconomic and cultural differentials are causally related to the second category of obstacles concerning the attitudes, learning behaviors, and cultural styles of the students themselves (Boykin & Toms, 1985; Fordham & Ogbu, 1986; Gordon, 1988; Steele, 1997). We think that these attitudes and behaviors can be made responsive to direct professional and social intervention. The two remaining categories—family support for academic learning and quality of pedagogical intervention—are perhaps the most widely recognized avenues of intervention. The quality of teachers and teaching has received the most systematic attention. Intervention to change the quality of family and home support for academic learning has been more or less neglected in communities of color and low income.

To overcome these obstacles, we see four possible lines of attack:

1. More equitable access to the human resource capital considered to be the essential preconditions of academic and personal development;

2. More universal access to appropriate and sufficient instruction and opportunity to learn;

3. More universal access to enabling and supportive contexts for academic learning in the communities and homes where children live; and

4.   The development of "agentic" learning attitudes and behaviors on the part of students who are now underrepresented among high academic achievers.

Given the ubiquitous association between access to the education-related forms of capital and quality of life (SES) on one hand and academic achievement on the other, we see no rational alternative to revolutionary change in the distribution of access to such capital. Human history is marked by continued movement toward broader participation in the political economy of societies. However, that natural movement may not be rapid and consistent enough for us to depend on such change, alone, to solve the problems of education for democratic living.

Gordon (1999) has advanced the concept of the affirmative development of academic ability as both relevant and informative to the efforts at optimizing success for all students and reducing the challenges of minority academic underachievement. As parallel to the affirmative action movement, Gordon first advanced the notion of affirmative development of academic ability more than 10 years ago (Gordon, 2001; Gordon & Meroe, 1989). Affirmative action was implemented to ensure that qualified individuals were not disqualified because of their ethnicity, gender, or race. Recent debate has questioned whether affirmative action is a program to privilege "unqualified" candidates over those who are qualified. While the affirmative action movement was established with a primary focus of expanding access to minority applicants to employment and to quality colleges and universities, increased access has not resulted in the reversal of the underrepresentation of minority students among students with higher levels of academic achievement. Hence, in their report, *Reaching the Top*, the College Board's National Task Force on Minority High Achievement (1999) recommended pursuing a policy of "affirmative development" in which various investments, actions, and public and private polices are pursued in order to create more opportunities for the intellective and personal development of minority students. Like affirmative action, the commitment to affirmative development emphasizes equitable opportunities to demonstrate one's competence despite one's identity, coupled with the deliberate creation, nurturance, and enhancement of intellective competence.

One of the most controversial topics in the field of psychology is the debate over the malleability of intelligence. Researchers have attempted to determine the extent to which heritability and environmental effects account for the quality of intelligence. For instance, it has been estimated that differences in cognitive abilities, as measured by tests, are approximately 50% associated with genetic variation (Martinez, 2000), but the remaining variation is significantly influenced by individual experiences

(Weinberg, 1989). But, these are crude estimates of influences that operate in reciprocal interactions that are reflected in phenotypes. The form taken by any specific phenotype can be explained by the fact that genetic material has very broad ranges of reactions depending on the environmental influences (Hirsch, 1969).

In addition to the impact of this controversy on policy and professional practice, beliefs with respect to the plasticity of intelligence have important implications for the academic performance of students. In her research with children and adolescents, Dweck (2000) examined students' beliefs about their intelligence and the consequences of those beliefs on academic achievement. Dweck found that students who believe that intelligence is fixed tend to give up in a class when their first test score was a D or an F. In contrast, when students are convinced that intelligence is malleable, they tend to persevere and eventually succeed. Negative expectations and giving up are associated with the idea that intelligence is static as opposed to malleable (Cain & Dweck, 1995).

Gordon argues that intellectual ability is malleable and can be modified through environmental influences. To ascribe intelligence solely to either nature or nurture is erroneous (Gordon, 1999; Martinez, 2000; Sternberg, 1982; Whimbey & Whimbey, 1975) and creates confusion for educators and parents who are interested in facilitating optimal learning environments. Intelligence, as with other complex behaviors, is best thought to have its origin in dialectical interactions between whatever is given genetically and the environments in which it is developed. According to Gordon (2001), academic abilities are not simply inherited aptitudes due to genetic differences (e.g., Herrnstein & Murray, 1994; Jensen, 1969) but are abilities that can be deliberately or incidentally developed through pedagogical and social interventions. He explains that individuals in our society, namely members of upper economic status groups, are exposed to economic, cultural, and social circumstances that predispose them to acquire high levels of intellective competence (attitudes, dispositions, appreciations, knowledge, skills, and habits of mind). For instance, in the households of high socioeconomic status families, children benefit from literate adults and the academic support of siblings and parents. High socioeconomic status families also have the financial capital to purchase intellectual resources (computers, books, magazines) that can help to enhance their child's education. In these families, children also have more access to community resources such as clubs, private lessons, summer experiences, and cultural activities. These enriching environments have cascading effects on academic achievement. That is, because children from these homes have more external resources (e.g., supplementary education), they tend to begin school better prepared than children from lower socioeconomic status groups.

Most minorities (e.g., blacks, Latinos, and Native Americans) in this country, on the other hand, have a history of being deprived of the same socioeconomic related educational and social opportunities. Those that live in urban and rural poverty are more likely to have less personal and social support for academic learning than their counterparts from more affluent families (Ianni, 1988). Thus, limited educational opportunities and access have made it more difficult for socioeconomically disadvantaged groups to develop intellective competencies and reach high levels of academic achievement. Consequently, a critical problem for educationists is the deliberate development of academic ability in those children whose natural life conditions do not predispose them to high levels of such achievement (Gordon, 1999). For this reason, Gordon (2001) has proposed that education stakeholders embark on a national effort, the affirmative development of academic ability, to develop academic abilities deliberately in students who are deprived of various capital resources. As conceived by Gordon, the goal of a national program of affirmative development would be to develop academic abilities in the lower and underclasses in our society through deliberate pedagogical and social interventions. Gordon has identified several components of such systematic intervention:

1. Early, continuous, and progressive exposure to rigorous preacademic and academic teaching and learning transactions. This should begin with high levels of language, literacy, and numeracy development.

2. Diagnostic, customized, and targeted assessment, instructional and remedial interventions.

3. The use of relational data management systems (systems that disaggregate data by specific input and outcome variables such as ethnicity, gender, and SES) to inform educational policy and practice decisions.

4. Explicit teaching of tacit knowledge and skills that are specific to the multiple cultural contexts in which the learner must function.

5. Exposure to high-performance learning communities (learning environments in which high achievement standards for teachers and all students are ubiquitous). Requires commitment and involvement from parents and community members.

6. Explication of tacit knowledge, meta-cognition, and meta-componential strategies.

7. Access to a wide range of supplementary educational experiences.

8. Connecting academic learning to the lives of subaltern communities of learners.

Edmund T. Gordon (in press) claims that he was not able to deal effectively with his high school experience until he gained awareness that he could map his academic experiences onto his personal political agenda. Now a professor of anthropology, he is developing an education intervention that incorporates explicit development of political and social action insights and skills into the high school curriculum. Reminiscent of Freire's (1970) concept of teaching as a subversive activity, Gordon's approach is designed to use involvement in political and social action as both a motivator for engagement with the academic experience, and as a vehicle for the study and mastery of specific academic content. This strategy is responsive to the paradox that adheres to the purposes of schooling as advanced by Anthony Wallace (1961), in which the official purposes of schooling are sometimes contradictory to the implicit purposes for which many young minority students might turn to schooling. Modern schools are more likely to see moral or skills development as their primary purpose, while these youth are more concerned with radical change or revolution. Rather than leaving these subaltern[1] groups on their own to develop alternative and resistant strategies with which to deal with schooling, the focus on political and social action, as a part of the academic experience, has the potential to channel antisocial and disruptive behavior into prosocial and developmentally productive activities. Unfortunately, empirical data are not yet available to disconfirm the implicit hypothesis. However, anecdotal, ethnographic, and some survey data strongly support this association between sense of power (Coleman, 1966), sense of purpose (Coles, 1967), responsible action (Sullivan, 1984), and effective human agency as expressed in academic and personal development.

One hardly needs to make the case here for the importance of access to appropriate and sufficient instruction and opportunity to learn. Darling-Hammond, Andrew Porter, Ronald Ferguson, Gordon and Shipman, Berliner and Biddle, James Coleman, and hosts of other investigators have repeatedly shown the association between quality of teaching, quality of teachers, adequacy of resources available to the school, time spent in school, and so on., and school achievement. This research supports the conclusion that such factors as the following are characteristic of effective instruction and opportunity to learn:

- Content and pedagogical knowledge and skill of teachers
- Richness, orderliness, and purposefulness of curriculum
- Adequacy of pedagogical resources
- Teacher knowledge of and adaptation of learning experiences to students

- Rigor of instructional demands in the presence of support for mastery

One of James Comer's (1997) recent books is titled *Waiting for a Miracle: Why Schools Can't Solve our Problems and How We Can*. In this insightful little book, Comer argues that it is folly for us to expect that schools alone will solve the problem of academic underproductivity in low-income students and students of color. He makes a case for greater participation on the part of parents in the education of their students. Gordon, Meroe, Bridglall, and Wang (in press) introduce the term *supplementary education* to refer to the formal and informal learning and developmental enrichment opportunities provided for students outside of school and beyond the regular school day or year. Some of these activities may occur within the school building but are beyond those included in the formal school curriculum. After-school care is, perhaps, the most widespread form of supplementary education. These supplements to schooling also include the special efforts that parents exert in support of the intellective and personal development of their children. These efforts may range from provisions for good health and nutrition to extensive travel and deliberate socialization to life in the academy, as well as to mediated exposure to selected aspects of both indigenous and hegemonic cultures. Many activities that are considered to be routine in the settings where they occur can implicitly cultivate the intellective and academic development of young people. These routines include reading to and with one's children; dinner table talk and inclusion in family discussion of important issues; exposure to adult models of behavior supportive of academic learning; active use of the library, museums, and community and religious centers as sources of information; help seeking from appropriate sources; as well as investments in reference and other education-related materials.

In addition, parents can exercise efforts directed at influencing children's choices of friends and peers; guiding and controlling use of their spare time; guiding and limiting time spent watching TV and playing video games; and encouraging participation in high-performance learning communities. We find a wide range of deliberate and incidental activities that serve to supplement the more formal and systematically structured academic learning provided through schooling. These more intentional child development practices are, no doubt, dually responsive to the folk knowledge of academically sophisticated families and the empirically derived knowledge of experts in child development and education.

DISCUSSION

Traditionally, resilience has been conceptualized as an individual process of "bouncing back" from adversity and/or traumatic experiences. Gordon and Song (1994) argue that the construct of "resilience" references a passive human trait. The construct of "defiance," on the other hand, connotes a dynamic process or active human agency—purposeful effort. The defiant individual does not simply "bounce back" but actively struggles against and/ or seeks solutions deliberately. In the case of a student who is faced with negative circumstances and is deprived of essential human resource capital (e.g., health, financial, etc.), it is not enough that the student be naturally resilient. What is required is that the student be enabled to defy these negative influences. Sullivan (1984) refers to acts of active navigation through or around challenges and toward more adaptive situations as human agency. Central to exercising agency is Bandura's (1989) concept of self-efficacy. According to this scholar, self-efficacy beliefs are important to human motivation, affect, and action. For instance, the higher the self-efficacy, the more challenging the goals individuals set for themselves and the stronger their commitment to achieve those goals. Bandura (2001) has also introduced the notion of an "agentic" perspective to refer to behavior that is intentionally creative of one's own experiences, and intentionally directed at the alteration of one's environment. It is in this context that we use *agentic learning* to refer to the deliberate, goal-directed, and efficacious activity of learners that is characterized by defiance.

Given the functional, situational, and structural forces that are arrayed against the likelihood of high levels of academic achievement and personal development for many minority students, it is remarkable that some of these students do succeed. In their study of the correlates of success, Gordon and Song (1994) sought to identify the common factors that appear to have contributed to individual achievement and the defiance of predictions of failure in black adults who were forecasted for failure because of their "at-risk" status. A retrospective construction of the lives of the "defiers" in the study indicated that they had achieved success against the odds through deliberate and fortuitous orchestrations of many personal, environmental, and situational factors. Findings from this study indicated that persons (e.g., African American men) who defy negative predictions of success have several factors in common. They include: (a) autonomy; (b) relationships with significant others; (c) attributions; (d) positive response to constraints; and (e) belief systems.

Autonomy—capability and disposition for autonomous action.
Instead of detaching from adverse situations, the defiers took deliber-

ate actions and they had the sense that such efforts were efficacious. They made decisive actions and consciously defined themselves as not being like their peers. This capability may be the essence of what Coleman and colleagues (1966) has called "sense of power."

Significant others—a meaningful relationship with a significant other or others who function as models, guides, providers of support, openers of opportunities, mentors, etc. High achievement seems seldom to be the result of individual effort alone.

Attributions—reality factors are important determinants of career development, but the personal perceptions or attributions assigned to specific phenomena are often of equal importance in determining life-course outcomes. Attributions individuals ascribe to difficult situations often determine the manner in which they will react to those experiences. Keeping stressful situations in perspective helps some individuals deal with adversity.

Positive response to constraints—constraining and negative factors do not necessarily depress development. They sometimes operate as catalytic agents of resistance or of more constructive responses. The perception of a negative situation as a challenge or an opportunity appears to be associated with these defiers of negative predictions who produce positive responses to constraints.

Belief systems—although belief in oneself (self-concept) and believing that something is worth doing and can be done (efficacy) are important, a system of beliefs that extends beyond oneself appears to be strongly associated with success against the odds. Such a belief system seems to provide anchorage and stability in the face of difficult experiences that challenge one's confidence and faith.

What then may be said of the relevance of the resilience/defiance construct for approaches to overcoming the obstacles to high academic achievement? It appears that there are individual differences in the behavioral proclivities of persons that may render some persons more disposed toward effective adaptation than are others. The work on temperament by Chess and Thomas (1977) clearly points in that direction. If resilience is the meta-expression of such characteristics, the task is to seek out such persons and to try to remove impediments to the expression of the trait. The persons who ran interference for the Gordon and Song defiers may have been doing just that. However, if the construct references the expression of human agency, it may be possible to develop that characteristic in persons. From our perspective, pedagogical interventions can foster defiance behavior by: (1) providing students with opportunities to develop close, productive, and rewarding relationships with supportive peers and adults; (2) increasing students' sense of efficacy through joyful and successful engagement of rigorous challenges, from which they gain praise and see their goals achieved; (3) encouraging participation in extracurricular and supplementary education activities that include service as well as being served; (4) encouraging participation in and reflection upon purposeful activities and rituals through which value and meaning can be understood; and (5) creating high performance learning communities and experiences in support of the development and reinforcement of intellective and social competence. In addition, teachers and parents can encourage students to develop habits of perseverance, patience, and concentration when working on academic tasks.

In all of these experiences we see elements of the process of defiance in such learned and learning behaviors as Carroll's (1963) time on task, Resnick's (1999) effort-based learning, Bandura's (2001) and Sullivan's (1984) agentic behavior, Nelson-LeGall's (1986) help-seeking behavior, Sternberg's (1982) meta-componential strategies, and Gordon's and DeStefano's (1984) task engagement and resource utilization strategies. Unlike resilience as a state that either exists or it does not, defiance involves processes and strategies that can be taught and learned. If having learned to be defiant, one chooses to claim to have arrived at a resilient state, so be it. But to understand the human adaptive processes by which obstacles to high academic achievement can be overcome, we find the defiance construct more dynamic and productive than the passive resilience construct. However, one need not choose either/or, both processes are likely to be operative in successful adaptations, but the former, *defiance* has the advantage of being capable of being taught and learned.

NOTE

1. Subaltern groups are persons who have been subordinated by the dominant class or culture while simultaneously have developed distinct strategies of opposition and resistance to the dominant culture (Gordon, in press).

REFERENCES

Ahlquist, R. (1991). Position and imposition: Power relations in multicultural class. *Journal of Negro Education, 60*(2), 133–146.

Asante, M. (1991). The Afrocentric idea of education. *Journal of Negro Education, 60*(2), 170–180.

Bandura, A. (1989). Human agency in social cognitive theory. *American Psychologist, 44*(9), 1175–1184.

Bandura, A. (2001). Social cognitive theory: An agentic perspective. *Annual Review of Psychology, 52*, 1–26.

Baron, R. M., Tom, Y. H., & Cooper, H. M. (1985). Social class, race, and teacher expectations. In J. B. Dusek (Ed.), *Teacher expectancies* (pp. 251–267). Hillsdale, NJ: Earlbaum.

Baumrind, D. (1978). Parental disciplinary patterns and social competence in children. *Youth and Society, 9*, 229–276.

Berliner, D., & Biddle, B. (1995). *The manufactured crisis: Myths, fraud, and the attack on American public schools*. Reading, MA: Addison-Wesley.

Blackwell, A. G., Stewart, K., & Pastor, M. (2002). *Searching for the uncommon common ground: New dimensions on race in America*. New York: Norton.

Bourdieu, P. (1986). The forms of capital. In J. Richardson (Ed.), *Handbook of theory and research for the sociology of education* (pp. 241–258). Westport, CT: Greenwood.

Boykin, A. W., & Ellison, C. (1995). The multiple ecologies of Black youth socialization: An Afrographic analysis. In R. Taylor (Ed.), *African American youth: Their social and economic status in the United States* (pp. 93–128). Westport, CT: Praeger.

Boykin, A. W., & Toms, F. (1985). Black child socialization: A conceptual framework. In H. McAdoo & J. McAdoo (Eds.), *Black children: Social, educational, and parental environments* (pp. 33–51). New York: Sage.

Bryson, S. (1998). Relationship between race and attitudes toward black men. Journal of *Multicultural Counseling and Development, 26*(4), 282–293.

Cain, K., & Dweck, C. (1995). The relation between motivational patterns and achievement cognitions through elementary school years. *Merrill-Palmer Quarterly, 41*, 25–52.

Campbell-Whatley, C. & Comer, J. (2000). Self-concept and African-American student achievement: Related issues of ethics, power and privilege, *Teacher Education and Special Education, 23*(1), 19–31.

Carroll, J. B. (1963). A model of school learning. *Teachers College Record*, pp. 723–733.

Carter, P. L. (2003). "Black" cultural capital, status positioning, and schooling conflicts for low income African American youth. *Social Problems, 50*(1), 136–155.

Chen, M., & Xitao, F. (1999, April). *Parental involvement and students' academic achievement: A meta-analysis*. Paper presented at the annual meeting of the American Educational Association, Quebec, Canada. (ERIC Document Reproduction Service No. ED 430048)

Chess, S., & Thomas, A. (1977). *Temperament and development*. New York: Brunner/Mazel.

Children's Defense Fund. (2003). *Key facts about education*. Retrieved July 23, 2003, from http://www.childrensdefense.org/keyfacts_education.htm

Clark, K. (1965). *Dark guetto*. New York: Harper & Row.

Coleman, J. S., Campbell, E. Q., Hobson, C. J., McPartland, J., Mood, A. M., Weinfield, F. D., et al. (1966). *Equality of educational opportunity*. Washington, DC: U.S. Government Printing Office.

Coles, R. (1967). *Children of crisis: A study of courage and fear*. Boston: Little, Brown.

The College Board. (1999). *Reaching the top: A report of the National Task Force on Minority High Achievement*. New York: Author.

Comer, J. P. (1997). *Waiting for a miracle: Why schools can't solve our problems and how we can*. New York: Dutton.

Cross, W. E., & Strauss, L. (1998). The everyday functions of African identity. In J. K. Swim & C. Stangor (Eds.), *Prejudice: Vol. 14. The target's perspective* (pp. 267–279). San Diego, CA: Academy Press.

Cruz, B. (2002). Don Juan and rebels under palm trees: Depictions of Latin Americans in US history textbooks. *Critique of Anthropology, 22*(3), 323–342.

Darling-Hammond, L. (1994). *Professional development schools: schools for developing a profession*. New York: Teachers College Press.

Darling-Hammond, L. (1999). *Teaching as the learning profession: Handbook of policy and practice*. San Francisco: Jossey-Bass.

Delpit, L. (1995). *Other people's children: Cultural conflict in the classroom*. New York: New Press.

Du Bois, W. E. B. (1969). *The souls of black folks*. New York: New American Library. (Original work published 1903)

Dweck, C. (2000). *Self-theories: Their role in motivation, personality, and development. Essays in social psychology*. Florence, KY: Psychology Press.

Epstein, J. L. (1991). Effects on student achievement of teachers' practices of parent involvement. In B. A. Hutson, T. G. Sticht, S. B. Silvern, F. R. Chang, & S. Wood (Eds.), *Advances in reading/ language research: Vol. 5. Literacy through family, community, and school interaction*. (pp. 261–276). Greenwich, CT: JAI Press.

Felice, L. (1981). Black student dropout behavior: Disengagement from school rejection and racial discrimination. *Journal of Negro Education, 50*(4), 415–424.

Ferguson, R. (1991). Paying for public education: New evidence on how and why money matters. *Harvard Journal on Legislation, 28*, 465–498.

Ferguson, R. (1998). Can schools narrow the black-white test score gap? In C. Jenks & M. Phillips (Eds.), *The black–white test score gap* (pp. 318–374). Washington, DC: Brookings Institution.

Ferguson, R. (2005). Why America's black–white school achievement gap exists. In G. Loury, T. Modood, & S. D. Tele (Eds.), *Social mobility in the U.S. and Great Britain*. New York: Cambridge University Press.

Fine, M. (1986). Why urban adolescents drop into and out of public high school. *Teachers College Record, 87*, 393–409.

Fordham, S., & Ogbu, J. (1986). Black students' school success: Coping with the burden of "acting white." *Urban Review, 18*, 17–206.

Franklin, V. P. (2002). Introduction: Cultural capital and African American education. *Journal of African American History, 87*,175–181.

Freire, P. (1970). *Pedagogy of the oppressed* (M. B. Ramos, Trans). New York: Herder and Herder.

Garmezy, N. (1991). Resilience in children's adaptation to negative life events and stressed environments. *Pediatrics, 20*, 459–466.

Gibbs, J. T. (1988). *Young, black, and male in America: An endangered species*. Westport, CT: Auburn House.

Goldhaber, D. D., & Brewer, D. J. (1997). Why don't schools and teachers seem to matter? Assessing the impact of unobservables on education. *Journal of Human Resources, 32*, 505–523.

Good, T. L. (1981). Teacher expectations and student perceptions: A decade of research. *Educational Leadership, 38*(5), 415–422.

Gordon, E. T. (in press). Supplementary education from black resistance? In E. W. Gordon, A. S. Meroe, B. L. Bridglall, & M. Wang (Eds.), *Supplementary education*. Boulder and New York: Rowman & Littlefield and The College Board.

Gordon, E. W. (1988). *Human diversity and pedagogy*. New Haven, CT: Center in Research on Education, Culture and Ethnicity, Institution for Social and Policy Studies, Yale University.

Gordon, E. W. (Ed.). (1999). *Education and justice: A view from the back of the bus*. New York: Teachers College Press.

Gordon, E. W. (Ed.). (2000). Production of knowledge and pursuit of understanding. In C. C. Yeakey (Ed.), *Edmund W. Gordon: Producing knowledge, pursuing understanding* (pp. 301–318). Stamford, CT: JAI Press

Gordon, E. W. (2001, September). Affirmative development of academic abilities. *Pedagogical Inquiry and Praxis, 2*. New York: Teachers College, Columbia University, Institute for Urban and Minority Education.

Gordon, E. W. (2002). Affirmative development: Looking beyond racial inequality. *College Board Review, 195*, 28–33.

Gordon, E. W., & Armour-Thomas, E. (1991). Culture and cognitive development. In L. O. Okagaki & R. J. Sternberg (Eds.), *Directors of development: Influences on the development of children's thinking* (pp.83–100). Hillsdale, NJ: Erlbaum.

Gordon, E. W., & DeStefano, L. (1984). Individual differences in development and learning. In J. E. Ysseldyke (Ed.), *School psychology: The state of the art*. Minneapolis, MN: National School Psychology In Service Training Network.

Gordon, E. W., & Meroe, A. S. (1989, January). Common destinies—continuing dilemmas. *Psychological Science, 2*(1), 23–30.

Gordon, E. W., Meroe, S., Bridglall, B. L., & Wang, M. (Eds.). (in press). *Supplementary education*. Boulder and New York: Rowman & Littlefield and The College Board.

Gordon, E. W., & Roberts, F. (1991). *One nation, many peoples: A declaration of cultural interdependence. The report of the New York State Social Studies Review and Development Committee*. Albany: State Education Department, University of the State of New York.

Gordon, E. W., & S. Shipman (1979). Human diversity, pedagogy, and educational equity. *American Psychologist, 34*(10), 1030–1036.

Gordon, E. W., & Song, L. D. (1994). Variations in the experience of resilience. In M.C. Wang & E. W. Gordon (Eds.), *Educational resilience in inner city America: Challenges and prospects* (pp. 27–43). Hillsdale, NJ: Erlbaum.

Grant, C. (1989, June). Urban teachers: their new colleagues and curriculum. *Phi Delta Kappan*, pp. 764–770.

Greenwald, R., Hedges, L., & Laine, R.D. (1996). The effects of school resources on student achievement. *Review of Educational Research, 66*, 361–396.

Haberman, M. (1989, June). More minority teachers. *Phi Delta Kappan*, pp. 771–776.

Heath, T. D. (1995). Parents' socialization of children. In B. B. Ingoldsby & S. Smith (Eds.), *Families in multicultural perspective* (pp. 161–184). New York: Guilford Press.

Herrnstein, R. J., & Murray, C. (1994). *The bell curve: Intelligence and class structure in American life.* New York: Free Press.

Highwater, J. (1981). The intellectual savage. In J. Highwater, *The primal mind: Vision and reality in Indian America* (pp. 205–215). HarperCollins.

Hirsch, J. (1969). Behavior-genetic analysis and its biosocial consequences. *IRCD Bulletin, 5*(4), 3–4, 16-20.

Ianni, F. A. J. (1988). *The search for structure: A report on American youth today.* New York: Free Press.

Jensen, A. R. (1969). How much can we boost IQ and scholastic achievement? *Harvard Educational Review, 39*, 1–23.

Jimenez, R. T. (2000). Literacy and the identify development of Latina/o students. *American Educational Research Journal, 37*(4), 971–1000.

Katz, J. (1999). *Tough guise: media images and the crisis of masculinity* [Videotape]. (Available at Media Education Foundation, 26 Center Street, Northhampton, MA 01060; 800–897–0089)

Kozol, J. (1991). *Savage inequalities: Children in America's schools.* New York: Crown.

Lipman, P. (1998). *Race, class, and power in school restructuring.* New York: State University of New York Press.

Luthar, S. S., Cicchetti, D., & Becker, B. (2000). The construct of resilience: A critical evaluation and guidelines for future work. *Child Development, 71*(3), 543–562.

Luthar, S. S., & Zigler, E. (1991). Vulnerability and competence: A review of research on resilience in childhood. *American Journal of Orthopsychiatry, 6*(1), 6–21.

Majors, R. & Billson, J. M. (1992). Cool pose: The dilemmas of African American manhood in America. New York: Lexington Books.

Martinez, M. E. (2000). *Education as the cultivation of intelligence.* Mahwah, NJ: Erlbaum.

Masten, A. S. (1994). Resilience in individual development: successful adaptation despite risk and adversity. In M.C. Wang & E. W. Gordon (Eds.), *Educational resilience in inner city America: Challenges and prospects* (pp. 3–25). Hillsdale, NJ: Erlbaum.

Mercer, J. (1973). *Labeling the mentally retarded: Clinical and social system perspectives on mental retardation.* Berkeley: University of California Press.

Miller, L. S. (1995). *An American imperative: Accelerating minority educational advancement.* New Haven, CT: Yale University Press.

Moses, R. (2001). *Radical equations: math literacy and civil rights.* Boston: Beacon Press.

NAACP. (2001). *Call for action in education.* Baltimore: NAACP Education Department.

Nelson-LeGall, S. (1986). *Help-seeking behavior in learning.* Pittsburgh, PA: Learning Research and Development Center, University of Pittsburgh. (ERIC Reproduction Service No. ED 275741)

Noguera, P. (2001). Racial politics and the elusive quest for equity and excellence in education. *Education and Urban Society, 34*(1), 27–42.

Ogbu, J. U. (1974). *The next generation: An ethnography of education in an urban neighborhood.* New York: Academic Press.

Ogbu, J. U. (1988). Class stratification, racial stratification, and schooling. In L. Weis (Ed.), *Class, race, and gender in American education* (pp.163–182). Albany: State University of New York Press.

Ogbu, J. U.(1992). Understanding cultural diversity and learning. *Educational Researcher, 21*(8), 5–14.

Payne, R. S. (1994). The relationship between teacher's beliefs and sense of efficacy and their significance to urban LSES minority students. *Journal of Negro Education, 63*(2), 181–194.

Peters, M. F. (1981). "Making it" Black family style: Building on the strengths of black families. In N. Stinnett (Ed.), *Family strengths: Roots of well being* (pp. 73-91). Lincoln: University of Nebraska Press.

Pincus, F. L. (1996). Discrimination comes in many forms: Individual, institutional, and structural. *American Behavioral Scientist, 40,* 186–195.

Porter, A. C. (1995). The uses and misuses of opportunity-to-learn standards. *Educational Researcher,* 24(1), 21-47.

Proctor, C. P. (1984). Teacher expectations: A model for school improvement. *Elementary School Journal, 84*(4), 469–481.

Recruiting New Teaching, Inc. (2000). A guide to today's teacher recruitment challenges. Belmont, MA: Author.

Resnick, L. B. (1999). From aptitude to effort. A new foundation for our schools. *American Educator, 23*(1), 14–17. (ERIC Document Reproduction Service No. EJ 587 016)

Singh, K., Bickley, P. G., Trivette, P., Keith, T. Z., Keith, P. B., & Anderson, E. (1995). The effects of four components of parental involvement on eighth grade student achievement: Structural analysis of NELS-88data. *School Psychology Review, 24,* 299–317.

Steele, C. M. (1997). A threat in the air: How stereotypes shape intellectual identity and performance. *American Psychologist, 52*(6), 613–629.

Steinberg, L., Dornbusch, S., & Brown, B. (1992). Ethnic differences in adolescent achievement: An ecological perspective. *American Psychologist, 47*(6), 723–729.

Sternberg, R. J. (1982). (Ed.). *Handbook of human intelligence.* New York: Cambridge University Press.

Sullivan, E. V. (1984). *A critical psychology: interpretation of the personal world.* New York: Plenum Press.

Tate, G. (1999). 15 arguments in favor of the future of hip-hop. In Vibe Magazine & A. Light (Eds.), The *Vibe history of hip-hop* (pp. 385–394). New York: Three Rivers Press.

Tettegah, S. (1996). The racial consciousness attitudes of White prospective teachers and their perceptions of the teachability of students from different racial/ethnic backgrounds: findings from a California study. *Journal of Negro Education, 65*(2), 151–163.

U.S. Department of Education, NCES. (2003, June). *The condition of education 2003* (NCES2003–067). Washington, DC: U.S. Government Printing Office.

Wallace, A. F. C. (1961). Schools in revolutionary and conservative societies. In F. D. Gruber (Ed.), *Anthropology and education* (pp. 25-54). Philadelphia: University of Pennsylvania Press.

Weinberg, R. (1989). Intelligence and IQ: Landmark issues and great debates. *American Psychologist, 44*(2), 98–104.

Weinstein, R. S. (2002). *Reaching higher: The power of expectations in schooling.* Cambridge, MA: Harvard University Press.

Whimbey, A., & Whimbey, L. S. (1975). *Intelligence can be taught.* New York: Dutton

Wolf, R. M. (1966). The measurement of environments. In A. Anastasi (Ed.), *Testing problems in perspective* (pp. 491-503). Washington, DC: American Council on Education.

Wolf, R. M. (1995). The measurement of environments: A follow-up study. *Journal of Negro Education, 64*(3), 354–359.

Young, I. M. (2000). Five faces of oppression. In M. Adams, W. Blumefield, R. Castaneda, H. W. Hackman, M. L. Peters, & X. Zuniga (Eds.), *Readings for diversity and social justice: An anthology on racism, anti-Semitism, sexism, heterosexism, ableism, and classism* (pp. 35–49). New York: Routledge.

PART III

RESPONSIBILITY

CHAPTER 9

ENHANCING STUDENTS' ACADEMIC RESPONSIBILITY AND ACHIEVEMENT

A Social-Cognitive Self-Regulatory Account

Barry J. Zimmerman

John W. Gardner (1963), a former Secretary of Health, Education, and Welfare, once noted that the ultimate goal of the American educational system is to shift to the individual the responsibility for pursuing his or her own education. Responsibility has been defined lexically as "account-ability for actions and their consequences" (English & English, 1958, p. 463), and academic responsibility refers to students' acceptance of accountability for their successes and failures in school. There is wide-spread agreement that students should be taught academic responsibility and encouraged to demonstrate this desirable personal quality both in and out of the classroom. Most current "responsibility" education pro-grams focus mainly on character and deportment rather than on aca-demic independence and personal shouldering of the responsibility for learning. However, there have been important discoveries in recent years

Optimizing Student Success in School With the Other Three Rs:
Reasoning, Resilience, and Responsibility, 179–197
Copyright © 2006 by Information Age Publishing
179

regarding the nature and role of key processes and beliefs underlying students' development of personal responsibility, such as attributions of personal causality, self-efficacy beliefs, and the development of self-regulation. This chapter considers theory and available research on the causes and effects of academic responsibility.

MONTESSORI'S EDUCATIONAL PROGRAM TO DEVELOP STUDENTS' ACADEMIC RESPONSIBILITY

Maria Montessori was an important pioneer in the development of a systematic program designed to teach academic responsibility to young children (Lillard, 1972). Key elements in her educational program are the presence of an underlying structure or order in the classroom environment. For example, there are designated places and methods for using educational materials, such as a wooden puzzle designed to teach seriation. The children are encouraged to choose their own activities but are informed that they must return the puzzle to the same place so that others might play with it later. To assist these youngsters in choosing among the instructional materials, teachers group the materials according to potential interests and arrange them in sequence according to difficulty. After children begin to interact with a specific educational material, no one else is permitted to interfere with their "work." When the children end the activity and return the materials to their special place, they complete the activity cycle and become a responsible partner in maintaining the order of the classroom. The matter-of-fact way in which these young children accept responsibility for their own learning is often a surprise to parents who fight daily battles over their offsprings' lack of tidiness in their bedrooms! Montessori's classroom environments do not remain fixed but rather are frequently altered to highlight unused educational tools better. Even then, the children are made aware that the educational materials should be returned to their proper resting place. Montessori also places growing things, such as a plant, in the classroom environment, and individual children are assigned responsibility for its daily care (Lillard, 1972).

Although children in a Montessori school are given the freedom to make personal activity choices, they are also exposed to consequences of their actions, such as complaints from classmates if they fail to return materials to their proper place. These consequences allow children to test themselves and to reflect upon their actions. In this way, they can develop the self-discipline needed to function responsibly on their own. From Montessori's perspective, these children are given educational choices but are also held accountable for their activities in a social and physical setting that has readily discernible rules. Although this instructional approach was developed at the dawn of the 20th century, it includes conditions for fostering academic responsibility that are consistent with current psychological research. For example, children see "responsible" behavior modeled by the teacher and peers in Montessori classrooms — namely how to select, interact with, and replace educational materials. The students' subsequent classroom activities are the result of personal choices and unimpeded personal interactions with the educational materials. These conditions are important for fostering *attributions* of personal control and responsibility.

THE ROLE OF ATTRIBUTIONS IN JUDGMENTS OF PERSONAL RESPONSIBILITY

Causal attributions refer to a posteriori judgments of responsibility for various outcomes, and these attributions have been classified according to key dimensions. Weiner (1986, 1992) has studied the dimensions of locus, stability, and control. In the case of students' academic functioning, *locus* refers to who is responsible for an outcome, such as a test score—the students themselves or others (e.g., classmates, teachers, or parents). A harmful locus attribution, called a self-serving bias, occurs when students attribute successes to themselves but failures to others when in fact students are partially responsible for both outcomes. Many children learn early in life that shifting causal responsibility for adverse outcomes away from themselves can deflect negative impressions that others might form of them (Graham, 1998). *Stability* refers to the changeability of a cause. For example, students' attributions of outcomes to personal effort are usually considered more changeable than attributions to personal ability or traits (Weiner, 1986). An adverse stability bias is to ascribe academic personal outcomes, such as a poor grade, to a fixed personal trait or ability when it is in fact an incrementally learnable skill (Dweck, 1988). *Control* refers to one's personal power to regulate outcomes. If students perceive that they have control over an event, they will take responsibility for the outcomes, even when they are unfavorable (Graham, 1998). An adverse control bias occurs when students underestimate their capability to effect outcomes, and they attribute negative results to uncontrollable factors, such as task difficulty or luck. It is important to note that the control dimension of attributions often interacts with the locus and stability dimensions because students who are confident about controlling academic outcomes are more likely to accept their personal role (i.e., locus) for these outcomes and to see any shortcomings as personally changeable (i.e., unstable). A key measure of self-confidence about control is students' self-efficacy, which is defined as a priori personal beliefs about one's capability to learn or perform at designated levels (Bandura, 1997).

INFLUENCE OF ATTRIBUTION TRAINING ON STUDENTS' PERCEPTIONS OF SELF-EFFICACY

A number of studies have taught elementary school children academic skills along with attributions designed to increase perceptions of personal efficacy. Dale Schunk (1998) and his colleagues have conducted more than a dozen intervention studies in various subject-matter areas, such as math, reading, or writing. The training sessions involved modeled demonstrations of the academic skill by an adult instructor, who verbalized the solution strategies. After the modeled demonstration, the students engaged in hands-on activity with materials and solved a few academic problems during an emulation phase. During this time, the instructor provided corrective feedback and training in the use of various self-regulatory processes, often including attribution training (Schunk, 1982, 1983, 1984; Schunk & Cox; 1986; Schunk & Rice, 1986). Then students engaged in self-directed practice.

The attribution training involved ability or effort feedback or some combination of these two attributions regarding students' academic successes. An example of the instructor's *ability* feedback attribution is, "You're good at this" and an example of the instructor's *effort* attribution feedback is, "You've been working hard." These researchers found that teachers' provision of ability attribution feedback for students' successes was more effective than effort feedback (Schunk, 1983, 1984). Although effort attribution feedback raised self-efficacy and promoted skill development compared to no feedback, its effects were weaker than ability attribution feedback (Schunk, 1982). Because an ability attribution implies stability and generality in one's level of skill, it is not surprising that attributing successes to ability leads to perceptions of greater self-efficacy. Redlich, Debus, and Walker (1986) studied the effects of attribution feedback regarding both successes and failures on students' acquisition of arithmetic skill. Learning-disabled students who displayed learned helplessness were exposed to modeled demonstrations of long division. Half of the students received attribution feedback reaffirming ability for success and stressing effort for overcoming failure (e.g., "That's incorrect; I know you have the ability but you just have to try harder"). Redlich and colleagues found that students who received attribution feedback displayed higher self-efficacy and arithmetic achievement and less helplessness. Clearly students' attributions regarding their errors are critical to their sense of personal control over their learning. Although attributions of errors to a lack of effort can enhance perceptions of self-efficacy, there is evidence that attributions of errors to poor strategy use may be more effective (Clifford, 1986; Zimmerman & Kitsantas, 1999). Growing evidence supports the fact that students' attributions regarding the causes of their performance outcomes depend not only on attribution feedback they receive from others, but also on their own self-regulatory processes and beliefs.

FORMING ATTRIBUTIONS OF PERSONAL RESPONSIBILITY: A SELF-REGULATORY PROCESS ANALYSIS

From a social-cognitive perspective, students' perceptions of academic responsibility depend on their use of key self-regulatory processes and their beliefs about the effectiveness of those processes. These motivational beliefs and learning processes are self-regulated in three cyclical phases: forethought, performance, and self-reflection (Zimmerman, 2000). Forethought phase processes and beliefs prepare students for learning whereas performance phase processes are designed to improve the quality of students' mental and physical activities. Self-reflection phase processes and beliefs occur after performance and influence students' reactions to those efforts. Self-reflection processes also influence forethought planning for subsequent efforts to learn in cyclical fashion. As noted in Figure 9.1, attribution judgments occur during the self-reflection phase.

Forethought Phase

Attribution judgments depend on forethought phase processes and beliefs, such as *goal setting*. Because expert learners set personal goals that are more specific, proximal, and challenging (Locke & Latham, 1990), they are more likely than nonexperts to view their learning outcomes as personally controllable (Cleary & Zimmerman, 2001). Students' attribution judgments are also affected by their forethought *strategic planning*. When expert learners encounter difficult tasks, they adopt or create specific strategies to assist them whereas novice learners rely on unsystematic discovery (Pressley, Borkowski, & Schneider, 1987). Because expert learners engage in strategic planning, they are more likely than nonexperts to attribute causation for their learning outcomes to these controllable methods (Kitsantas & Zimmerman, 2002).

Students' self-reflective phase attributions are also influenced by learners' forethought self-motivational beliefs, such as self-efficacy, outcome expectations, task interest or valuing, and a learning goal orientation.

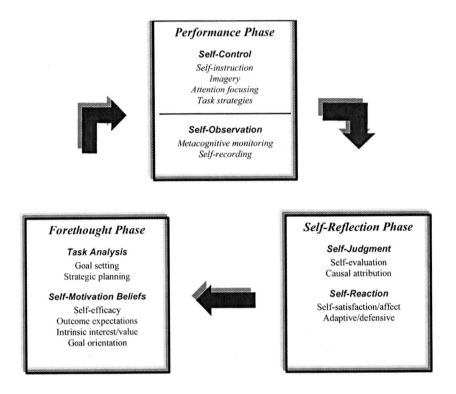

Figure 9.1.   Phases and subprocesses of self-regulation. From Zimmerman and Campillo (2003). Copyright (2003) by Cambridge University Press. Reprinted with permission.

Students who are *self-efficacious* about controlling or regulating their learning beforehand are more likely to judge their learning outcomes as personally controllable (Bandura, 1997). Regarding *outcome expectancies*, students who expect favorable learning outcomes and subsequently receive them are more likely to attribute causality to themselves than students who receive them unexpectedly (Fiske & Taylor, 1991). Concerning *intrinsic interest*, students who value a task skill, such as spelling accuracy, will put forth greater effort to learn this skill and will be more likely to attribute their successes to their effort (Lepper & Hodell, 1989). A student's learning *goal orientation* refers to his or her valuing of learning as a process in its own right rather than as a source of outcome-related success. Students who focus their goals on learning processes rather than learning outcomes are more likely to attribute causation to personal control (Zimmerman & Kitsantas, 1997, 1999).

Performance Phase

Attribution judgments are also hypothesized to be dependent on self-control processes, which involve use of specific learning methods or strategies such as *self-instructions, imagery, attention focusing,* and *task strategies.* As mentioned earlier, students who intentionally use specific strategies to control their learning are more likely to attribute outcomes to this strategy use rather than to other personal or impersonal variables, such as ability or task difficulty (Zimmerman & Kitsantas, 1997, 1999).

Students' attributions are also dependent on their self-observation processes during performance. *Meta-cognitive self-monitoring* refers to mentally tracking one's performance whereas *self-recording* refers to keeping a physical record of one's performance, such as a graph for the completion of homework assignments. Because of superior meta-cognitive monitoring and self-recording, expert learners track their learning progress more effectively (Ericsson & Kintsch, 1995) and are more likely to attribute personal causality to those efforts. By contrast, novice learners seldom track their learning progress systematically and are more likely to attribute causality to uncontrollable events, such as task difficulty or luck. These limitations in self-observation undermine novice learners' assumption of personal responsibility for unfavorable academic outcomes.

Self-Reflection Phase

Attribution judgments are also hypothesized to depend on another self-reflection phase process, *self-evaluation.* Because learners can often select their own self-evaluative criteria, they often differ in the way they interpret the same performance. Expert learners, such as professional writers (Cowley, 1959), tend to adopt a self-improvement or mastery criterion because these criteria provide direct feedback regarding the effectiveness of their learning processes, and these students are more likely to attribute causation for errors to controllable factors, such as their learning of specific techniques (Kitsantas & Zimmerman, 2002). By contrast, novice learners tend to self-evaluate using a social comparative criterion because they lack specific goals, and this social criterion leads them to attribute causation to normative causes, such as mental ability.

Students' attribution judgments regarding their academic performance outcomes affect their self-reactions. For example, attributions of errors to uncontrollable sources, such as a fixed mental ability, can undermine students' perceptions of *self-satisfaction* with their prior academic performance and can influence their future courses of action (Zimmerman & Kitsantas, 1997, 1999). Attributions of errors to uncontrollable factors, such as task difficulty, can also lead to *defensive* self-reactions intended to protect a person from dissatisfaction and aversive affect. These inferences lead to procrastination, task avoidance, cognitive disengagement, and apathy (Boekaerts & Niemivirta, 2000; Garcia & Pintrich, 1994). By contrast, causal attributions of errors to controllable sources, such as one's learning method, can sustain self-satisfaction and can lead to *adaptive* self-reactions, such as modifying or changing a strategy (Kitsantas & Zimmerman, 2002).

This cyclical model of perceived responsibility delineates how students' post-performance attributions of personal responsibility depend on their prior self-regulatory processes and beliefs, especially perceptions of self-efficacy. Although all children self-regulate to some degree (Winne, 1997), those who self-regulate *proactively* are much more effective than those who self-regulate *reactively*. For example, proactive students scan text passages for organizational cues before engaging in reading whereas reactive students read the text first and try to figure out the meaning afterward. From a cyclical perspective, proactive students engage in high-quality forethought, such as goal setting, which is designed to optimize their performance phase efforts and their self-reflections—including attributions to personally controllable sources. By definition, reactive learners must play "catch up" regarding events that initially had their own inertia, such as trying to figure out the meaning of a text after it was read. Such students feel victimized by learning events that are not under their control. These experiences undermine their sense of self-regulation and erode their willingness to shoulder responsibility for outcomes. This leads to the question of what types of personal experiences can limit students' development of self-regulatory processes, undermine their willingness to accept responsibility for learning outcomes, and place them at academic risk?

STUDENTS AT ACADEMIC RISK

Although children living in Western societies enjoy many freedoms, significant numbers of these children fail to develop effective self-regulatory skills. Because of their freedom and affluence, these youngsters often make choices that can lead to many personal problems, such as binge television watching or video game playing. The unfortunate consequences of students' lack of self-regulation, such as limited studying and poor report card grades, often leads these students to deny personal responsibility and to blame other people or unfortunate circumstances. Although some level of freedom of choice is essential to self-regulatory development, it is an insufficient condition. As was noted by Montessori, young children acquire a sense of personal responsibility when the classroom environments have a clear structure—with freedoms and duties spelled out in detail. In these environments, students know what is expected of them, how to meet those expectations, and what the consequences are. With school-age students, homework assignments can impart the same self-regulatory lessons if it is structured and monitored carefully, an issue that will be discussed in greater detail later.

What prevents a child or youth from acquiring and using proactive methods to self-regulate their academic functioning? A deficiency in *social experience* is a major problem. Many key self-regulatory processes are difficult to learn by individuals who grow up in homes or communities where these processes are not taught, modeled, or rewarded. Brody and his colleagues (Brody & Flor, 1998; Brody, Stoneman, & Flor, 1996) have found that parental processes play an important role in children's self-regulatory development and that significant numbers of children fail to develop sufficient self-regulatory skill to manage personal problems and achieve consistently in school. Parents who set clear "no nonsense" standards and who closely monitor their children's school activity and achievement were more successful in increasing not only their offspring's self-regulation but also their levels of social and cognitive development. Brody and colleagues' empirical research, which focused on the role of parents, came to similar conclusion to those reached by Montessori regarding teachers: Self-regulation emerges in structured environments where duties and consequences were structured ahead of time for children. These conditions assist students to set realistic goals and choose effective strategies during forethought phase functioning. The important lesson to be drawn from this research is that students have difficulty learning to self-regulate in environments that are poorly structured. Teachers and parents can impose order within microenvironments under their control, such as the classroom or the home, and when this is obtained, students can see self-regulatory behavior modeled by others in those settings, and they can experience a sense of control when they can emulate.

A deficiency in *motivation* is another major problem. Students often fail to acquire or use proactive self-regulatory methods because of a lack of interest or persistence. Proactive self-regulatory techniques require planning and anticipation during forethought, concentration and self-monitoring during performance, and mindful self-evaluation and attribution during self-reflection—all of which depend on high levels of self-motivation. If an academic skill or its outcomes are not perceived as personally valuable, there is little incentive to self-regulate. Unfortunately, Steinberg, Brown, and Dornbusch (1996) found significant numbers of students who displayed apathy or disinterest regarding participation in class or completion of homework. Because of their low self-confidence and lack of intrinsic interest in school, these students disengaged themselves from active efforts to learn and instead relied on reactive methods of self-regulation, such as self-evaluating their academic performance by social comparison with classmates. As the students' academic functioning and sense of self-efficacy spiraled downward, they often sought membership in deviant peer groups, which sanctioned further disengagement from proactive efforts to learn and abdication of responsibility for the academic results.

Disabilities in learning and emotional functioning, such as cognitive problems in concentration, recall, reading, and writing, are a third major problem. Because these *learning disabilities* are widely believed to have neurological origins, these students tend to attribute causation for their academic difficulties to fixed biological limitations. This leads to dissatisfaction and defensive reactions and cyclically to decreases in self-motivation and proactive forms of forethought. For example, learning-disabled students often set lower academic goals for themselves and struggle to control their impulses and to self-assess their capabilities accurately (Borkowski & Thorpe, 1994). The learning disabled are often more self-critical and less self-efficacious about their performance and tend to give up more easily than nondisabled students (Schunk, 1985). These students were also prone to attribute responsibility for their outcomes to uncontrollable causes, such as ability (Schunk & Cox, 1986). However, efforts to teach learning-disabled students compensatory self-regulatory methods to overcome their reading and writing dysfunctions including attributions to controllable causes, such as effort or strategy use, have proven effective (Butler, 1998; Graham & Harris, 1994; Schunk, 1998).

Although researchers of academic self-regulation include targeted measures of students' attribution of responsibility for academic outcomes in their studies, such as for writing, they also use comprehensive scales of students' attributions of personal responsibility in diverse areas of intellectual functioning.

ASSESSING STUDENTS' ACADEMIC RESPONSIBILITY

The most widely used scale for assessing students' academic responsibility has been the Intellectual Achievement Responsibility (IAR) questionnaire (Crandall, Katkovsky, & Crandall, 1965). This scale consists of 34 forced-choice items. Each item stem describes either a positive or a negative achievement experience that routinely occurs in children's daily lives, such as "When you do well on a test at school, it is more likely to be . . ." This stem is followed by two alternative attributions: (1) one indicating that someone or something else was responsible for the test result, such as "because the test was especially easy," or (2) the other indicating that the student him- or herself was responsible, such as "because you studied for it." The stems of the items fell into two categories, *successes* or *failures*, such as doing well or poorly on a test in school; these two categories were separately scored as subscales. The test items dealt with *school-related experiences*, such as being promoted to the next grade, studying, subject-matter competence, and understanding the teacher, or *general experiences*, such as playing games, solving puzzles, appearing dumb or bright, and attaining successful careers. When the scales were administered to students ranging in grade from elementary school to high school seniors, the authors found that students before the third grade had trouble understanding the logical structure of the items and that students, below the sixth grade should be tested orally to compensate for reading deficiencies.

The internal consistency measure of the IAR was moderate, ranging between .54 and .60, and relatively low correlations emerged between the success and failure subscales, indicating that the two scales were measuring quite different phenomena (Crandall et al., 1965). After the sixth grade, girls surpassed boys in mean scores of intellectual responsibility. The IAR subscale scores were relatively independent of social class or social desirability influences. In the sixth grade and above, IAR scores were found to correlate poorly with test results. However, below the sixth grade, there were significant correlations with the total IAR scores and achievement as well as with report card grades. In other research (Crandall, Kotkovsky, & Preston, 1962), total scale IAR scores were found to correlate with the amount of time that boys spent in intellectual activities during free play and the intensity with which they engaged in these activities. Crandall and her colleagues concluded that the children who feel responsible for their intellectual successes and failures showed greater initiative in seeking rewards and greater persistence in the face of difficulty.

During the ensuing years since the IAR was developed, it has been used in numerous studies. The scale has demonstrated moderate correlations with a wide variety of other motivational constructs, such as locus of control and personal independence. Of particular interest is the relation between students' perceived level of self-regulation and their intellectual responsibility using the IAR. In a key study, Arlin and Whitley (1978) developed a scale to measure students' perceptions of self-management choices, such as "I have enough chances to work at my own speed" and "I have enough chances to work on special things that interest me." Using a cross-lagged correlation design with fifth, sixth, and seventh graders, these researchers found that perceived opportunity for self-management during class at the beginning of the school year was significantly more predictive of students' acceptance of responsibility at the end of the school year than the reverse (i.e., responsibility measures from the fall predicting self-management perceptions in the spring). The relative size of the two cross-lagged correlations was interpreted as quasi-experimental evidence of causality of self-management experiences on students' willingness to accept responsibility for their actions. Arlin and Whitley concluded that when students perceived their classroom as a place where they can manage their own instruction, they are more likely to accept responsibility for their academic successes.

DOES COMPLETING HOMEWORK ASSIGNMENTS ENHANCE STUDENTS' ACADEMIC RESPONSIBILITY?

Educators of school-age children have historically relied upon homework experiences to develop academic responsibility. One popular homework guide for parents put it this way:

> For many children, homework is the first time they have responsibility all their own.... From the moment the teacher gives the assignment to the moment it is turned in again, the responsibility rests on your children's shoulders. (Canter & Hausner, 1987, p. 6)

The parental guide also discusses the role of homework in teaching academic self-regulation:

> Homework is about children's making choices: When to do homework, how to do homework, where to do homework, and even if they do homework. (Cantor & Hausner, 1987, p. 137)

Similar to Montessori's recommendations, students complete homework assignments under conditions where they perform with minimal interruption by teachers and other students, and they are exposed to the consequences of their actions in the form of an assignment grade. In recent publications, researchers have reaffirmed an interest in the question of whether homework enhances students' development as independent learners with better study skills, more positive academic attitudes, and greater responsibility toward learning (Cooper & Valentine, 2001).

Anastasia Kitsantas and I recently conducted a study of the relation between homework experiences and students' perceptions of academic responsibility and achievement in an all-girls' high school that emphasizes homework as a key part of the curriculum (Zimmerman & Kitsantas, 2005). The girls, who were drawn from the 9th through the 12th grades, averaged more than 3 hours of homework daily. The impact of teachers' assignments on the quality and quantity of the girls' homework and their academic achievement was investigated along with two key intervening variables: self-efficacy for learning beliefs and perceived responsibility.

A new Perceived Academic Responsibility (PAR) scale was developed that involved students' rating of responsibility for various academic outcomes according to a Likert scale that ranged from "mainly students' responsibility" to "mainly teachers' responsibility" (i.e., the locus attribution dimension). These academic outcomes included deficiencies in students' motivation (e.g., going through the motions without trying), deportment (e.g., fooling around in class), and learning processes (e.g., not taking notes in class). We expected that homework completion experiences would predict increased perceptions of academic responsibility. The internal consistency measure of reliability for this Likert scale was very high at .97. Unlike the IAR, which included a variety of outside factors besides teachers, Zimmerman and Kitsantas's scale focused on students' perceptions of their academic responsibility in comparison to their teachers' responsibility.

We assessed self-efficacy for learning with a new scale of students' certainty about regulating various academic problems or contexts associated with reading, note taking, writing, and test taking, as well as general studying. This self-efficacy scale was validated by its high correlation with a teacher rating measure of students' self-regulated learning ($r = .72$). Based on the cyclical model of self-regulation described earlier, it was hypothesized that the girls' self-efficacy to regulate learning beliefs would be predictive of their perceptions of academic responsibility. The internal consistency measure of reliability for this scale was also very high at .99.

Path analysis procedures assessed whether the girls' homework practices were predictive of their self-efficacy for learning beliefs and perceptions of academic responsibility as mediators of their grade point average (GPA) in school. A measure of the girls' achievement prior to their entrance into high school was included in the path model as a control variable. These analyses revealed that the effect of the girls' homework completion on their GPA was in fact mediated through their self-efficacy and academic responsibility beliefs. In addition, the effect of self-efficacy on GPA was mediated primarily through perceived responsibility, although it did exert a significant direct effect on GPA as well. These results indicate that the girls' homework experiences influenced their self-efficacy beliefs about learning, which in turn led them to shoulder greater academic responsibility for their academic outcomes.

Another issue concerns the impact of the girls' achievement prior to high school on the GPA during high school. Although the correlation between girls' prior achievement and their GPA was quite high ($r = .57$), path decomposition analyses revealed that the direct effect of prior achievement on GPA was small in comparison to its indirect effect via the girls' homework practices and self-efficacy beliefs. This indicates that higher prior achievement led the girls to improve their homework practices and to enhance their perceptions of self-efficacy to learn during high school in a self-regulated fashion.

SELF-REGULATORY TRAINING AND STUDENTS' ATTRIBUTIONS OF PERSONAL RESPONSIBILITY

A key question emerging from research on self-regulation and attributions of personal responsibility is whether instruction in self-regulatory processes can directly lead to improvements in students' attributions of personal responsibility, especially for unfavorable outcomes. In a study that was conducted using a writing revision task (Zimmerman & Kitsantas, 1999), high school girls were asked to revise a series of sentences from commercially available sentence-combining workbooks. These exercises involved transforming a series of simple and often redundant sentences into a single nonredundant sentence. For example, the sentences: "It was a fish. The fish was silver. The fish squirmed when it landed in the boat" could be rewritten as "The silver fish squirmed when it landed in the boat." The girls were taught a three-step strategy for revising these multi-sentence problems through modeling that involved identifying key information, deleting duplicate information, and combining the remaining elements. An objective scoring system was developed to assess whether the sentences were rewritten briefly but accurately. Finally, the girls were asked to practice this skill on their own using two key self-regulatory processes: goal setting and self-recording.

The effects of two types of goals were studied: those dealing with process and outcomes. As was discussed earlier, goal orientation theorists hypothesize that proactive self-regulators focus on learning processes, such as use of a strategy, rather than on outcomes, such as getting higher grades in writing. However, social-cognitive researchers (Zimmerman & Schunk, 2004) have hypothesized that outcome expectations also motivate learning but that focusing on outcomes before automaticity is attained can be detrimental. Automaticity refers to the point in acquisition when a learning process can be executed flawlessly. Once a strategy is internalized, an outcome goal can enhance personal adaptation. One of the expected advantages of a learning "process" orientation is that it should prompt students to attribute causation for errors to controllable factors, such as to strategy use or practice. Thus, three instructional groups were studied (i.e., process goals, outcome goals, and shifting goals [process goals followed by outcome goals]) as well as a no-goal control group.

During a practice session following training, girls in a process goal group focused on strategic steps for revising each writing task, whereas girls in an outcome goal group focused on decreasing the number of words in the revised passage. The optimal group shifted from process goals to outcome goals when automaticity was achieved. Some of the girls in each goal group were asked to self-record. Girls in the process-monitoring group recorded strategy steps they missed on each writing task, whereas girls in the outcome-monitoring group wrote down the number of words used in each writing task. Girls in the shifting goal group changed their method of self-monitoring when they shifted goals. Thus, the experiment compared the effects of process goals, outcome goals, and shifting goals as well as self-recording during self-directed practice.

Immediately after the practice period, the girls were asked why they did not do better when revising the last problem. Their attributions were classified into six categories: strategy use, ability, effort, practice, task difficulty, and "don't know." The results revealed that girls who shifted goals from processes to outcomes surpassed the writing revision skill of girls who adhered exclusively to process goals or to outcome goals. Girls who focused on outcomes exclusively displayed the least writing skill, and those who self-recorded reported significantly more writing regardless of their goal-setting group. Girls who focused on process goals throughout learning or during the first part of learning (the shifting goal group) attributed their outcomes primarily to strategy use. By contrast, girls in the outcome group or control group attributed their limited effectiveness primarily to a lack of effort, low ability, high task difficulty, or "don't know." The cyclical impact of these self-reflective phase attributions on the girls' self-motivation for further learning was profound. Strategy attributions (i.e., a controllable learning process) were highly predictive of increases in the girls' self-satisfaction reactions, self-efficacy beliefs, intrinsic valuing of the writing task, and performance on the writing revision posttest. Interestingly, attributions to ability and effort were negatively predictive of the girls' self-satisfaction, self-efficacy beliefs, intrinsic interest, and posttest writing skill. Clearly, students who were instructed in the use of self-regulatory processes, such as goal setting, attributed lower-level performance to strategy deficiencies rather than uncontrollable sources, such as a lack of ability. These attributions in turn were cyclically predictive of enhanced self-motivation to continue learning. In contrast to this self-enhancing cycle of learning displayed by proactive self-regulators, reactive self-regulators who attribute limited learning outcomes to uncontrollable sources display a self-defeating cycle of learning.

CONCLUSION

Research now demonstrates that students' willingness to accept responsibility for their academic performance and outcomes is very dependent on their perceptions of self-efficacy as well as their self-regulatory skill. Classroom and home environments that are structured so that tasks, roles, and consequences are well understood appear to contribute to students' sense of self-control. Attribution researchers have shown that students' perceptions of personal control play a major role in their willingness to accept responsibility for their academic outcomes, especially for their errors or shortcomings. Students who proactively self-regulate their academic functioning are more willing to shoulder responsibility for adverse outcomes and to persist in an adaptive way to improve their academic learning.

This is a vital quality for students in the 21st century, who will be expected to utilize various forms of technology (e.g., computers and telecommunications) to learn in a self-directed fashion during their school years as well as later when they enter the employment market. As John Gardner recognized 40 years ago, schools must expand their scope beyond coursework proficiency to the development of transportable learning skills and motivational beliefs that enable students to assume responsibility for pursuing their own learning. To prepare students to learn efficiently and self-confidently on their own, teachers will need to shift their focus. Maria Montessori (1964, p. 285) described this pedagogical orientation in the following way: "What is the greatest sign of success for a teacher thus transformed? It is to be able to say, 'The children are now working as if I did not exist.'"

ACKNOWLEDGMENT

I would like to thank Robert J. Sternberg and Rena Subotnik for their helpful comments on an earlier draft of this chapter.

REFERENCES

Arlin, M., & Whitley, T. W. (1978). Perceptions of self-managed learning opportunities and academic locus of control: A causal interpretation. *Journal of Educational Psychology, 70,* 988–992.

Bandura, A. (1997). *Self-efficacy: The exercise of control.* New York: W. H. Freeman.

Boekaerts, M., & Niemivirta, M. (2000). Self-regulated learning: Finding a balance between learning goals and ego-protective goals. In M. Boekaerts, P. Pintrich, & M. Zeidner (Eds.), *Handbook of Self-Regulation* (pp. 417–451). San Diego, CA: Academic Press.

Borkowski, J., & Thorpe, P. K. (1994). Self-regulation and motivation: A life-span perspective on underachievement. In D. H. Schunk & B. J. Zimmerman (Eds.), *Self-regulation of learning and performance: Issues and educational applications* (pp. 45–73). Hillsdale, NJ: Erlbaum.

Brody, G. H., & Flor, D. (1998). Maternal resources, parenting practices and child competence. *Child Development, 69,* 803–816.

Brody, G. H., Stoneman, Z., & Flor, D. (1996). Parental religiosity, family processes, and youth competence in rural, two-parent African American families. *Developmental Psychology, 32,* 696–706.

Butler, D. L. (1998). A strategic content learning approach to promoting self-regulated learning by students with learning disabilities. In D. H. Schunk & B. J. Zimmerman (Eds.), *Self-regulated learning: From teaching to self-reflective practice* (pp. 160-183). New York: Guilford Press.

Cantor, L., & Hausner, L. (1987). *Homework without tears: A parent's guide for motivating children to do homework and to succeed in school.* New York: HarperPerennial.

Cleary, T., & Zimmerman, B. J. (2001). Self-regulation differences during athletic practice by experts, non-experts, and novices. *Journal of Applied Sport Psychology, 13,* 61–82.

Clifford, M. (1986). Comparative effects of strategy and effort attributions. *British Journal of Educational Psychology, 56,* 75–83.

Cooper, H., & Valentine, J. C. (2001). Using research to answer practical questions about homework. *Educational Psychologist, 36,* 143–154.

Cowley, M. (1959). *Writers at work: The Paris review interviews.* New York: Compass Books.

Crandall, V. C., Katkovsky, W., & Crandall, V. J. (1965). Children's beliefs in their own control of reinforcements in intellectual-academic achievement situations. *Child Development, 36,* 91–109.

Crandall, V. J., Katkovsky, W., & Preston, A. (1962). Motivation and ability determinants of children's intellectual achievement behaviors. *Child Development, 33,* 643-661.

Dweck, C. S. (1988). Motivational processes affecting learning. *American Psychologist, 41,* 1040–1048.

English, H. B., & English, A. C. (1958). *A comprehensive dictionary of psychological and psychoanalytical terms.* New York: David McKay.

Ericsson, K. A., & Kintsch, W. (1995). Long-term working memory. *Psychological Review, 102,* 211–245.

Fiske, S., & Taylor, S. (1991). *Social cognition.* New York: McGraw-Hill.

Garcia, T., & Pintrich, P. R. (1994). Regulating motivation and cognition in the classroom: The role of self-schemas and self-regulatory strategies. In D. H. Schunk & B. J. Zimmerman (Eds.), *Self-regulation of learning and performance: Issues and educational applications* (pp. 127–53). Hillsdale, NJ: Erlbaum.

Gardner, J. (1963). *Self-renewal.* New York: Harper & Row.

Graham, S. (1998). Social motivation and perceived responsibility in others: Attributions and behavior of African American boys labeled as aggressive. In J. Heckhausen & D. S. Dweck (Eds.), *Motivation and self-regulation across the life span* (pp. 137–158). New York: Cambridge University Press.

Graham, S., & Harris, K. R. (1994). The role and development of self-regulation in the writing process. In D. H. Schunk & B. J. Zimmerman (Eds.), *Self-regulation of learning and performance: Issues and educational applications* (pp. 203-228). Hillsdale, NJ: Erlbaum.

Kitsantas, A., & Zimmerman, B. J. (2002). Self-regulation of volleyball players. *Journal of Applied Sport Psychology, 14*, 91–105.

Lepper, M. R., & Hodell, M. (1989). Intrinsic motivation in the classroom. In C. Ames & R. Ames (Eds.), *Research on motivation in education* (Vol. E, pp. 255–296). Hillsdale, NJ: Erlbaum.

Lillard, P. P. (1972). *Montessori: A modern approach.* New York: Schocken Books.

Locke, E. A., & Latham, G. P. (1990). *A theory of goal setting and task performance.* Englewood Cliffs, MNJ: Prentice Hall.

Montessori, M. (1964). *The absorbent mind.* Wheaton, IL: Theosophical Press.

Pressley, M., Borkowski, J. & Schneider, W. (1987). Cognitive strategies: Good strategy users coordinate metacognition and knowledge. In R. Vasta & G. Whitehurst (Eds.), *Annals of child development* (Vol. 5, pp. 89–129). Greenwich, CT: JAI Press.

Redlich, J. D., Debus, R. L., & Walker, R. (1986). The mediating role of attribution and self-efficacy variables for treatment effects on achievement outcomes. *Contemporary Educational Psychology, 11*, 195–216.

Schunk, D. H. (1982). Effects of effort attributional feedback on children's perceived self-efficacy and achievement. *Journal of Educational Psychology, 74*, 548-556.

Schunk, D. H. (1983). Ability versus effort attributional feedback: Differential effects on self-efficacy and achievement. *Journal of Educational Psychology, 75*, 848-856.

Schunk, D. H. (1984). Sequential attributional feedback and children's achievement behaviors. *Journal of Educational Psychology, 74*, 548–556.

Schunk, D. H. (1985). Participation in goal setting: Effects on self-efficacy and skills of learning disabled children. *Journal of Special Education, 19*, 307–317.

Schunk, D. H. (1998). Teaching elementary students to self-regulate practice of mathematical skills with modeling. In D. H. Schunk & B. J. Zimmerman (Eds.), *Self-regulated learning: From teaching to self-reflective practice* (pp. 137–159). Performance Phase New York: Guilford Press.

Schunk D. H., & Cox, P. D. (1986). Strategy training and attributional feedback with learning disabled students. *Journal of Educational Psychology, 78*, 201–209.

Schunk, D. H., & Rice, J. M. (1986). Extended attributional feedback: Sequence effects during remedial reading instruction. *Journal of Early Adolescence, 6*, 55–66.

Steinberg, L., Brown, B. B., & Dornbusch, S. M. (1966). *Beyond the classroom.* New York: Simon & Schuster.

Weiner, B. (1986). *An attributional theory of motivation and emotion.* New York: Springer-Verlag.

Weiner, B. (1992). *Human motivation Metaphors, theories, and research.* Newbury Park, CA: Sage.

Winne, P. H. (1997). Experimenting to bootstrap self-regulated learning. *Journal of Educational Psychology, 88*, 397–410.

Zimmerman, B. J. (2000). Attainment of self-regulation: A social cognitive perspective. In M. Boekaerts, P. Pintrich, & M. Zeidner (Eds.), *Self-regulation: Theory, research, and applications* (pp. 13–39). Orlando, FL: Academic Press.

Zimmerman, B. J., & Kitsantas, A. (1997). Developmental phases in self-regulation: Shifting from process to outcome goals. *Journal of Educational Psychology, 89,* 29–36.

Zimmerman, B. J., & Kitsantas, A. (1999). Acquiring writing revision skill: Shifting From process to outcome self-regulatory goals. *Journal of Educational Psychology, 91,* 241–250.

Zimmerman, B. J., & Kitsantas, A. (2005). Homework perceptions and academic achievement: The mediating role of self-efficacy and perceived responsibility beliefs. *Contemporary Educational Psychology.*

Zimmerman, B. J., & Schunk, D. H. (2004). Self-regulating process and outcomes: A social cognitive perspective. In D. Y. Dai & R. J. Sternberg (Eds.), *Motivation, emotion, and cognition: Perspectives on intellectual development and functioning* (pp. 323-349). Mahwah, NJ: Erlbaum.

CHAPTER 10

A MOTIVATIONAL PERSPECTIVE ON SCHOOL ACHIEVEMENT

Taking Responsibility for Learning, Teaching, and Supporting

Jacquelynne S. Eccles

Understanding individual and group differences in school achievement is critical to designing educational environments that maximize each student's learning. Scholars from many different disciplines have worked on increasing this understanding. In this chapter, I focus on a subset of factors linked to expectancy–value theories of achievement motivation and task engagement, stressing the importance of these factors in explaining race and ethnic group differences in school achievement within the United States. On average, students from African American, Hispanic, and Native American families perform more poorly than children from Asian American and European American families throughout their school careers (Berry & Asamen, 1989). Many explanations have been offered

Optimizing Student Success in School With the Other Three Rs:
Reasoning, Resilience, and Responsibility, 199–224
Copyright © 2006 by Information Age Publishing
199

for these differences (see Connell, Halpern-Felsher, Clifford, Crichlow, & Usinger, 1995; Connell, Spencer, & Aber, 1994; Lee & Smith, 2001). I believe that at least part of the difference lies in the impact of discriminatory experiences at school both on students' confidence in their own ability to master the school material (the expectancy component of expectancy–value models) and on the value they place on being fully engaged in the learning tasks provided in their schools. It is very unlikely that students will decide to take responsibility for their own learning if they believe their teachers lack confidence in their academic abilities due to their race or ethnic group. It is also unlikely that they will take responsibility for their own learning if they themselves come to place little value on being fully engaged in the learning agenda of their schools because of racial discriminatory experiences at school. I elaborate this argument throughout the chapter and discuss one set of ethnic-identity-related constructs that have been shown to help these young people cope with discriminatory experiences in school and suggest ways that schools might help to support these protective psychological processes.

I believe my approach relates directly to two of the Other Three Rs stressed in this book: responsibility and resiliency. It relates to responsibility in two ways. First, my approach stresses two sets of individual motivational constructs that impact on students' willingness to engage in school tasks and accept the responsibility for their own learning. Second, I stress the importance of teachers and schools accepting responsibility both for facilitating all students' motivation for learning and for preventing experiences likely to undermine some students' desire to fully engage in the learning agenda at school.

My approach also relates to resiliency through the importance I place on psychological processes linked to experiences of either racial or ethnic discrimination. Those experiences at school are likely to undermine their confidence in themselves and their sense of belonging in the school. The conceptual framework of resiliency is a useful tool for understanding students' response to ethnic and racial discriminatory experiences at school for two reasons: First, personal experiences of ethnic or racial discrimination are a major source of risk that can increase the probability of negative developmental outcomes (Essed, 1990; Jackson et al., 1994; Phelan, Yu, & Davidson, 1994). Being in an uncaring and unsupportive environment where individuals do not feel a sense of relatedness is an important developmental risk factor (Jessor, Van Den Bos, Vanderryn, Costa, & Turbin, 1995). If experiences of racial/ethnic discrimination can lead individuals to conclude that they are devalued and not an integral part of the "in group" because of their racial/ethnic group membership, then these experiences are likely to undermine individuals' sense of belonging at school, as well as their own psychological well-being (Feagin, 1992). Racial/ethnic discrimination can also convey the message that the teachers do not have high expectations for the students' academic efficacy (Wong, Eccles, & Sameroff, 2003). To the extent that these messages are internalized by a student, he or she is likely to lose confidence in his or her own academic efficacy. Second, the framework of resiliency (e.g., linking the response to risks to protective factors) stresses agentic components that can facilitate positive development in the face of risky experiences.

One type of racial/ethnic devaluation that has received tremendous attention in social psychology is the phenomenon of stereotype threat (Steele & Aronson, 1995). Stereotype threat occurs when individuals' awareness of society's negative stereotypes about their social group leads them to be anxious about engaging in behaviors that confirm those stereotypes, particularly those pertaining to intellectual abilities. Research with African American college students has shown that these anxieties result in decreases in valuing of school, effort to do well on academic tasks, and performance on standardized tests. A few studies with adolescents have replicated these findings. For example, there is a negative relation between Hispanic high school students' awareness of ethnic discrimination and their evaluation of their own ethnic group (Phinney, 1996a, 1996b). Similarly, qualitative research has shown that perceived ethnic discrimination at school affects participation in school and socioemotional adjustment for some high school students of color (Phelan et. al., 1994).

There is also some research on adolescents' perception of future discriminatory barriers. Many adolescents of African American, Mexican American, and Native American origins are aware that they may encounter educational and job discrimination in the future (e.g., job ceilings). Findings from qualitative research indicate that some African American and Hispanic adolescents respond to this awareness by disengaging from mainstream institutions, such as school (Ogbu, 1992). Their academic disidentification includes: (1) disaffection with school, including low educational expectations and poor academic motivation; (2) association with friends who support negative attitudes toward school; and (3) poor school performance and attainment (Fordham & Ogbu, 1986; Mickelson, 1991; Ogbu, 1992; Taylor, Casten, Flickinger, Roberts, & Fulmore, 1994).

If experiences of racial/ethnic devaluation at school can assault students' sense of relatedness to their surroundings, as well as their confidence in their own abilities and their anxieties about their own academic performance, then protective factors are needed to compensate for and/or buffer against the potential threats posed by racial/ethnic stigma (Connell, 1990; Goodenow & Grady, 1993). One potential protective factor is students' identification with their racial/ethnic group. Different theories of racial/ethnic identity suggest that a healthy identification with one's racial/ethnic group can buffer against prejudice and discrimination (e.g., Cross, 1991; Phinney, 1996a; Sellers, Smith, Shelton, Rowley, & Chavous, 1998). In particular, researchers have suggested that attachment to one's racial/ethnic group (i.e., feeling a strong sense of connection to one's racial/ethnic group) can play a key role in maintaining psychological health in the face of experiences of racial/ethnic devaluation.

Although some studies have shown that feeling a sense of relatedness to one's ethnic group is associated with higher self-esteem and better mental health for Asian Americans, Hispanic/Latinos, and African Americans (Crocker, Luhtanen, Blaine, & Broadnax, 1994; Phinney, 1996b), few studies have directly examined whether racial/ethnic identification is a protective factor against the potential threats of school-based racial/ethnic discrimination for school engagement and achievement. Wong and colleagues (2003) conducted a longitudinal study of African American adolescents living near Washington, DC to assess these hypotheses. First, they examined whether perceived discrimination by teachers and peers is negatively related to changes in academic, socioemotional, and behavioral indicators of psychological adjustment among African American adolescents. Based on prior research on developmental risks and on ethnic devaluation, they predicted that perceived racial discrimination would be related to decreases in both academic motivation and school performance (Fordham & Ogbu, 1986; Mickelson, 1991; Ogbu, 1992; Steele & Aronson, 1995; Taylor et al., 1994). Both of these predictions were confirmed: Those African American youth who reported the highest levels of racial discriminatory experiences during their eighth-grade school year showed the greatest decreases in their grades, their interest in school, and their confidence in the ability to master mathematics and other school subjects.

Second, Wong and colleagues (2003) tested whether racial identification could act as a protective factor against the academic threats posed by experiences of school-based racial discrimination. They defined racial identification in terms of the adolescents' belief that being African American made them a part of a rich and supportive cultural group (i.e., did they feel close to friends because of similar race/ethnicity, did they believe that people of their race/ethnicity had a rich heritage and they had rich traditions because of their race/ethnicity, and did they feel supported by people of their own race/ethnicity). As predicted, this form of racial identification did moderate the impact of racial discrimination on the school engagement and achievement of these African American adolescents: Those youth who reported a strong ethnic group identification did not show the negative impact of experiences of racial discrimination over time on their academic grade point average and their confidence in their ability to do well in their school subjects.

In the next sections, I provide an overview of the Eccles and colleagues expectancy–value model of academic achievement motivation and discuss how this model can help us understand both individual and group differences in school achievement. First, I discuss how both positive expectations of academic success and placing high value on learning at school are critical for students' taking responsibility for their own learning. Second, I discuss how experiences of racial/ethnic discrimination and race/ethnic-related low teacher expectations can undermine students' confidence in their academic abilities, students' academic aspirations, and the value students' place on being fully engaged in the learning agenda of school. Finally, I make some recommendations for school interventions that might facilitate rather than undermine the value students place on taking responsibility for their own learning.

EXPECTANCY–VALUE MODEL OF ACADEMIC ACHIEVEMENT MOTIVATION

Most currently popular motivational perspectives on school achievement are linked theoretically to classic expectancy–value models of motivation (Eccles & Wigfield, 2002) in that most perspectives stress the importance of either confidence in one's ability to master the learning tasks, or the value one attaches to mastering these tasks, or both. Eccles and Wigfield (2002) argued that classic expectancy–value models of motivation can be conceptualized in terms of two fundamental questions: Can I do the task? and Do I want to do the task? I believe that the answers to these two questions determine students' engagement in school-based learning tasks, as well as their willingness to take full responsibility for their own learning. If the answer to the first question (Can I do the task?) is no, then the students are unlikely to take responsibility for their own learning. Instead they are likely to engage in a variety of self-protective strategies designed to maintain their sense of self-worth (Covington, 1992). Too often, the consequences of these strategies include academic failure and withdrawal from the school's learning agenda.

But even if the answer to the first question is yes, full and sustained engagement depends on the answer to the second question, Do I want to do the task? If the answer to this question is no, then it is unlikely that the students will take responsibility for implementing self-regulated learning strategies. Instead, it is likely that they will either engage in a variety of avoidance strategies or put forth the minimal amount of effort necessary to minimize the negative consequences of lack of engagement. I believe that effective school reform initiatives must take into account both of these two determinants of school academic motivation. I also believe that experiences of racial and ethnic discrimination at school influence academic achievement through their impact on the answers to both of these two questions.

Can I Do the Task?

Several theories, and a great deal of recent research, focus on a variety of constructs related to the question "Can I do this task?", including individuals' beliefs about their academic competence and self-efficacy, individuals' expectancies for academic success or failure, individual's educational aspirations, and individuals' sense of control over their academic outcomes. In general, when students answer this question affirmatively, they perform better and are motivated to select more challenging tasks. For example, Bandura's (1994) social-cognitive model emphasizes human agency and perceptions of efficacy (defined as individuals' confidence in their ability to organize and execute a given course of action to solve a problem or accomplish a task) in determining individuals' achievement strivings. Bandura characterizes self-efficacy as a multidimensional construct that can vary in strength (i.e., positive or negative), generality (relating to many situations or only a few), and level of difficulty (feeling efficacious for all tasks or only easy tasks). High levels of academic self-efficacy predict subsequent academic performance, course enrollment, and occupational choice (see Bandura, 1994; Eccles & Wigfield, 2002; Kao & Tienda, 1995; Pajares & Miller, 1994; Zimmerman, Bandura, & Martinez-Pons, 1992). Most importantly for this chapter, personal efficacy regarding academic work has been shown to be an important predictor of academic achievement among African American adolescents (e.g., Gurin & Epps, 1974; Hale-Benson, 1989).

Several scholars have focused on the importance of high domain specific ability self-perceptions and expectations for success for academic achievement in particular school subjects (e.g., Eccles & Wigfield, 2002; Harter, 1998; Marsh, 1990). These scholars argue that individuals who think they are very good at specific school subjects will earn higher grades and be more invested in working hard to master the associated learning tasks even after controlling for prior achievement levels. By and large the evidence is consistent with these predictions.

Because this set of constructs is discussed more fully in other chapters in this volume, I will not say a great deal more here. I will, however, reiterate the fact that negative racial and ethnic stereotypes can lead teachers and school districts to communicate low expectations for the academic achievements of some groups of students. Research has shown that this can be done through a variety of means, including differential teacher–student face-to-face daily interactions (see Brophy & Good, 1974; Graham, 1984, 1994; Jussim, Eccles, & Madon, 1996), tracking into low-ability groups and then providing inferior educational experiences in these groups (Gamoran & Mare, 1989; Pallas, Entwisle, Alexander, & Stluka, 1994; Rosenbaum, 1980), failure to provide encouragement for high educational aspirations, and failure to provide high-quality educational experiences that promote both current achievement levels and confidence and lay the groundwork for continued success in future courses (Bryk, Lee, & Holland, 1993).

Many school intervention experiments have focused on increasing students' sense of personal academic efficacy. By and large, these studies show that one must simultaneously teach students the skills necessary for academic success and provide efficacy training in order to increase continued school achievement (Fosterling, 1985; Kulik, Kulik, & Bangert-Drowns, 1990). Efficacy training alone can actually set the students up for future academic failure. Teachers also need to develop and then maintain high academic expectations for all of their students and need to provide all of their students with opportunities to develop high educational aspirations. Finally, teachers and principals need to make sure that racial/ethnic discriminatory experiences that communicate low academic expectations are not tolerated at school.

Do I Want to Do the Task?

Taking responsibility for one's own learning requires a desire to do the task (Eccles & Wigfield, 2002; Meece, 1994; Pintrich & Schunk, 1996: Schunk & Zimmerman, 1994). Thus it is critical that the answer to this question be yes if students are going to take personal responsibility for their own learning and their full engagement in the learning agenda of the school. Most motivational theorists have tried, either directly or indirectly, to identify the beliefs and experiences that increase the probability of a yes answer. Eccles and her colleagues have explicitly tackled this issue in their expectancy–value model of achievement-related choices (Eccles & Wigfield, 2002; Eccles Parsons et al., 1983; see also Feather, 1992). In this section, I summarize the Eccles and colleagues perspective on subjective task value (STV), linking group differences in school achievement to specific aspects of STV, and suggest ways that educational reform might address group differences in school achievement by increasing the STV all students attach to taking responsibility for their own learning.

Over the past 25 years, my colleagues and I have studied the motivational and social factors influencing such long- and short-range achievement goals and behaviors as school grades, course selections, persistence on difficult tasks, and the allocation of effort across various achievement-related activities. Drawing upon the theoretical and empirical work associated with decision making, achievement theory, and attribution theory (see Crandall, 1969; Weiner, 1992), we elaborated a comprehensive theoretical model of achievement-related choices that could be used to guide our subsequent research efforts. This model links achievement-related choices most directly to two sets of beliefs: the individual's expectations for success and the importance or value the individual attaches to the various options perceived by the individual as available. The model also specifies the relation of these beliefs to cultural norms, experiences, aptitudes, and to those personal beliefs and attitudes that are commonly assumed to be associated with achievement-related activities (see Eccles, 1994; Eccles, Wigfield, & Schiefele, 1998). In particular, the model links achievement-related beliefs, outcomes, and goals to interpretative systems like causal attributions and other meaning-making beliefs linked to achievement-related activities and events, to the input of socializers (primarily parents and teachers), to various social roles and other culturally based beliefs about both the nature of various tasks in a variety of achievement domains and the "appropriateness" of participation in such tasks, to self-perceptions and self-concept, to one's perceptions of the task itself, and to the processes and consequences associated with identity formation. Each of these factors are assumed to influence both the expectations one holds for future success at the various achievement-related options and the subjective value one attaches to these various options. These expectations and the value attached to the various options, in turn, are assumed to influence choice among these options.

For example, let us consider taking responsibility for one's own learning in school. The model predicts that people will be most likely to invest time and energy in tasks that they think they can master and that have high task value for them. Expectations for success (and a sense of domain-specific personal efficacy) were discussed earlier. The STV of particular achievement tasks like learning in school is influenced by several factors. For example, does the person enjoy doing the subject material? Is the learning activity required? Is the learning activity seen as instrumental in meeting one of the individual's long- or short-range goals? Is the person anxious about his or her ability to successfully master the learning material being presented? Does the person think that the learning task is appropriate for people like him or her? Finally, does working on the learning task interfere with other more valued options?

Four features of our approach are particularly important for understanding both individual and group differences in school achievement. First, we have focused on the choice dimension of achievement-related behavior. We believe that the conscious and nonconscious choices people make about how to spend time and effort lead, over time, to marked differences between groups and individuals in school achievement. Focusing attention on achievement-related choices reflects a second important component of our perspective; namely, the issue of what becomes a part of an individual's field of possible choices. Although individuals do choose from among several options, they do not actively, or consciously, consider the full range of objectively available options in making their selections. Many options are never considered because the individual is unaware of their existence or the individuals think these options are not realistically available to them. For example, as I discuss later, one reason to engage fully in school learning tasks is that what one will learn by this investment of time and energy will increase future educational and occupational options. If students' visions of the future do not include continued education and the types of occupations linked to college education, then spending a lot of time mastering what is being taught in primary and secondary school in order to gain access to these future options is not likely to provide a positive motivational incentive. Similarly, if doing well in school itself is not seen as part of one's social or personal identities, then putting in the time and effort to do well in school is likely to have relatively low STV.

A third important feature of our perspective is the explicit assumption that achievement-related decisions, such as the decision to invest large amounts of time and energy into one's schoolwork, are made within the context of a complex social reality that presents each individual with a wide variety of choices, each of which has both long-range and immediate consequences. Furthermore, the choice is often between two or more positive options or between two or more options that each has both positive and negative components. For example, the decision to invest time in studying and mastering one's schoolwork is typically made in the context of other important decisions such as whether to spend time with one's friends, spend time perfecting other skills, or help out at home. The critical issue is the relative personal value of each option. Given high likelihood of success, we assume that people will then choose those tasks or behaviors that have relatively higher personal value. Thus it is the hierarchy of STVs that matter rather than the absolute values.

A true life experience with my daughter provides an excellent example of these choices. In the third grade, she did not do very well on her report card. I asked her why she was doing so poorly in her schoolwork. In her first reply, she said other children also were doing poorly. I reacted by saying I really did not care how the other children were doing, I was only concerned with her poor performance. To which she replied, "But I would have to work harder to do better." I agreed and asked why she wasn't working harder. She replied "What do you want me to do? Waste my childhood doing schoolwork?" Clearly, she had no problems with her sense of personal efficacy. Instead, she just did not value doing schoolwork as much as she valued other ways of spending her time. These two examples point to the importance of the value component of the Eccles and colleagues expectancy–value model. I focus on this component in this chapter.

The fourth feature of our approach is that the processes linked to both expectancies and STVs are both developmental and dynamic. Like many researchers interested in self processes, we assume that both personal states and situational characteristics make the various components of the self system more or less salient at different times. As such the immediate STV of various behaviors will fluctuate depending on the salience of different components of the self system. We also assume that the components of the self system also change across developmental time in response to experience with specific tasks, changing cognitive abilities and interpretative beliefs, changing socialization pressures, and changing sociocultural influences.

In summary, my colleagues and I assume that achievement-related choices (e.g., educational and occupational choices), whether made consciously or nonconsciously, are guided by the following: (1) one's expectations for success on, and sense of personal efficacy for, the various options, as well as one's sense of competence for various tasks; (2) the relation of the options both to one's short- and long-range goals and to one's core personal and social identities and basic psychological needs; (3) the individual's culturally based role schemas such as those linked to gender, social class, religious group, and ethnic group; and (4) the potential cost of investing time in one activity rather than another. All of these psychological variables are influenced by one's experiences and one's interpretation of these experiences, by cultural norms, and by the behaviors and goals of one's socializers and peers.

COMPONENTS OF SUBJECTIVE TASK VALUE (STV)

We conceptualize STV in terms of four components: (1) intrinsic or interest value (i.e., expected enjoyment of engaging in the task); (2) attainment value or the value an activity has because engaging in it is consistent with one's self-image; (3) the utility value of the task for facilitating one's long-range goals or in helping the individual obtain immediate or long-range external rewards; and (4) the cost of engaging in the activity. In this section, I describe each of these components and discuss how they might be related to discriminatory experiences.

Intrinsic and Interest Value

My colleagues and I reserve the term "intrinsic value" to either the enjoyment one gains from doing the task or the anticipated enjoyment one expects to experience while doing the task. In this sense, our notion of intrinsic value is similar to the idea of flow proposed by Csikszentmihalyi (1988), who discussed intrinsically motivated behavior as the immediate positive and exhilarating subjective experience that occurs when people are engaged in an activity. Flow is only possible when people feel that the opportunities for action in a given situation match their ability to master the challenges. The challenge of an activity may be something concrete or physical like the peak of a mountain to be scaled, or it can be something abstract and symbolic, like a set of musical notes to be performed, a story to be written, or a puzzle to be solved. Recent research has shown that both the challenges and skills must be relatively high before a flow experience becomes possible (Massimini & Carli, 1988). For us, an anticipated sense of flow would add to the intrinsic value of the task and increase the likelihood of taking responsibility for fully engaging in the task. In contrast, many aspects of evaluative techniques and teacher–student interactions can undermine students' intrinsic motivation to do schoolwork (e.g., Lepper & Cordova, 1992; Mac Iver & Reuman, 1993; Mac Iver, Stipek, & Daniels,1991).

Also related to our notion of intrinsic task value is the idea of interest value as evident in the work of people like Hidi, Renninger, and Schiefele (Hidi, 1990; Renninger, Hidi, & Krapp, 1992; Schiefele, 1991). These researchers differentiate between individual and situational interest. Individual interest is a relatively stable evaluative orientation toward certain domains that one enjoys doing; situational interest is an emotional state aroused by specific features of an activity or a task.

We know little about the origins of either within-individual or between-individual differences in interest. In some ways, individual differences in patterns of interest are related to the issues I discuss later under attainment value: The attraction to, or enjoyment of, particular types of activities are undoubtedly linked to core aspects of the self such as temperament, personality, and motivational orientations. Also, it is likely linked to both genetic propensities and to classical learning associated with either positive or negative emotional experiences during initial encounters with particular activities.

Over the last 30 years, educational psychologists have become interested in trait-like individual differences in what might be referred to as the desire to learn (see Gottfried, 1990; Harter, 1998; Nicholls, 1984, 1989; Schiefele, 1996). These researchers define this enduring learning orientation in terms of three components: (1) preference for hard or challenging tasks, (2) learning that is driven by curiosity or interest, and (3) striving for competence and mastery. Empirical findings suggest that the three components are highly correlated and that high levels of a trait-like desire to learn is related to a mastery-oriented coping style for dealing with failure, high academic achievement, and the use of appropriate self-regulated learning strategies (Benware & Deci, 1984; Pintrich & Schrauben, 1992; Schiefele, 1996).

We know much more about the task characteristics linked to situational interest in part because the research on school-related situational interest has focused on the characteristics of academic tasks that create interest (e.g., Hidi & Baird, 1986). Among others, the following text features arouse situational interest: personal relevance, both familiarity and novelty, high activity level, and comprehensibility (Hidi & Baird, 1986). We also know that there is strong empirical support for the relation of both individual and situational interest with text comprehension and recall, as well as with deep-level learning (see Renninger et al., 1992; Schiefele, 1996).

All of these findings suggest that it is important to do all one can to increase the interest value of school learning tasks if we want to optimally motivate our students to engage fully in the learning agenda of school and to take responsibility for their own learning. Several intervention studies have demonstrated that attempts to increase the interest value of academic achievement tasks do increase school engagement and performance (e.g., Bateson & Johnson, 1976; Blumenfeld et al., 1991).

Attainment and Utility Value

My colleagues and I identified two more psychological sources of value: attainment and utility value. As they grow up, individuals develop an image of who they are and what they would like to be. This image is made up of many component parts, including (1) conceptions of one's personality and capabilities, (2) long-range goals and plans, (3) schema regarding the proper roles of men and women, (4) instrumental and terminal values (Rokeach, 1973), (5) motivational sets, (6) ideal images of what one should be like; and (7) social scripts regarding proper behavior in a variety of situations. We conceptualize attainment value in terms of the needs and personal values that an activity fulfills. Those parts of an individual's self-image that are central or critical to self-definition should influence the value the individual attaches to various activities; these differential values, in turn, should influence the individual's desire to engage fully in school-based learning activities (Eccles, 1994). For example, if doing well in school is a central part of an individual's self-image, then that person should place higher value on investing time and energy in doing well in school than in other pursuits because doing well in school has high attainment value for this.

Utility value is determined by how well a task fits into an individual's goals and plans or fulfills other basic psychological needs. For example, if a student plans to become an engineer, then mastering arithmetic in elementary school will have high utility value because it will allow him or her to take college-track mathematics in secondary school.

What might influence both the centrality and usefulness of doing well in school and taking responsibility for one's own learning in school? Connell and Wellborn (1991) proposed that there are three basic human needs that might relate to both the centrality and usefulness of taking responsibility for one's own learning: the needs for competence, relatedness, and autonomy. Connell and Wellborn argued that people's motivation to engage in a task is influenced by the extent to which the task provides opportunities to experience autonomy, social relatedness, and a sense of competence. If tasks do not provide these opportunities, then individuals will not become engaged or will try to disengage by whatever means are available to them. Harter (1998) and other more classic theorists (e.g., White, 1959) also pointed to the centrality of effectance, competence, and social relatedness needs. If classroom experiences provide opportunities for students to fulfill these basic needs, then the attainment value of fully engaging in the learning agenda of school should be increased. Eccles and her colleagues documented this prediction (Eccles, Early, Frasier, Belansky, & McCarthy, 1997).

The importance of competence needs, in particular, has received a great deal of attention in the achievement literature. For example in her model of mastery or effectance motivation, Harter (1998) described the effects of both success and failure experiences on mastery motivation. She proposed that successful mastery attempts that (initially) are positively reinforced lead to internalization of the reward system. They also enhance perceptions of competence and perceived internal control over outcomes, give the individual pleasure, and ultimately increase mastery motivation. In contrast, when mastery attempts fail, the need for approval by others persists, with a corresponding increase in external control beliefs, lower competence beliefs, higher anxiety in mastery situations, and, ultimately, lower mastery motivation. This model is important because it includes the effects of both success and failure on subsequent motivational orientations, which we believe influence the attainment value of various types of activities. If an individual has had a history of school mastery attempts being both successful and rewarded by key individuals, then the value of school-based learning tasks that provide opportunities for mastery and competence development will be high because the person has come to value feelings of mastery and competence. In contrast, if the individual has failed at mastery attempts on particular tasks and feels incompetent at those tasks, then individuals are likely to lower the value they attach to being competent at these particular types of tasks because such tasks will not be seen as providing the opportunity to feel competent. In this way, prior successes and failures can influence the value of future tasks through their impact on the attainment value of those tasks.

Given this perspective, it is essential that teachers set up their instructional practices in ways that allow all children to experience success at their mastery attempts. Researchers in the area of achievement goal theory (e.g., Anderman & Maehr, 1994; Maehr & Midgley, 1996; Pintrich & Schunk, 1996) have explored the importance of mastery-oriented classrooms quite extensively. Achievement goal theory researchers hypothesize that school learning tasks vary along at least two important dimensions: (1) the extent to which mastery or improvement is stressed (i.e., a mastery focus); and (2) the extent to which doing better than others is stressed (i.e., a performance focus). They argue that the greater the focus on mastery instead of performance, the greater the likelihood that all students will feel competent and will have repeated experiences of mastery. Maehr and Midgely (1996) conducted an extensive school intervention effort to test these ideas. They worked with a middle school for several years to help the teachers create new forms of evaluation and new learning opportunities that focused attention on mastery of new material and reduced focus on socially comparative grading systems based on one's relative performance compared to other students. The results were quite positive. Other work by Midgely and her colleagues has also shown that age-related declines in both the value students attach to doing their schoolwork and their confidence in their ability to master their school subjects are linked to teachers' increasing stress on doing better than other students rather than on working for one's own increased understanding and competence (e.g., Midgley, Anderman, & Hicks, 1995).

Being successful at taking responsibility for one's own learning also requires having the meta-cognitive skills necessary to engage in self-directed learning (Pintrich & Schunk, 1996) including the ability to assess one's current competence and to seek out help in developing new competencies, as well as the ability to control one's behavior in a planful manner designed to "get the job done." Some students come to school with these skills already in place; some do not. If students are to have the kinds of mastery experiences necessary to increase the attainment value of engaging fully in school-based learning tasks, teachers must make sure they have these meta-cognitive skills and that their use of these skills is supported.

Although less research has been done on the other two basic needs (i.e., social relatedness and autonomy), evidence is beginning to accumulate supporting their importance for school engagement. As I noted in the introduction to this chapter, research based in a variety of subfields has pointed to the critical importance of social relatedness and a sense of belonging for human development. Individuals are likely to enjoy being in contexts that provide opportunities for the fulfillment of this basic need and the activities that are central to such contexts are likely to take on high attainment and utility value. Both Goodenow (1993) and Roeser (Roeser, Midgley, & Urdan, 1996) have shown that feelings of belongingness in classrooms and schools predict increased engagement and school learning. Similar results have been reported by Anderman (1999), Birch and Ladd (1997), Furrer and Skinner (2003), and Wentzel (1997). Finally, one of the major benefits of cooperative learning structures is that they increase all students' sense of belonging in their classroom's agenda (Stevens & Slavin, 1995).

Racial and ethnic discrimination are likely to undermine minority students' sense of belonging at school. As noted earlier, Wong and colleagues (2003) showed that experiences of racial discrimination predicted declines in school achievement. It seems likely that part of this relation reflects the negative impact of experiences of racial discrimination on students' feelings of social relatedness to both their teachers and the other students at school (i.e., their feelings of belonging at school). For example, Steele and his colleagues argue that students who believe that their teachers have low expectations for their academic performance will disidentify with school learning as a way of coping with experiences of racial and ethnic discrimination at school (e.g., Steele & Aronson, 1995). Qualitative studies of ethnic minority youth in various schools also support the hypothesis that experiences of racial and ethnic discrimination undermine African American, Hispanic, and low-achieving students' engagement in learning activities at school through their impact on these students' sense of belonging at school (e.g., Phelan et al., 1994; Suarez-Orozco & Suarez-Orozco, (2001).

Deci, Ryan and their colleagues have done most of the work on the importance of support for autonomy in classrooms for students' motivation to fully engage the learning agenda of the classroom (Deci & Ryan, 1985; Pajares & Miller, 1994). They argue that individuals need to feel personally responsible for their behavior and their goals. To the extent that teachers create opportunities for this to be true, students are more motivated to do their schoolwork and learn the material better. The longitudinal work that I have done with my colleagues also illustrates the importance of perceived opportunities for autonomous control over one's learning behaviors. We have found that students' interest in schoolwork declines as they move from elementary schools into secondary schools (see Eccles et al., 1993, for review of this work). In part, this decline is mediated by declines in the students' perceptions of the opportunities provided for autonomous decision making regarding learning behaviors (Midgley & Feldlaufer, 1987). Declines in teachers' sense of efficacy as teachers and declines in the perceived social support from teachers also contribute to these declines in students' motivation as they make the transition to secondary school (see Eccles et al., 1993; Roeser & Eccles, 1998).

My colleagues and I have become quite interested in another possible basic need: mattering. We believe that people need to feel like they are considered to be valuable contributors to their social groups and institutions. Researchers interested in service learning also stress the importance of opportunities to make meaningful contributions to ones' school and community for maintaining the motivation to take responsibility for one's academic learning (see Eccles & Templeton, 2002). One very impressive intervention study was done based on this need: the Coca-Cola study (cited in Eccles & Templeton, 2002). In this project, at-risk adolescents were assigned to give cross-age peer tutoring in reading to first graders. Those adolescents who had this experience over an extended period of time showed an increased commitment to their own academic performance as evidenced by increases in their grades and high school graduation rates. Again, such opportunities are likely to be especially important during the secondary school years because adolescents are quite sensitive developmentally to increases in such opportunities (Eccles et al., 1993). Evidence from the field of service leaning supports these hypotheses (see Eccles & Templeton, 2002).

Individual differences in school motivation are also likely to be linked to individual differences in self-schema and both personal and social goals and identities. As noted above, these differences should be directly related to the perceived attainment value of various activities. Our gender research is an excellent example of these processes for both group-level and individual-level differences in school-related achievement choices. Our work on gender and individual differences in high school math and science course enrollment is an excellent example of the importance of the perceived utility value of various course options. In our first longitudinal study of the math course enrollment decisions of intellectually able, college-bound high school students, gender differences in students' decisions to enroll in advanced mathematics were mediated primarily by gender differences in the value that the students attached to mathematics (Eccles, Adler, & Meece, 1984). More specifically, the young women were less likely than the young men to enroll in advanced mathematics primarily because they felt that math was less important, less useful, and less enjoyable than did the young men. We also found clear evidence of gender differences in the value attached to various school subjects and activities in our study of elementary school-age children enrolled in a gifted program (Eccles & Harold, 1992). Even though there was no gender differences in expectations for success in mathematics, these girls reported liking math less than the boys and rated math as less useful than the boys. In addition, the boys also attached greater importance to sports than did the girls. Not surprisingly, the boys were much more likely to be engaged in sports activities throughout their elementary school years than the girls. Finally, we have now followed a sample through high school and found that both gender and individual differences in enrollment in advanced math courses and physics courses are mediated by the perceived utility of these courses for the individual's long-range educational and occupational goals (Vida & Eccles, 2003; Updegraff, Eccles, Barber, & O'Brien, 1996). Furthermore, interventions based on making physics more interesting to females by using more human biological examples of physical principles have been quite successful at increasing females' engagement in physics classes (Hoffmann & Haeussler, 1995; Lehrke, Hoffmann, & Gardner, 1985).

The work by Markus, Oyserman, and their colleagues (Markus & Nurius, 1986; Oyserman, Gant, & Ager, 1995) also illustrates the importance of group and individual differences in possible selves for students' willingness to take responsibility for their own learning. Oyserman and Markus (1990) found that individuals are more motivated to invest time and energy in mastering school learning materials if they included academic success in their future possible selves and academic failure in their feared future possible selves. Oyserman extended this idea by looking at the extent to which African American adolescents included academic success in their view of what it means to be a successful African American (Oyserman et al., 1995). Her survey studies have supported this hypothesis. Subsequently, Oyserman has conducted several interventions designed to increase the salience of academic achievement in both individuals' possible selves and ethnic identity. For example, using a randomized treatment intervention design, Oyserman, Terry, and Bybee (2002) provided a group of African American adolescents with a series of experiences designed to help them expand both their views of themselves in various future occupations and the means of obtaining these various occupational goals. These means included increased commitment to educational success. Those students who were part of the treatment reported greater bonding with school and greater concern with doing well in school than the controls. They also evidenced better school attendance.

Given the relation of both perceived importance and the utility value of mastering school-based learning materials to school performance, my colleagues and I were very surprised at how rarely we heard teachers provide any explanation for why the students might want to do their schoolwork other than to do well on the next test in our many hours of math classroom observations. In our early work, we observed for 10 hours in each of 60 secondary math classrooms and coded every public teacher–student interaction. The model number of times these teachers provided any explanation for the utility of doing the math work other than to do well on tests was zero. I had always enjoyed doing math and so had sufficient intrinsic reasons to motivate my engagement in the math being taught by my teachers. As I watched other students who did not enjoy doing math, I had to wonder what would provide them with sufficient motivation for them to answer yes to the question "Do I want to do this work?" Clearly, most of these teachers provided little information to increase the probability of a yes answer.

Perceived Cost

According to our model, the value of a task should also depend on a set of beliefs that can best be characterized as the cost of participating in the activity. Cost is influenced by many factors, such as anticipated anxiety; fear of failure; fear of the social consequences of success, such as rejection by peers or anticipated racial discrimination or anger from one's parents or other key people; and fear of loss of a sense of self-worth.

This conceptualization of cost is similar to the kinds of dynamics discussed by Covington in his self-worth theory. Covington (1992) defined the motive for self-worth as the desire to establish and maintain a positive self-image, or sense of self-worth. Because children spend so much time in classrooms and are evaluated so frequently there, Covington argued that protecting one's sense of academic competence is likely to be critical for maintaining a positive sense of self-worth. However, school evaluation, competition, and social comparison can make it difficult for some children to maintain the belief that they are competent academically. Covington outlined various strategies children develop to avoid appearing to lack ability, including procrastination, making excuses, avoiding challenging tasks, and not trying. The last two strategies are particularly interesting. Covington and Omelich (1979) referred to effort as a "double-edged sword" because, although trying is important for success (and is encouraged by both teachers and parents), if children try and fail, it is difficult to escape the conclusion that they lack ability. Therefore, if failure seems likely, some children will not try, precisely because trying and failing threatens their ability self-concepts. Avoiding challenging tasks is a good way to avoid or minimize failure experiences. Thus, it is not surprising that it is used by even high-achieving students who are failure avoidant.

Rather than responding to a challenging task with greater effort, these students try to avoid the task altogether in order to maintain both their own sense of competence and others' perceptions of their competence. Similarly, recent work by Newman and his colleagues demonstrates that students may be reluctant to ask for help in classrooms because they think that this will make them appear stupid (Newman, 1994; Newman & Goldin, 1990; Newman & Schwager, 1995).

Cost can also be conceptualized in terms of the loss of time and energy for other activities. People have limited time and energy. They cannot do everything they would like. They must choose among activities. To the extent that one loses time for Activity B by engaging in Activity A and to the extent that Activity B is high in one's hierarchy of importance, then the subjective cost of engaging in A increases. Alternatively, even if the subjective value of A is high, the value of engaging in A will be reduced to the extent that the subjective value of B is higher and to the extent that engaging in A jeopardizes the probability of successfully engaging in B. Thus, cost refers to what the individual has to give up to do a task (e.g., Do I do my math homework or call my friend?), as well as the anticipated effort one will need to put into task completion. Is working this hard to get an A in math worth it? My colleagues and I have emphasized that cost is especially important to choice and that sociocultural processes linked to social identity formation and cultural socialization should have a big influence of the perceived cost of the various activities competing for young people's time and energy (e.g., Eccles, 1994). Schools need to provide young people with genuine reasons for attaching higher subjective task value to taking responsibility for one's own learning than taking responsibility for one's behavior in other aspects of their daily lives.

CONCLUSION

In this chapter, I have reviewed the relation of psychological constructs of expectancy–value models of achievement behaviors linked to students' taking responsibility for their own learning. I have also stressed the importance of teachers' taking responsibility for providing students with the types of experiences likely to increase both their own expectations for success and to the subjective task value that they attach to engaging fully in their school's learning agenda. A large body of research supports the importance of expectations for success and students' sense of personal efficacy to master school materials. Far less research has focused on documenting the importance of subjective task value as well as establishing effective interventions to increase the subjective task value students attach to taking responsibility for their own learning. Such research is badly needed.

ACKNOWLEDGMENTS

The writing of this chapter was supported in part by grants from the National Institute for Child Health and Human Development and the Spencer Foundation.

REFERENCES

Anderman, L. H. (1999). Classroom goal orientation, school belonging, and social goals as predictors of students' positive and negative affect following transition to middle school. *Journal of Research and Development in Education, 32(2)*, 89–103.

Anderman, E. M., & Maehr, M. L. (1994). Motivation and schooling in the middle grades. *Review of Educational Research, 64*, 287–309.

Bandura, A. (1994). *Self-efficacy: The exercise of control*. New York: W. H. Freeman.

Bateson, C. D., & Johnson, A. (1976). Arousing intrinsic motivation as a goal for introductory classes: A case study. *Teaching of Psychology, 3*, 155–159.

Benware, C. A., & Deci, E. L. (1984). Quality of learning with an active versus passive motivational set. *American Educational Research Journal, 21*, 755–765.

Berry, G. L., & Asamen, J. K. (Eds.). (1989) *Black students: Psychosocial issues and academic achievement*. Newbury Park, CA: Sage.

Birch, S. H., & Ladd, G. W. (1997). The teacher-child relationship and children's early school adjustment. *Journal of School Psychology, 35(1)*, 61–79.

Blumenfeld, P. C., Soloway, E. Marx, R. W., Krajcik, J. S., Guzdail, M., & Palincsar, A. (1991). Motivating project-based learning: Sustaining the doing, supporting the learning. *Educational Psychologist, 26*, 369–398.

Brophy, J. E., & Good, J. L. (1974). *Teacher–student relationships*. New York: Holt, Rinehart & Winston.

Bryk, A. S., Lee, V. E., & Holland, P.B. (1993). *Catholic schools and the common good*. Cambridge, MA: Harvard University Press.

Connell, J. P. (1990). Context, self, and action: A motivational analysis of self-system processes across the life span. In D. Ciccetti & M. Geeghly (Eds.), *The self in transition: Infancy to childhood* (pp. 61–97). Chicago: University of Chicago Press.

Connell, J. P., Halpern-Felsher, B. L., Clifford, E., Crichlow, W., & Usinger, P. (1995). Hanging in there: Behavioral, psychological, and contextual factors affecting whether African-American adolescents stay in high school. *Journal of Adolescent Research, 10*, 41–63.

Connell, J. P., Spencer, M. B., & Aber, J. L. (1994). Educational risk and resilience in African American Youth: Context, self, and action outcomes in school. *Child Development, 65*, 493–506.

Connell, J. P., & Wellborn, J. G. (1991). Competence, autonomy, and relatedness: A motivational analysis of self-system processes. In R. Gunnar & L. A. Sroufe (Eds.), *Minnesota symposia on child psychology* (Vol. 23, pp. 43–77). Hillsdale, NJ: Erlbaum.

Covington, M. V. (1992). *Making the grade: A self-worth perspective on motivation and school reform.* New York: Cambridge University Press.

Covington, M. V., & Omelich, C. L. (1979). Effort: The double-edged sword in school achievement. *Journal of Educational Psychology, 71,* 169–182.

Crandall, V. C. (1969). Sex differences in expectancy of intellectual and academic reinforcement. In C. P. Smith (Ed.), *Achievement -related motives in children* (pp. 11–45). New York: Russell Sage Foundation.

Crocker, J., Luhtanen, R., Blaine, B., & Broadnax, S. (1994). Collective self-esteem and psychological well-being among White, Black, and Asian college students. *Personality and Social Psychology Bulletin, 20,* 503–513.

Cross, W. E. (1991). *Shades of black: Diversity in African-American identity.* Philadelphia: Temple University Press.

Csikszentmihalyi, M. (1988). The flow experience and its significance for human psychology. In M. Csikszentmihalyi & I. S. Csikszentmihalyi (Eds.), *Optimal experience* (pp. 15–35). Cambridge, MA: Cambridge University Press.

Deci, E. L., & Ryan, R. M. (1985). *Intrinsic motivation and self-determination in human behavior.* New York: Plenum Press.

Dewey, J. (1913). *Interest and effort in education.* Boston: Riverside Press.

Dornbusch, S. M. (1994). *Off the track.* Presidential address at the biennial meeting of the Society for Research on Adolescence, San Diego, CA.

Eccles, J. S. (1994). Understanding women's educational and occupational choices: Applying the Eccles et al. model of achievement-related choices. *Psychology of Women Quarterly, 18,* 585–609.

Eccles, J. S., Adler, T. F., & Meece, J. L. (1984). Sex differences in achievement: A test of alternate theories. *Journal of Personality and Social Psychology, 46*(1), 26–43.

Eccles, J. S., Early, D., Frasier, K., Belansky, E., & McCarthy, K. (1997). The relation of connection, regulation, and support for autonomy in the context of family, school, and peer group to successful adolescent development. *Journal of Adolescent Research, 12,* 263–286.

Eccles, J. S., & Harold, R. D. (1992). Gender differences in educational and occupational patterns among the gifted. In N. Colangelo, S. G. Assouline, & D. L. Amronson (Eds.), *Talent development: Proceedings form the 1991 Henry B. and Jocelyn Wallace National Research Symposium on Talent Development* (pp. 3–29). Unionville, NY: Trillium Press.

Eccles, J. S., Midgley, C., Buchanan, C. M., Wigfield, A., Reuman, D., & Mac Iver, D. (1993). Developmental during adolescence: The impact of stage/environment fit. *American Psychologist, 48,* 90–101.

Eccles, J. S., & Templeton, J. (2002). Extracurricular and other after-school activities for youth. In W. S. Secada (Ed.), *Review of educational research* (Vol. 26, pp. 113–180). Washington, DC: American Educational Research Association Press.

Eccles, J. S., & Wigfield, A. (2002). Motivational beliefs, values, and goals. In S. T. Fiske, D. L. Schacter, & C. Zahn-Waxler (Eds.), *Annual review of psychology* (Vol. 53, pp. 109–132). Palo Alto, CA: Annual Reviews.

Eccles, J. S., Wigfield, A., & Schiefele, U. (1998). Motivation. In N. Eisenberg (Ed.), *Handbook of child psychology* (5th ed., Vol. 3, pp. 1017–1095). New York: Wiley.

Essed, P. (1990). *Everyday racism: Reports from women of two cultures.* Claremont, CA: Hunter House

Feagin, J. R. (1992). The continuing significance of racism: Discrimination against black students in white colleges. *Journal of Black Studies, 22,* 546–578.

Feather, N. T. (1992). Values, valences, expectations, and actions. *Journal of Social Issues, 48,* 109–124.

Furrer, C., & Skinner, E. (2003). Sense of relatedness as a factor in children's academic engagement and performance. *Journal of Educational Psychology, 95,* 148–162.

Fordham, S., & Ogbu, J. U. (1986). Black students' school success: Coping with "the burden of 'acting white'". *The Urban Review, 18,* 176–206.

Fosterling, F. (1985). Attributional retraining: A review. *Psychological Bulletin, 98,* 495–512.

Gamoran, A., & Mare, R. D. (1989). Secondary school tracking and educational inequality: Compensation, reinforcement, or neutrality? *American Journal of Sociology, 94,* 1146–1183.

Goodenow, C. (1993). Classroom belonging among early adolescent students: Relationships to motivation and achievement. *Journal of Early Adolescence, 13*(1), 21–43.

Goodenow, C., & Grady, K.E. (1993). The relationship of school belonging and friends' values to academic motivation among urban adolescent students. *Journal of Experimental Education, 62,* 60–71.

Gottfried, A. E. (1990). Academic intrinsic motivation in young elementary school children. *Journal of Educational Psychology, 82,* 525–538.

Graham, S. (1984). Communicating sympathy and anger to black and white children: The cognitive (attributional) consequences of affective cues. *Journal of Personality and Social Psychology, 47,* 14–28.

Graham, S. (1994). Motivation in African Americans. *Review of Educational Research, 64,* 55–117.

Gurin, P., & Epps, E. (1974). *Black consciousness, identity, and achievement.* New York: Wiley.

Hale-Benson, J. (1989). The school learning environment and academic success. In G. L. Berry & J. K. Asamen (Eds.), *African American students: Psychosocial issues and academic achievement* (pp. 83–97). Newbury Park, CA: Sage.

Harter, S. (1998). The development of self-representations. In W. Damon (Series Ed.) & N. Eisenberg (Vol. Ed.), *Handbook of child psychology* (5th ed., Vol. 3, pp. 553–617). New York: John Wiley and Sons.

Hidi, S. (1990). Interest and its contribution as a mental resource for learning. *Review of Educational Research, 60,* 549–571.

Hidi, S., & Baird, W. (1986). Interestingness—A neglected variable in discourse processing. *Cognitive Science, 10,* 179–194.

Hoffmann, L., & Haeussler. (1995, April). *Modification of interests by instruction.* Paper presented at annual meeting of the AERA, San Francisco.

Jackson, J. S., Brown, T. N., Williams, D. R., Torres, M., Sellers, S. L., & Brown, K. (1994). Racism and the physical and mental health status of African Americans: A thirteen year national panel study. *Ethnicity and Disease, 4.*

Jessor, R., Van Den Bos, J., Vanderryn, J., Costa, F. M., & Turbin, M. S. (1995). Protective factors in adolescent problem behavior: Moderator effects and developmental change. *Developmental Psychology, 31,* 923–933.

Jussim, L., Eccles, J., & Madon, S. (1996). Social perception, social stereotypes, and teacher expectations: Accuracy and the quest for the powerful self-fulfilling prophecy. In L. Berkowitz (Ed.), *Advances in experimental social psychology* (pp. 281–388). New York, Academic Press.

Kao, G., & Tienda, M. (1995). Optimism and achievement: The educational performance of immigrant youth. *Social Science Quarterly, 76,* 1–19.

Kulik, C. L. Kulik, J., & Bangert-Drowns, R. (1990). Effectiveness of mastery learning programs: A meta-analysis. *Review of Educational Research, 60,* 265–299.

Lee, V. E., & Smith, J. B. (2001). *Restructuring high schools for equity and excellence: What works.* New York City: Teachers College Press.

Lehrke, M., Hoffmann, L., & Gardner, P. L. (Eds.). (1985). *Interests in science and technology education.* Kiel: Institut fur die Padagogik der Naturwissenschaften.

Lepper, M. R., & Cordova, D. (1992). A desire to be taught: Instructional consequences of intrinsic motivation. *Motivation and Emotion, 3,* 187–208.

Mac Iver, D. J., & Reuman, D. A. (1993). Giving their best: Grading and recognition practices that motivate students to work hard. *American Eduation, 17,* 24–31.

Mac Iver, D. J., Stipek, D. J., & Daniels, D. H. (1991). Explaining within-semester changes in student effort in junior high school and senior high school courses. *Journal of Educational Psychology, 83,* 201–211.

Maehr, M. L., & Midgley, C. (1996). *Transforming school cultures.* Boulder, CO: Westview Press.

Markus, H., & Nurius, P. (1986). Possible selves. *American Psychologist, 41,* 954–969.

Marsh, H. W. (1990). The causal ordering of academic self-concept and academic achievement: A multiwave, longitudinal analysis. *Journal of Educational Psychology, 82.*

Massimini, F., & Carli, M. (1988). The systematic assessment of flow in daily experience. In M. Csikszentmihalyi & I. S. Csikszentmihalyi (Eds.), *Optimal experience: Psychological studies of flow in consciousness* (pp. 266–287). Cambridge, MA: Cambridge University Press.

Meece, J. L. (1994). The role of motivation in self-regulated learning. In D. H. Schunk & B. J. Zimmerman (Eds.), *Self-regulation of learning and performance* (pp. 25–44). Hillsdale, NJ: Erlbaum.

Mickelson, R. A. (1991). The attitude–achievement paradox among black adolescents. *Sociology of Education, 63,* 44–61.

Midgley, C., Anderman, E., & Hicks, L. (1995). Differences between elementary and middle school teachers and students: A goal theory approach. *Journal of Early Adolescence, 15,* 90–113.

Midgley, C., & Feldlaufer, H. (1987). Students' and teachers' decision-making fit before and after the transition to junior high school. *Journal of Early Adolescence, 7*, 225–241.

Newman, R. S. (1994). Adaptive help-seeking: A strategy of self-regulated learning. In D. H. Schunk & B. J. Zimmerman (Eds.), *Self-regulation of learning and performance: Issues and educational applications* (pp. 283–301). Hillsdale, NJ: Erlbaum.

Newman, R. S., & Goldin, L. (1990). Children's reluctance to seek help with schoolwork. *Journal of Educational Psychology, 82*, 92–100.

Newman, R. S., & Schwager, M. T. (1995). Students' help-seeking during problem solving: Effects of grader, goal, and prior achievement. *American Educational Research Journal, 32*, 352–376.

Nicholls, J. G. (1984). Achievement motivation: Conceptions of ability, subjective experience, task choice, and performance. *Psychological Review, 91*, 328–346.

Nicholls, J. G. (1989). *The competitive ethos and democratic education*. Cambridge MA: Havard University Press.

Ogbu, J. G. (1992). Understanding cultural diversity and learning. *Educational Researcher, 21*, 5–14.

Oyserman, D., Gant, L. & Ager, J. (1995). A socially contextualized model of African American identity: social persistence and possible selves. *Journal of Personality and Social Psychology, 69*, 1216–1232.

Oyserman, D., & Markus, H. (1990) Possible selves and delinquency. *Journal of Personality and Social Psychology, 59*, 112–125.

Oyserman, D. Terry, K., & Bybee, D. (2002). A possible selves intervention to enhance school involvement. *Jouranl of Adolescence, 25*, 313–326.

Pajares, F., & Miller, M. D. (1994). Role of self-efficacy and self-concept beliefs in mathematical problem solving: A path analysis. *Journal of Educational Psychology, 86*, 193–203.

Pallas, A. M., Entwisle, D. R., Alexander, K. L., & Stluka. M. F. (1994). Ability-group effects: Instructional, social, or institutional? *Sociology of Education, 67*, 27–46.

Patrick, B. C., Skinner, E. A., & Connell, J. P. (1993). What motivates children's behavior and emotion? Joint effects of perceived control and autonomy in the academic domain. *Journal of Personality and Social Psychology, 65*, 781–791.

Phelan, P., Yu, H. C., & Davidson, A. L. (1994). Navigating the psychosocial pressures of adolescence: The voices and experiences of high school youth. *American Educational Research Journal, 31*, 415–447.

Phinney, J. S. (1996a). Understanding ethnic diversity: The role of ethnic identity. *American Behavioral Scientist, 40*(2), 143–152.

Phinney, J. S. (1996b). When we talk about American ethnic groups, what do we mean? *American Psychologist, 51*, 918–927.

Pintrich, P. R., & Schrauben, B. (1992). Students' motivational beliefs and their cognitive engagement in classroom academic tasks. In D. H. Schunk & J. L. Meece (Eds.), *Student perceptions in the classroom* (pp. 149–183). Hillsdale, NJ: Erlbaum.

Pintrich, P. R., & Schunk, D. H. (1996). *Motivation in education: Theory, research, and applications*. Englewood Cliffs, NJ: Merrill-Prentice Hall.

Renninger, K. A., Hidi, S., & Krapp, A. (Eds.). (1992). *The role of interest in learning and development*. Hillsdale, NJ: Erlbaum.

Roeser, R.W., & Eccles, J. S. (1998). Adolescents' perceptions of middle school relation to longitudinal changes in academic and psychological adjustment. *Journal of Research on Adolescence, 8*, 123–158.

Roeser, R.W., Midgley, C., & Urdan, T. (1996). Perceptions of the school psychological environment and early adolescents' psychological and behavioral functioning in school: The mediating role of goals and belonging. *Journal of Educational Psychology, 88*, 408–422.

Rokeach, M. (1973). *The nature of human values*. New York: Free Press.

Rosenbaum, J. E. (1980). Social implications of educational grouping. *Review of Research in Education, 7*, 361–401.

Schiefele, U. (1991). Interest, learning, and motivation. *Educational Psychologist, 26*, 299–323.

Schiefele, U. (1996). Topic interest, text representation, and quality of experience. *Contemporary Educational Psychology, 21*, 3–18.

Schunk, D. H., & Zimmerman, B. J. (Eds.). (1994). *Self-regulation of learning and performance*. Hillsdale, NJ: Erlbaum.

Sellers, R. M. Smith, M. A., Shelton, J. N., Rowley, S. A., & Chavous, T. M. (1998). Multidimensional model of racial identity: Are conceptualization of African American racial identity. *Personality and Social Psychology Review, 2*(1), 18–39.

Steele, C. M., & Aronson, J. (1995). Stereotype threat and the intellectual test performance of African Americans. *Journal of Personality and Social Psychology, 69*, 797–811.

Stevens, R. J., & Slavin, R. E. (1995). The cooperative elementary school: Effects on students' achievement, attitudes, and social relations. *American Educational Research Journal, 32*, 321–351.

Suarez-Orozco, C., & Suarez-Orozco, M. (2001). *Children of immigration*. Cambridge: Harvard University Press.

Taylor, R.D., Casten, R., Flickinger, S., Roberts, D., & Fulmore, C.D. (1994). Explaining the school performance of African-American adolescents. *Journal of Research on Adolescence, 4*, 21–44.

Updegraff, K. A., Eccles, J. S., Barber, B. L., & O'Brien, K. M. (1996). Course enrollment as self-regulatory behavior: Who takes optional high school math courses. *Learning and Individual Differences, 8*, 239–259.

Vida, M., & Eccles, J. S. (2003, March). *Predicting mathematics-related educational and career choices*. Paper presented at the biennial meeting of the Society of Research on Adolescence, Baltimore, MD.

Weiner, B. (1992). *Human motivation: Metaphors, theories, and research*. Newbury Park, CA: Sage.

Wentzel, K. R. (1997). Student motivation in middle school: The role of perceived pedagogical caring. *Journal of Educational Psychology, 89*(3), 411–419.

White, R. H. (1959). Motivation reconsidered: The concept of competence. *Psychological Review, 66*, 297–333.

Wong, C. A., Eccles, J. S., & Sameroff, A. J. (2003). The influence of ethnic discrimination and ethnic identification on African-Americans adolescents' school and socioemotional adjustment. *Journal of Personality, 71*, 1197–1232.

Zimmerman, B. J., Bandura, A., & Martinez-Pons, M. (1992). Self-motivation for academic attainment: The role of self-efficacy beliefs and personal goal setting. *American Educational Research Journal, 29*, 663–676.

PART IV

MODEL

CHAPTER 11

INTEGRATING THE OTHER THREE Rs INTO THE CURRICULUM

A Model for Improving Academic Achievement

Jeanine C. Cogan, Robert J. Sternberg, and Rena F. Subotnik

Enhancing student learning and improving academic achievement for all children is a primary goal of educators. Some schools are responding to this goal by implementing character education or life skills programs based on promising research findings on the efficacy of such programs (Berkowitz & Bier, 2004; Greenberg et al., 2003). For example, a recent study of 681 elementary schools found that instruction in character education was associated with higher academic scores (Benninga, Berkowitz, Kuehn, & Smith, 2003).

Although there are many core values or life skills associated with effective character education programs, we propose that an integrated model of *reasoning*, *resilience*, and *responsibility* (the Other Three Rs) holds great

Optimizing Student Success in School With the Other Three Rs:
Reasoning, Resilience, and Responsibility, 227–238
Copyright © 2006 by Information Age Publishing
227

promise for enhancing student learning and achievement. In this chapter we discuss the Other Three Rs Model for Student Learning, designed to help teachers convey three key skills applicable to students' academic and general life pursuits: how to (1) *reason* well, (2) be *resilient* in the face of challenges, and (3) take *responsibility* for one's own learning.

BACKGROUND

The Other Three Rs Model began as an American Psychological Association (APA) initiative, sponsored by Robert J. Sternberg, Dean of Liberal Arts at Tufts University and former IBM Professor of Psychology and Education at Yale University and past president of the APA. A diverse team of experts he organized identified reasoning, resilience, and responsibility as three learnable skills that, taken together, have great potential for increasing academic success. APA applied for and received a grant from the James S. McDonnell Foundation to conduct a pilot study examining the impact on learning and achievement of teaching elementary students the Other Three Rs. The grant supported a collaborative of key stakeholders to design the process for infusing the concepts of reasoning, resilience, and responsibility into the elementary curriculum with an eye toward improving student learning. The collaborative[1] consisted of experts from a broad range of fields, including:

- Research on reasoning, resilience, and responsibility
- Professional development of elementary school teachers
- Curriculum development, including local and state curriculum standards
- Program implementation and evaluation
- Elementary school teaching

FUNDAMENTAL ASSUMPTIONS OF THE OTHER THREE RS MODEL

Three fundamental assumptions form the basis for the Other Three Rs Model for Student Learning:

1. Reasoning, resilience, and responsibility can be learned.
2. Once learned and internalized, reasoning, resilience, and responsibility lead to measurable increases in academic achievement.
3. The Other Three Rs derive their greatest power through their interaction with each other.

WHY THE OTHER 3Rs

The following section outlines the research on reasoning, resilience, and responsibility that lays the foundation for the Other Three R's Model for Student Learning.

Reasoning

Reasoning, critical thinking, or good general intellectual functioning is one of the strongest predictors of academic success and resilience (Sternberg, 2003a, 2004). Teaching children problem solving—how to figure things out—is key to successful learning, and problem solving is characterized by the ability to generate possible strategies, analyze those strategies, and anticipate their possible consequences. Skills that a child learns to master under the heading of problem solving include planning, flexibility, resourcefulness, and critical thinking (Bernard, 2004):

Planning entails looking ahead, anticipating possible outcomes, and making healthy choices.

Flexibility entails shifting plans when one's original strategy does not work out.

Resourcefulness involves seeking help when needed, using resources intelligently, and developing "street smarts."

Critical thinking refers to higher-order thinking skills that go beneath surface impressions and opinions to offer understanding and deeper meaning to an event or situation.

The collaborative developed the Other Three Rs model around problem-solving skills, since problem solving is central to academic achievement and incorporates important components of reasoning

Resilience

Resilience provides individuals with skills to surmount life's challenges competently, to persevere, and even to capitalize on setbacks. Being resilient is part of what distinguishes those who thrive in adverse circumstances from those who do not (see Brabeck & Walsh, Chapter 7, this volume). In the past decade, resilience research has moved from exclusive focus on addressing negative phenomena such as dropout rates and depression by considering indices of positive development and well-being. This research concludes that resilience is important for improving academic achievement and for success in life (e.g., Bernard, 1995; Greenberg et al., 2003; Sternberg & Grigorenko, 2000; Waxman et al, 1997).

Both external and internal factors determine individuals' levels of resilience. Some important external factors that contribute to resilience in children are positive relationships with an adult, higher socioeconomic status, and positive school environment (Bernard, 2004). Internal or individual factors that contribute to resilience in children are many, and include good intellectual functioning, perseverance, problem solving, self-efficacy, self-regulation, optimism, and high goals, among others (Seligman & Csikszentmihalyi, 2000; Sternberg, 2003a; Weinstein, 2002).

The prevailing understanding among researchers in the field is that everyone has the capacity to be resilient. Learning these skills is not only beneficial in and of itself; the skills are associated with increased academic performance, a high priority for educational administrators, parents, teachers, and policymakers alike.

Responsibility

Responsibility, taking accountability for one's actions and their consequences, is associated with heightened academic achievement (Masten & Coatsworth, 1998). Research points to the following key processes underlying students' development of academic responsibility (Zimmerman, Chapter 9, this volume):

1. *Attributions* of success or failure for finding the best strategy, technique, or method of learning. Attributions that increase students' personal responsibility for their achievement are ones that allow students to feel that they have control over the outcomes of their efforts. Research indicates that attributing success or failure to effort is effective, but not as effective as attributions associated with finding the best strategy, technique, or method of learning (Zimmerman, this volume).

2. *Self-efficacy.* Self-efficacy describes a sense that one is competent and has the ability to affect personal life outcomes (Bandura, 1995). Believing that one is prepared to accomplish what he or she wants to can be more potent than innate ability in determining success (Maddux, 2002). Perceived self-efficacy plays a major role in educational success as it leads students to set challenging goals, employ various cognitive strategies, and persist when facing obstacles (Schunk, 1991; Zimmerman, 1995).

3. *Self-regulation.* Students' perceptions of academic responsibility depend on their use of key self-regulatory processes and their beliefs about the effectiveness of those processes. When students

use self-regulated learning strategies, they experience increased academic success (Zimmerman & Martinez-Pons, 1986).

The concept of responsibility within our model also incorporates *social responsibility* because of its relevance to life skills and the judicious application of academic knowledge. Social responsibility includes the wisdom to be responsible for others as well as oneself—seeking outcomes that reflect the common good (Sternberg, 1999, 2003b).

AN INTEGRATED MODEL OF THE OTHER THREE RS

As is illustrated in Figure 11.1, the crux of the Other Three Rs Model is a new problem-solving model in which reasoning, resilience, and responsibility are practiced in tandem. A challenge for many teachers is how to get their students to implement a problem-solving model on a regular basis. Those models miss explicit reference to resilience and responsibility, which students need to access in order to use the model in the first place and persist with problem solving until a solution is found.

The first step in using a problem-solving model requires the student to take responsibility for the problem and wanting to solve it. Additionally, the student needs to take responsibility for completing each step of the problem-solving model. Students exercise resilience when the steps of the problem-solving model prove to be challenging for them. When encountering a step in the problem-solving model that is difficult to complete, rather than giving up or skipping the step, the Other Three Rs Problem-Solving Model urges students to use their creative and critical thinking skills until they come up with an alternative. Thus, in the Other Three Rs Problem Solving Model, responsibility and resilience are integral components to every step. Refer to Figures 11.2 and 11.3 for the exact definitions and descriptions of reasoning, resilience, and responsibility.

THE ABCS OF PROBLEM SOLVING

After reviewing the literature and many problem-solving models, we synthesized aspects of these successful models to create a new model that would be accessible to a third-grade population (refer to Figure 11.1). This model includes the key components that decades of research have shown to be integral to successful problem solving: understanding the problem, devising a plan, implementing the plan, and looking back to learn from and evaluate the plan (e.g., Bransford & Stein, 1993; Polya, 1945).

The following section is a short summary of the ABC's of the problem-solving model.

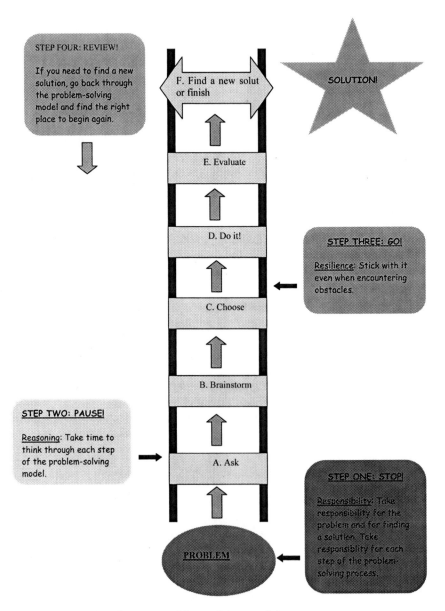

Figure 11.1.   The other 3Rs problem-solving model.

- *Reasoning:* Thinking that utilizes explicit and/or implicit rules focusing on effective problem solving, particularly with regard to academic challenges.
- *Resilience*: Competently surmounting challenges, both inside and outside of school.
- *Responsibility*: Being accountable for one's own actions and inactions and the social and academic consequences of those actions and inactions.

Figure 11.2.   Definitions of the Other 3 Rs.

Resilience
   ✓ **Challenges and difficulties are a normal part of life:**
     "Challenges are normal. We all have them."
   ✓ **Persistence/Determination**
     "If at first I don't succeed, I will try again."
     Caveat: If a certain strategy doesn't work with necessary effort, then try a different strategy.
   ✓ **View obstacles as challenges to be overcome** (approach challenges by keeping things in perspective and seeing them as opportunities for learning).
     "What can I learn from this?"
     "How can I approach this challenge?"

Responsibility
   ✓ **Personal responsibility**
     "It's up to me to create the results I want."
     "It's up to me to make it happen."
     "How I act matters."
   ✓ **Academic responsibility:** Being accountable for one's academic effort and achievement.
     "Good grades result from my efforts."
     "If I want to learn, it is up to me."
     "If I don't understand, I have to ask."
   ✓ **Social responsibility**
     • Seeing and caring about other peoples' points of view.
      "I will listen and care about what you have to say."
     • Concern for the common good.
      "I care about what is good for all of us, not just for me."
     • Giving help and seeking help.
      "I will help you."
      "I need help."

Reasoning
   ✓ **Developing multiple strategies**
     "What strategies can help me here?"

Figure 11.3.   Explanations of the Other Three Rs in accessible language for young students.

A is for Ask. In this first step students are encouraged to clearly define the problem to be solved by asking questions like "What is the problem?" or "What needs to be accomplished?"

Asking the right question involves *reasoning*. At times the process of defining the problem will be simple and straightforward. Other times there may be multiple problems embedded in one problem. If there is more than one problem, then students are encouraged to disentangle individual problems by clearly defining each, prioritizing them, and then using this model to solve them one at a time.

The second component of this step involves asking, "What strategies could I use in order to solve this problem successfully?" Students are reinforced for coming up with multiple strategies for finding the solution rather than focusing immediately on one.

B is for Brainstorming possible strategies. Brainstorming is frequently underutilized in problem solving. Students often come up with only one possible strategy before implementing it. The strength and the challenge of this model is in teaching students how to generate many possible approaches on a continuous basis. Without brainstorming, students may choose the most readily available or familiar strategy rather than a more creative or optimal one. In this step students are encouraged to develop a wide range of options, even ones that they may find implausible at first. Whereas brainstorming is a common technique used with groups, in this model individual brainstorming is encouraged as a first step to group brainstorming so that all students may practice and learn the skill of developing multiple strategies for solving a problem.

C is for Choosing a strategy from the brainstormed list that has promise for solving the problem with the fewest undesirable side effects.

The *Choose* step requires *reasoning* in the form of forward thinking—the ability to anticipate outcomes that different approaches may bring about. When students anticipate possible negative consequences to strategies, they learn to choose ones that will likely generate positive outcomes. The following four-step procedure was developed by our team for students to practice choosing an optimal strategy:

1. **Pick.** Students are asked to pick their top three strategies from their brainstormed list.

2. **Possible outcomes.** Students are encouraged to anticipate and record at least three possible outcomes (both positive and negative) for each strategy.

3. **Discard.** When recognizing possible negative outcomes students may then discard a strategy that had otherwise appeared to be a good idea.

4. **Choose**. After this process of anticipating outcomes, students then choose a strategy to implement.

D is for Do it. Once a strategy is chosen, students are to carry out that strategy with 100% effort. *Doing it* 100% requires responsibility for solving the problem and resilience to stick with the steps of the model until the problem is solved.

E is for Evaluate the strategy that was tried. After students carry out their chosen strategy with 100% effort, they evaluate the results by asking themselves questions like: "Is the problem solved? Did the strategy work well? Was there a strategy that might have worked even better?" Such evaluation requires *reasoning*.

F is for Find another strategy. If, after students evaluate the effectiveness of their strategy, they conclude that the problem was not solved to their satisfaction, they need to review the entire process. In this step students are encouraged to think through the steps of the model from the bottom up (from D to A) until they find the appropriate entry point to start over again (e.g., "Did I put 100% effort into my chosen strategy?" "Did I choose a good strategy?" "Did I brainstorm enough ideas?" "Did I ask the right questions and define the problem correctly?").

F is also for Finished! If students find a good strategy and solve the problem, they can congratulate themselves for successfully finishing with this application of the problem-solving model.

A SAMPLE APPLICATION OF THE MODEL TO A MATHEMATICS PROBLEM

Lollipop Cookies: A Mathematics Problem

Last year for *Grandma's Bake Sale* Sally and John made 3-dozen lollipop cookies to sell. They sold so fast that this year they plan to make 9-dozen.

Lollipop Cookies

Ingredients needed:

1 1/2 Cup sugar
3/4 Cup (1-1/2 sticks) margarine
2 eggs
1 1/2 teaspoons vanilla
3 Cups flour
1 teaspoon baking powder
1/2 teaspoon salt

To make 9-dozen cookies they will need to change the recipe. The directions will not change. Only the amount of each ingredient needs to be changed. How much of each ingredient will Sally and John need to make 9-dozen cookies?

An Application of the ABCs Model of Problem Solving

The students' first step for solving this problem is to *ask* what the questions are that need to be answered. In this case the question was outlined fairly explicitly in the math problem, "How much of each ingredient is needed to make 9-dozen cookies?" The students then follow this up with the next key question that leads them into the brainstorming step, "What are some strategies we can use to determine how much of each ingredient is needed to make 9-dozen cookies?" The second step is to *brainstorm* possible strategies for solving the problem. One strategy is to multiply each ingredient by three. This is an efficient approach and requires a basic understanding of how to multiply fractions. Another strategy is to convert all ingredients into decimals and then multiply by three. This is a two-step process, which requires an understanding of how to translate fractions into decimals. A third strategy is to add each ingredient three times. This strategy requires knowing how to add fractions together but it does not allow a student to practice and learn the multiplication of fractions.

After listing these three or other possible strategies and thinking through possible outcomes, the students *choose* a strategy. In this case, let us say the students choose the first one, multiplying the ingredients by three.

Now the students *do* the chosen strategy. In this step the students may conclude the chosen strategy didn't work: "We tried to multiply by three but got a goofy answer." This is one of the places in the model where both responsibility and resilience are key for success. The students must take responsibility for doing the strategy and show determination to make that strategy work or find another one until the problem is solved.

The next step is for students to *evaluate* the strategy: "Did we get the right answer? Did we multiply the fractions by three successfully?" If the answer is "no," then the students need to *find* another strategy to use, such as changing the fractions to decimals and then multiplying by three. Alternatively, if the students evaluate the answer as correct, then the problem-solving task is *finished*.

CONCLUSION

The Other Three Rs Model of Student Learning builds on the research based wisdom of prior problem-solving models by incorporating key skills needed for optimal problem solving. The model is currently being piloted in third grade classrooms randomly assigned to this intervention in a large school district in the Washington DC region.

The Other Three Rs model was tested in 17 Montgomery County, Maryland public elementary schools with 43 third grade teachers and 724 students. Third grade teachers from the 17 schools, balanced on school characteristics, were randomly assigned to receive either the Other Three Rs training intervention or an alternative intervention that focused on teaching and learning mnemonics. Both the Other 3Rs and the mnemonics trainings were composed of five sessions, 3 hours in length and were conducted from October, 2004 to January, 2005. Teachers learned skills and content that they then incorporated into their daily instruction. Each session of the trainings included the same four components: (1) review and discussion, (2) hands on practice, (3) application, and (4) strategies for taking the lessons in the classroom. Results of this pilot will be available soon though initial analyses suggest the feasibility and benefits of teaching the Other Three Rs as a mechanism for enhancing student learning.

Learning how to "stick with it" when strategies for solving a problem fail is imperative so that students will not abandon using the model and finding a solution. Additionally, when students take responsibility for the problem, they commit to generating strategies and finding a solution. They also become more involved in their own learning and take responsibility for their academic success. Lastly, students practice critical and analytical thinking by continually generating multiple strategies for solving a problem. The benefits to students of repeatedly practicing this model include learning the skill of generating effective strategies, increased resilience, and practicing taking responsibility for their academic success.

ACKNOWLEDGMENTS

The project described in this chapter was supported by a grant from the McDonnell Foundation. We would like to thank all those who contributed to this project, including (in alphabetical order) Diane Blyer, Carol Dwyer, Rose Furr, Linda Jarvin, Suzanne Morrow, Debra Rog, Debra Reynolds, Sandra Shmookler, Vivian Sonnenborn, Joanne Steckler, Connie Sullivan, Mary Walsh, Roger Weissberg, Priscilla Waynant, Greg White, Russell Wright, and Barry Zimmerman.

REFERENCES

Bandura, A. (1995). *Self-efficacy in changing societies*. Cambridge, UK: Cambridge University Press.

Benninga, J. S., Berkowitz, M. W., Kuehn, P., & Smith, K.(2003). The Relationship between character education and academic achievement. *Journal of Research in Character Education, 1*(1), 19–32.

Berkowitz, M. W., & Bier, M. C. (2004). Research-based character education. *Annals of the American Academy of Political and Social Science, 591*, 72–85.

Bernard, B. (2004). *Resiliency: What we have learned.* San Francisco: WestEd.

Bransford, J. D., & Stein, B. S. (1993). *The ideal problem solver: A guide to improving thinking, learning, and creativity.* New York: Worth.

Greenberg, M. T., Weissberg, R. P., O'Brien, M. U., Zins, J. E., Fredericks, L., Resnik, H., & Elias, M. J. (2003). Enhancing school-based prevention and youth development through coordinated social, emotional and academic learning. *American Psychologist, 58*, 466–474.

Maddux, J. (2002). Self-efficacy: The power of believing you can. In C. Synder & S. Lopez (Eds.), *Handbook of positive psychology* (pp. 277–287). New York: Oxford University Press.

Masten, A. S., & Coatsworth, J. D. (1998). The development of competence in favorable and unfavorable environments: Lessons from research on successful children. *American Psychologist, 53*(2), 205–220.

Polya, G. (1945). *How to solve it: A new aspect of mathematical method.* Princeton, NJ: Princeton University Press.

Schunk, D. (1991). Self-efficacy and achievement motivation. *Educational Psychologist, 26*, 207–231.

Seligman, M., & Csikszentmihalyi, M. (2000). Positive psychology: An introduction. *American Psychologist. 55*(1), 5–14.

Sternberg, R. J. (1999). The theory of successful intelligence. *Review of General Psychology. 3*(4), 292–316.

Sternberg, R. J. (2003a). The Other 3 Rs: Part two: Reasoning. *Monitor on Psychology, 34*(4), 5.

Sternberg, R. J. (2003b). Responsibility: One of the Other Three Rs. *Monitor on Psychology, 34*(3), 5.

Sternberg, R. J. (2004). *Psychology* (4th ed.). Belmont, CA: Thomson.

Sternberg, R. J., & Grigorenko, E. L. (2000). *Teaching for successful intelligence to increase student learning and achievement.* Arlington Heights, IL: Skylight.

Waxman, H. C., Huang, S. L., & Padron, Y. N. (1997). Motivation and learning environment differences between resilient and non-resilient middle school students. *Hispanic Journal of Behavioral Sciences, 19*, 137–155.

Weinstein, R. (2002). *Reaching higher: The power of expectations in schools.* Cambridge, MA; Harvard University Press.

Zimmerman, B. J. (1995). Self-efficacy and educational development. In A. Bandura (Ed.), *Self-efficacy in changing societies* (pp. 202–231). Cambridge, UK: Cambridge University Press.

Zimmerman, B. J., & Martinez-Pons, M. (1988). Construct validation of a strategy model of student self-regulated learning. *Journal of Educational Psychology, 80*(3), 284–290.

PART V

SUMMARY

CHAPTER 12

THE OTHER 3 Rs

Implications for the Design of Learning Environments, Research, and Policy

Susan R. Goldman

The emphasis of the present volume on reasoning, resilience, and responsibility as the "Other" three Rs is both a timely and welcome contribution to discussions about the goals and outcomes of schooling. This is especially so in the context of the No Child Left Behind legislation (NCLB, 2001) and its use of once-a-year testing in reading, mathematics, and science for school accountability. NCLB is creating a great deal of pressure on practitioners to focus on what is tested to the exclusion of other aspects of children's education. In fact, research indicates that an overemphasis on high-stakes accountability assessments often leads to a narrowing of the curriculum to focus only on what the tests measure (Haney, 2000; Kohn, 2000; McNeill, 2000; Valencia & Bernal, 2000). Producing high achievement and sufficient average yearly gains to meet the criteria set forth by NCLB could well leave little room in formal schooling for reasoning, resilience, and responsibility. Yet, the contributions to this volume give strong voice to the need for children to emerge from schooling as knowledgeable, resilient, and responsible individuals.

Optimizing Student Success in School With the Other Three Rs:
Reasoning, Resilience, and Responsibility, 241–260
Copyright © 2006 by Information Age Publishing

A second reason that this volume is timely concerns the societal shift from an industrial society to a knowledge society. The traditional three Rs (reading, 'riting, and 'rithmetic) may have been sufficient for agrarian and industrial societies, but they are clearly inadequate for successful functioning in the knowledge society of the 21st century. To be successful, individuals need mathematical and language literacy competencies that exceed those needed in the past. They must be able to understand and manipulate complex text and mathematical relationships in a variety of media forms and across a range of subject-matter domains. Digital media and resources, most notably the World Wide Web, require that individuals be able to evaluate and select from among a vast array of potential sources of information and to relate multiple sources of information to one another (Goldman, 2004). Having selected a source, learners need to be able to ascertain whether the information is trustworthy, reliable, and relevant to their purposes. They need to make sense of the information so that they understand the concepts and their interrelationships. Cognitive psychologists refer to the need for learners to construct coherent mental models from these sources. Mental models are one form in which some types of knowledge are represented (Mayer, Chapter 4, this volume). Constructing coherent models requires that learners adopt a critical stance toward the information—that they question it and hold up the claims and evidence to critical analysis and examination. The research indicates, however, that critical processing of information sources is very difficult for individuals to do, either on or off the Web (e.g., Norris & Phillips, 1994; Palincsar & Magnusson, 2001; Wiley, Goldman, & Graesser, 2004).

Some of the reasons it is difficult to take a critical stance toward information sources are cognitive but some are social and emotional. It seems obvious that complex thinking and reasoning about ideas is central to making sense and evaluating credibility, reliability, and relevance. However, also involved are issues of identity and confidence (Bloome & Egan-Robertson, 1993). That is, questioning the information in a text presumes that one has the right to question. It requires that individuals see themselves as having the authority to analyze a text and decide what to believe and what not to. In some social situations and organizations (e.g., bible class, the army, or indeed, in any hierarchically organized system) it may take quite a lot of courage to say "I disagree." Ensuring that children have the opportunity to learn and achieve these fundamental literacies for the 21st century demands that the goals of schooling go well beyond the traditional three Rs. Schools must support children in developing resilience in the face of disagreements from others and in taking responsibility for active construction of meaning.

The foregoing analysis of what graduates of educational systems need to know and be able to do to assume productive roles in the knowledge society of the 21st century is consistent with other voices calling for the integration of academic, social, and emotional learning in formal educational contexts (Greenberg et al., 2003; Zins, Bloodworth, Weissberg, & Walberg, 2004). Efforts to create such integration need to also address issues of within- and cross-grade instructional coherence, a characteristic of high-performing schools (Greenberg et al., 2003; Newman, Smith, Allensworth, & Bryk, 2001). But how can we design educational contexts to ensure these outcomes? Luce and Thompson (Chapter 6, this volume) propose that the selection of instructional practices be based on identifying areas of strength and areas that need strengthening based on achievement performance patterns over time at individual, class, school, and district levels. To address needs, districts can consult various compendia of need-specific practices that others have found effective and select those that match their current needs. The success of this process for improving achievement depends on a number of factors, most especially the alignment of the achievement performance indicators and instructional practices. If the two do not align, the practice may be effective but have little or no impact on the achievement indicators. As well, the indicators themselves need to align with district standards for knowledge and reasoning. A second important factor stems from the fact that no two educational contexts are exactly alike. The new district context might differ from the original on a number of dimensions. For the practices found to be effective in the original district context to be effective in a new district context, adaptations are often necessary, but the knowledge to make these adaptations is often lacking (Goldman, 2005). Finally, this approach can improve the achievement of social and emotional competencies only if there are appropriate performance indicators of them. At present, achievement indicators typically address reading, mathematics, and other specific subject-matter areas. Thus, effective implementation of the Luce and Thompson approach requires that attention be paid to some complex underlying issues. It is only in the doing that these complexities are revealed.

The other chapters in the volume contribute to an increasing knowledge base for addressing the complexities involved in improving achievement in cognitive, social, and emotional arenas. The material in the chapters ranges from descriptive research on correlates of achievement (Eccles, Chapter 10; Mayer, Chapter 4; Nuñes, Chapter 5; Brabeck & Walsh, Chapter 7; Zimmerman, Chapter 9) to research that establishes causal connections between attitudes toward intellectual functioning and achievement, social and emotional development (Good & Dweck, Chapter 3). Other chapters take a more systemic perspective. For example, Gordon and Mejia redefine resilience as active defiance of constraints imposed by the sociopolitical power structure. Sternberg likens wisdom to responsible uses of knowledge and discusses the importance of resilience for creativity. The final chapter of the volume presents a school-based intervention designed to connect and integrate reasoning, resilience, and responsibility so that students practice all three together (Cogan, Sternberg, & Subotnik, Chapter 11). I briefly elaborate on these characterizations of the chapters before relating them to a framework for the design of learning environments.

LESSONS FROM DESCRIPTIVE AND EXPLANATORY RESEARCH

There has been a great deal of research over the last several decades that is relevant to issues of what cognitive, social, and emotional conditions are correlated with performance in laboratory tasks and with achievement outcomes obtained from students' educational histories. Two major lessons from the research reported in this volume and from the related literature are that (1) although an individual's achievement in school can be talked about as an attribute of the individual, academic outcomes for individuals are determined as much by the practices and norms of the institutions and communities in which that individual is situated, and (2) efforts to improve achievement need to be comprehensive if they are to be successful, long-term, and self-sustaining.

Reasoning. Successful reasoning involves multiple forms of knowledge. Mayer outlines four of the forms commonly cited in the cognitive literature: strategic, conceptual, factual, and procedural. Many students demonstrate the best competence with procedural knowledge, but often their command of that is inadequate because it is not related appropriately to other forms of knowledge and the isolated nature of it limits when students use it. They frequently fail to use procedures unless the surface form of the task matches the circumstances under which they learned the procedure. In addition, many of the tasks students are presented with in formal educational contexts are relatively simplistic. Students are expected to answer them quickly. As a result, students apply the procedures they know, and do so quickly, often giving little thought to the reasonableness of the answer. Indeed, students—both high and low achieving—often express the view that if you can't solve it immediately, it can't be solved (Cognition and Technology Group at Vanderbilt [CTGV], 1997). Students' views about math problems illustrate Mayer's fifth form of knowledge, attitudinal, and show how students' attitudes toward mathematics impact their solution strategies.

An important issue in performance on reasoning tasks is whether students have access to the task and content knowledge to perform well. Nuñes emphasizes that for deaf children verbal information places high demands on processing resources. As a result, they may not have access to the critical task information or may fail to access content they know. However, deaf children demonstrate strong visual and spatial processing. Nuñes's research indicates that deaf children's performance improves when mathematical reasoning tasks are presented in visual and spatial formats rather than verbal. She refers to an ongoing project that is looking at the impact of systematically increasing the visual and spatial modalities in instruction.

Social and emotional development in context. The several chapters that deal with social and emotional development and its relation to achievement make clear that academic outcomes for individuals are determined as much by the practices and norms of the institutions and communities in which that individual is situated as by characteristics typically attributed to the individual. Note that there is also increasing emphasis on the context of learning by those who focus on cognitive aspects of learning.

Brabeck and Walsh examine social context variables in relation to resilience. Their main claim is that multiple variables determine resilience and its opposite, risk. These variables operate at multiple levels, in multiple spheres, and may have differential impacts at different points in development. For example, they discuss the impact of poverty on a range of variables, including biological, social, and psychological, and across multiple contexts, including family, school, and the larger community. While there are numerous effects of poverty that make it difficult for children to do well in school, there are nevertheless many cases in which children demonstrate resilience in overcoming risk factors and succeed. They argue that we need to understand what variables are associated with resilience and use this information to create contexts that will foster it. Toward that end, they indicate that academic resilience is correlated with feeling oneself a part of a school community and with having relationships with teachers who set high expectations for students and provide the support students need to meet those expectations.

Recognizing the complexity and multileveled nature of the variables affecting academic as well as social and emotional outcomes, Brabeck and Walsh argue that the current way in which support services are provided is itself a major obstacle to improving outcomes. They contend that a comprehensive services model is necessary to support the development of healthy socioemotional functioning and academic success. They briefly describe encouraging but preliminary findings from just such a model that is in its early years of implementation. One of the difficulties in assessing the comprehensive support services model will be the specification of the appropriate time frame for observing change in the outcome variables, academic as well as social and emotional.

Although self-efficacy, motivation, and responsibility are often conceived of as attributes of an individual, Zimmerman places responsibility for their development squarely in the learning context. He indicates that students need to take on challenging tasks, but with appropriate levels of structure and support so that they can succeed. In unstructured situations, students may find it difficult to self-regulate their activity. In addition to success at challenging tasks, developing a strong sense of self-efficacy involves a variety of additional processes and constructs, including attributions of agency and locus of control, and self-regulatory and meta-cognitive processes. When students perceive that they are in control of outcomes, they are more likely to take on responsibility for academic performance. If the perception is that school is "done to me" rather than something "I do," students have little investment in the tasks, and hence, little personal responsibility for doing them.

A similar relationship to the context is critical in Eccles's expectancy–value model. When faced with an academic—or indeed any—task, the individual must ask: Can I do the task? (expectancy) and Do I want to do the task? (value). If the answer to these questions—either or both—is no, students will be less likely to take responsibility for their own learning and achievement, and will be less likely to engage with, and persist at, these tasks. Giving up on school tasks stands in the way of the positive cognitive, social, and emotional experience of mastering a challenging task, an experience that contributes to resilience. Eccles contends that how individuals answer these questions is related to the expectations that others set for them and that task value results from a variety of social and cultural influences.

Eccles uses the constructs in her model to explain the lower achievement of students of color who may experience discrimination in school settings. That experience may in turn lower students' own expectations that they can do well in school, and the value they place on doing well. When society at large and the local school community communicate lowered achievement expectations for students of color and engage in other forms of discriminatory behavior, these messages are incorporated into students' beliefs and attitudes toward engaging in school tasks and caring about the outcomes of their performance. Included among the variables contributing to task value are input from socializers (parents, teachers, peers), experiences in achievement-related events, social roles and culturally based beliefs about specific tasks, appropriateness of the task for the individual, self-concept, self-efficacy, processes and consequences associated with identity formation, and the personal values and needs of the individual. In discussing these, Eccles points out that different variables take on different weights at different time spans in development. Thus, the "same" variable may have a different impact when the individual is 10 years old as compared with 16 years old. Any of the numerous psychoso-cial variables that Eccles discusses can be an obstacle to high achievement for students of color. Whether it is an obstacle depends on other variables in the context, leading to quite a complex set of predictions. Eccles does a very good job of describing these sets of interlinked dependencies. The expectancy–value model provides a compelling descriptive account of motivation, and the complex interactions needed to explain an individual's expectancy and valuation of any given learning task. Less clear are the implications of the model for the design of learning environments that support high achievement for all students. However, one implication that Eccles herself states is that for high achievement to occur, students need opportunities to work on, and be successful at, challenging and interesting tasks.

Attitudes toward learning connect the Other 3 Rs. Students' beliefs about the nature of learning are systematically related to reasoning, resilience, responsibility, and to learning outcomes. That is the clear conclusion from several decades of work by Carol Dweck and colleagues, summarized by Good and Dweck in this volume. Individuals who hold entity views of intellect see it as a fixed ability whereas those who hold incremental views see intellectual functioning as subject to change through learning. In a variety of studies, Dweck and colleagues have demonstrated correlational and causal relationships between these two views of intellect, task–goal orientation, and long-term achievement in challenging subject-matter areas, such as mathematics. They have consistently found that those who hold entity views are performance oriented (emphasis on getting the right answer) whereas those with incremental views are learning oriented (emphasis on mastery and the processes of learning). In one study, they found that incrementalists paid attention to feedback that would help them learn in the future whereas those holding entity orientations focused on just the "right or wrong" feedback and ignored the feedback information that would help them learn in the future. The work thus suggests a cognitive mechanism contributing to differences in achievement over the longer term.

In the mathematics work, Dweck and colleagues induced incremental, learning orientations in two groups of women, African Americans, and Hispanics. The long-term impact was higher levels of achievement in mathematics when compared to students from these gender and ethnic groups who were provided with neutral or entity/performance orientations. This is an impressive result, especially because the experimental manipulation of orientation allows the conclusion that orientation caused the achievement results.

Entity as compared to incremental beliefs about intellect are also related to persistence. Research in the mathematics domain showed that women with incremental orientations were more likely to persist in mathematics than were those who held entity orientations. They were thus more resilient in the face of negative stereotypes about women and math achievement. Finally, Grant and Dweck (2003) found that students with incremental, learning goal orientations took more responsibility for their own learning and the learning of others.

Good and Dweck present very strong evidence of the impact of an individual's beliefs on their academic performance, responsibility for their learning, and persistence in the face of tasks that are challenging from intellectual, personal, and identity perspectives. What is critical about persistence is that it is intellectually challenging tasks that require it, along with critical thinking, deep reasoning, and meaningful problem solving. Thus, if students do not tackle such tasks, they will not have an opportunity to benefit intellectually, socially, or emotionally from having met the challenge. Exercising choice to engage with challenging tasks illustrates that students are exercising responsibility for their educational activities, choosing those that will benefit them in the long run by pushing their reasoning skills. Thus, when learning environments that serve underachieving students do not provide challenging tasks, they do these students a disservice in multiple ways.

Interconnections among the Other 3 Rs and social context. Gordon and Mejia provide a sociopolitical framework for understanding the complex relationships among social, emotional, and cognitive development and achievement outcomes in formal educational settings. Although they discuss obstacles to academic achievement that are similar to those mentioned by Walsh and Brabeck and by Luce and Thompson, such as poverty, Gordon and Mejia reframe the discussion in terms of the unequal power distribution among those who achieve and those who are less likely to. Rather than poverty, they talk about inequality of access to relevant resources. Rather than attitudes and forms of knowledge, they talk about attitudes and behaviors that are not explicitly taught in school but that are assumed and necessary for success. These include meta-cognitive strategies, energy deployment, resource utilization, and time on task. If these academic literacies are presumed and students who do not have them are not taught them, they become obstacles to success in school. The community social context is critical for several reasons. It provides the first source of appropriate knowledge and attitudes toward learning and schooling. If those are different from the forms of knowledge and attitudes expected by the school, and the school conveys a negative attitude toward the home community, students may experience expectancy and value messages (ala Eccles) that result in their either not undertaking, or undertaking and giving up on, complex and challenging intellectual tasks. The family and community are also important because they provide the individual with the first opportunity to learn and to understand the ways in which support is distributed over individuals. In high poverty communities, there tends to be low capital for family or community support. Schools and teachers thus serve an especially important role in providing opportunity to learn for these students. However, many teachers are underprepared for those conditions that limit what students can achieve. When there is low capital in the community, the absence of highly qualified teachers has an even greater impact on student achievement.

In the context of unequal distribution of power as a root cause of underachievement, Gordon and Mejia reject the notion of resilience as too passive. Instead, overcoming challenging obstacles requires an active stance against the forces that place individuals at risk. They argue that what needs to be examined is the defiance of youth who succeed despite overwhelming constellations of risk variables. They also point out that the circumstances that foster defiance may be at odds with the broader aims of schooling, as traditionally conceived. They argue for the "affirmative development of academic ability" through means that foster defiant behavior, such as greater opportunities for relationships with adults and peers who are supportive of academic goals, creating high performance learning communities, and opportunities to engage in challenging academic tasks in which students achieve their goals and increase their sense of self-efficacy.

That resilience is actually defiance is also manifest in Sternberg's effort to connect the Other 3 Rs to his WICS mode of higher mental processes—wisdom, intelligence, and creativity synthesized. He connects reasoning to intelligence, creativity to resilience, and wisdom to using knowledge responsibly. The discussion of creativity and resilience cogently makes the point that creative ideas are often defiant, in the sense used by Gordon and Mejia. That is, creative ideas are often disparaged, dismissed, and denounced. Putting forth a creative idea takes courage, a willingness to take risks, and persistence in the face of resistance. Being resilient requires many of these same characteristics, especially persistence.

An intervention environment for connecting the Other 3 Rs. Cogan and colleagues propose an initial integrative model of reasoning, resilience, and responsibility that translates these concepts into a classroom-friendly implementation. In this model, typical academic activities (e.g., solving math or social studies problems) are intertwined with strategies for developing responsibility and resilience in the course of solving the problem. There are not yet empirical data that establish the validity of the model or whether the classroom activities produce changes or improvements in the "Other 3 Rs." This effort is to be commended on a number of dimensions. First, it brought a variety of researchers to the table for the purpose of designing instructional units that would have explicit learning objectives in academic, social, and emotional areas plus explicit strategies for achieving them. The unique contributions of this effort are the explicitness of the three kinds of learning objectives and the provision of specific strategies. Other problem- and project-based curriculum development efforts have shown effects on complex problem solving in mathematics and science as well as changes in several motivational dimensions (e.g., interest, self-confidence, feelings about math challenges) (e.g., Brown & Campione, 1996; Cognitive and Technology Group at Vanderbilt, 1992; Linn & Hsi, 2000). However, in many of these cases only the academic objectives have been well specified; the social and emotional ones have been attended to in the design features more so than in the instructional strategies. For example, problems are selected to be interesting, authentic, and meaningful to children but strategies designed to encourage completion of the problem, even in the face of difficulties, have largely been absent.

A challenging aspect of putting the Cogan and colleagues intervention model to the test, as with most of the other models discussed in this volume, is defining concepts sufficiently well that they can be measured and the definitions agreed upon by members of the community. In the specific model proposed by Cogan and colleagues, all three concepts are heavily situated in a specific problem-solving situation. That is, reasoning is thinking through each step; responsibility means assuming responsibility for each part of the problem; and resilience is sticking with it when obstacles to solution are encountered. These are more constrained definitions of the constructs than those identified in other chapters. However, for purposes of creating concrete, actionable constructs that classroom teachers and their students can address, this narrowing is needed. Assuming that the intervention is successful with these narrowed definitions, a next step will be to connect the more constrained definitions to the broader senses in which they are used in models discussed in this volume. A second issue concerns the degree to which the problems themselves meet the "challengingness" criteria that emerges as a theme across the chapters (discussed below). Not only do problems need to be challenging, but they need to demand the kind of critical literacy skills needed to succeed in the 21st century knowledge society. The results of the pilot should provide much useful data on a number of the critical issues raised by the chapters in this volume. Thus, the intervention is certainly a good starting point for designing systematic approaches to integrating reasoning, resilience, and responsibility in a single task.

In summary, the theoretical and empirical perspectives in this volume converge on several principles that need to be operationalized in creating educational environments that develop and integrate complex reasoning, resilience, and responsibility. My synthesis of these principles goes as follows.

- Students need challenging tasks and environments that support them doing these well and in ways in which they can feel in control of the outcomes.
- Challenging tasks require students to reason critically, to weigh information, and to make choices based on intrinsic and sometimes extrinsic task variables.
- Support comes in the form of individuals and communities of individuals in which students feel a sense of belonging and relationship.
- Connections to these individuals provide the emotional, social, and cognitive supports that can sustain an individual through a challenging task.

It is one thing to put forth a set of principles and quite another to implement them in the design of learning environments. The task may be made more tractable in the context of a framework that makes explicit the multiple relationships among knowledge, learners, and the contexts in which they live and learn. That framework is the one proposed in *How People Learn* (HPL; Bransford, Brown, & Cocking, 2000).

THE HPL FRAMEWORK FOR THE DESIGN OF LEARNING ENVIRONMENTS

The design framework put forth in *How People Learn* (Bransford et al., 2000) emerged from a consideration of the lessons learned from the past 40 years or so of cognitive and developmental research on learning. Although the volume considered work on motivation and self-efficacy, the research coverage was heavily weighted on the cognitive side. The explication and discussion of the HPL design framework emphasized the cognitive much more so than the social and emotional. Nevertheless, the HPL design framework is general enough to accommodate a weightier treatment of social and emotional aspects of learning environments. One valuable contribution of the chapters in this volume is that they help elaborate a number of aspects of the HPL framework.

The HPL model identifies four dimensions of learning environments, all of which interact (in twos, threes, and fours) in important ways: knowledge, learner, assessment, and community. The descriptions of each that I provide here incorporate important concepts from the initial conceptu-

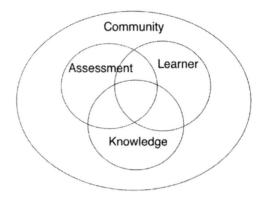

Figure 12.1.   The *How People Learn* framework for the design of learning environments.
Adapted from Bransford, Brown, and Cocking (2000).

alization of the model, refinements developed by our research team (Carney, Oney, Goldman, & Pellegrino, 2004), and elaborations suggested by
the chapters in the present volume. Figure 12.1 depicts the basic organization of the model as depicted in Bransford and colleagues (2000).

A learning environment is *knowledge-centered* if it emphasizes the
important concepts in a domain or discipline, how they are organized,
the big principles that relate concepts, and the epistemology of the
domain. *Learner-centered* refers to what students bring to the learning situation: cognitions (including any preferences for processing specific kinds
of information), emotions, cultural norms and values, attributions, and
sense of self as learner. *Assessment-centered* refers to ways of measuring
learning and change. Particularly important from an HPL point of view is
assessment for learning as well as assessment of learning (Pellegrino,
Chudowsky, & Glaser 2002). *Community-centered* refers to the social context of learning, as well as to the broader contexts within which the learning takes place. It encompasses features of formal learning environments
such as instructional grouping; opportunities for scaffolding; norms and
values regarding collaboration, cooperation, and competition; and expectations regarding participation. Based on the importance of the socio-
demographic and socioeconomic variables for achievement, as discussed
in several chapters in the present volume, community-centered also
extends beyond formal educational contexts to learners' home and out-
of-school communities, as well as the values, norms, attitudes, and beliefs
reflected in those contexts. Learners' identities are shaped by the contexts
in which they live, as reflected in several of chapters of this volume (e.g.,

Eccles; Good & Dweck; Brabeck & Walsh; Zimmerman) and are as central in what they bring to formal learning situations as their conceptions of the physical world.

The symbolism of the HPL learning environment diagram is critical for understanding how learning environments are orchestrated to support activities that afford all children opportunities to achieve. As is evident in Figure 12.1, the HPL model is represented as a Venn diagram, with three intersecting circles (knowledge, learner, assessment) set inside a fourth (community). The two- and three-way overlaps draw attention to more local aspects of learning environments. For example, the overlap of knowledge and learner reflects the need for developmentally appropriate goals for learning in the disciplines, as well as analyses of how learners of different ages are likely to respond to different concepts, tasks, and types of instruction. The learner–assessment overlap taps into the need to use developmentally appropriate forms of feedback as well as outcome assessments. Just as deaf students do better with visual and spatial information during instruction, such strengths need to be taken into account for assessment. English language learners may understand more than they can produce in English. Thus, comprehension assessment needs to be done in a way that production limitations do not affect estimates of understanding (Goldman, Reyes, & Varnhagen, 1984).

The overlap of community and knowledge speaks to epistemology. Discipline-based communities of practice set the norms for what counts as evidence and what is taken to be "known" within the discipline. With the expanded scope of community set forth here, the overlap also captures out-of-school norms, values, and epistemologies with respect to different disciplinary areas. Likewise, the community–assessment overlap draws attention to differences in potential value, legitimacy, and meaning of traditional achievement measures, whether students do well or poorly on them. From a sociohistorical perspective on mathematics learning, Martin (2000) found that some parents did not see the importance of pursuing mathematics in high school even when their children were performing at high levels on district achievement tests. To these parents, higher mathematics was not relevant to the career paths open to their children. In the face of these parental attitudes and expectations, continuing to do well in mathematics represents a form of defiance, as Gordon and Mejia (this volume) define it.

The intersection of knowledge, learner, and community speaks to cultural relevance, value, and potential interest of different topics and tasks within a domain for specific groups of learners. The intersection of assessment, knowledge, and learner speaks to the issue of the appropriateness of particular forms of assessment for the discipline and learners. It also reflects feedback on learning, and how learners process and use that feedback cognitively, socially, and emotionally.

Finally, the knowledge, learner, assessment overlap is embedded in community. This embedding captures considerations of how different communities use and interpret the results of assessments of specific learners in specific domains, and the meaning of these outcomes to community members as well as to learners-as-members of classroom, school, family, and larger, societal communities. That community acts as a backdrop indicates its permeating effect on the whole of the learning environment. The learner comes to learning situations in different disciplines with expectations formed through interactions with members of communities both in and out of formal educational contexts. These interactions shape learners' approaches to assessment and learning regardless of the discipline or kind of assessment. These experiences may be positive and conducive to engagement with learning or negative and resistant to engagement. The out-of-school community is a source of stereotypes, cultural values and norms, and expectations that impact learners' approaches to discipline-based tasks, assessments of learning, and views of themselves as competent and capable learners. These are juxtaposed with the values, culture, and norms of the school community. The research on individual and contextual variables that is reported in this volume indicates that there are complex interactions and, perhaps, compensatory effects among these variables and with achievement. The enhanced HPL framework suggests that the integration of cognitive, social, and emotional dimensions of learning requires that we design learning environments that make serious attempts to be simultaneously centered on knowledge, learner, assessment, and community.

IMPLICATIONS FOR RESEARCH AND POLICY

There are a number of implications for research and policy regarding the design of learning environments that take seriously the challenge of integrating cognitive, social, and emotional development and learning. In closing, I consider four: (1) the kind of settings in which we do research on learning and achievement; (2) the time frame over which we conduct the research; (3) the definition and coherence across investigators of the key constructs we study; and (4) the relationship between policy and research.

Research Settings

From a research perspective, we need to move beyond studying learning in artificially created environments if we wish our results to generalize to authentic contexts of learning. Most artificially created situations assign differences among individuals to the "error" term—the noise making it harder to find significance for the one or two variables that we intentionally manipulate. It is precisely the variance among individuals in the "same" environment that we need to make the subject of our research. That is, as some of the findings in the chapters in this volume show, we need much deeper understanding of the resilient and defiant individuals who succeed despite the odds, of the ways in which interactions in combination with success on difficult academic tasks lead to the formation of identities as learners. We have largely correlational data for many of the social context variables and achievement. Such data produce rich descriptions and complex models of a host of interdependent and interacting variables. However, the models allow only limited predictions of impact because it is typically not possible to identify causal leverage points. Causal leverage points are places in the models where changing the value of one or two variables would dramatically change the outcomes. The manipulation of orientation to learning (Good & Dweck, this volume) is an exception in that it has been possible to show that orienting individuals toward learning orientations produces improvements in learning outcomes.

An approach to research that may have more traction for impacting outcomes for students is one that draws its problems from the world of practice, with a commitment to contributing to the solution of those problems as well as to furthering the knowledge base. This approach, identified by Stokes (1997) as research in Pasteur's Quadrant, is a way to create bridges between the world of research and the world of formal educational environments. A second approach to research is to examine learning as it occurs in out-of-school contexts. What motivates and keeps people engaged in learning in such settings? Are there parallels in in-school environments that would allow learners to use what they learn outside on the inside of school? Lee's (2001) research on cultural modeling in literary study demonstrates the power of this approach.

The Time Frame of Research

Correlated with where and how we do research on cognitive, social, and emotional dimensions of learning is the time frame over which we study the phenomena. Short-term laboratory studies (an hour or two) may accurately reflect the time course over which we can memorize lists of items or understand one or two texts but they are far too short to capture many authentic learning situations. The cognitive literature on the development of expertise, for example, suggests that most experts have spent many years developing their expertise. Furthermore, short-term laboratory or laboratory-like studies limit the kind of reasoning that can be studied and are totally inadequate to capture the development of identity, expectancy, values, and attitudes. Indeed, these constructs are typically talked about as developmental outcomes rather than outcomes of learning. The contrast relates to the distinction between learning and development in terms of the length of time over which the process takes place. If we accept the fact that complex reasoning and deep understanding are more like traditional developmental than traditional learning outcomes, we need to adjust the time course over which we conduct research on learning. Multiyear, longitudinal studies will be needed to capture complex learning processes. On the positive side, this puts constructs from the cognitive domain on a time scale similar to that of social and emotional constructs, potentially making it more likely that researchers will attempt to study all three simultaneously.

The Constructs We Study

As an outsider looking in on research on social and emotional sides of learning, I am always awestruck by the sheer number of concepts that are put forth by different researchers. I have always struggled with the similarities and differences among concepts such as self-efficacy, self-confidence, and locus of control; self-regulated learning and meta-cognition; task interest and task value; identity as a learner and self-efficacy; effort, persistence, perseverance, and time-on-task. The present volume is no exception and presented a new set of terms with which to grapple. Responsibility is the wise use of knowledge as compared with taking initiative for one's own learning. Resilience is perseverance on the same task even in the face of repeated failure as compared with adapting to feedback and modifying goals and tasks so one can succeed. In part, the profusion of labels for various constructs is an epiphenomenon of the research traditions on social and emotional phenomena. Many motivational researchers define their constructs with respect to self-report questionnaires and surveys from which various scales are developed. Thus, to take a hypothetical (at least to my knowledge) case, whether a person is described as happy or unhappy depends on the patterns of responses to a set of questions that have face validity for the construct in question. Reputable scales are those that have been subjected to rigorous development efforts and that conform to expected reliability and validity criteria. I applaud these efforts because we have learned many important and useful principles from this work.

However, making progress in the study of social and emotional learning seems to require that some effort be made to at least align clusters of constructs that are highly similar in their consequential meaning. I freely admit that the same problem plagues constructs in the cognitive area. Alas, the distinctions are "perfectly clear" to me, and I leave it to those who consider themselves to be outside the cognitive realm to construct a similar litany of cognitive constructs that seem highly interchangeable and in need of clearer differentiation.

The Relationship Between Policy and Research

We live in an era of evidence-based decision making. And why not? There is so much information available. Shouldn't we be able to find evidence on which to base policy recommendations and decisions? Unfortunately—or perhaps fortunately—the evidence is rarely so cut and dry that only one decision or policy can be derived from the data. Evidence must be weighed and evaluated against a set of criteria to determine trustworthiness and credibility, replicability, and limits of generalizability. These processes are guided by complex sets of political, social, and personal forces. Indeed, people tend to believe the evidence that accords with their prior beliefs and are slow to change these beliefs. Thus, policymaking is a complex process in which the use of evidence to make decisions about policies and actions is mediated by values, norms, beliefs, and political exigencies (Ferrero, 2005).

The derivation or justification of policies about the education of children is further complicated by the time frame over which it is legitimate to look at the impact of existing policies and practices. The research on teacher learning indicates that it takes 3 to 5 years for teachers to change their classroom instructional practice, even with fairly intensive professional development (Cochran-Smith & Lytle, 1999). Learning to teach well is probably one of the most difficult kinds of expertise to acquire. Not only do teachers need to know content and pedagogical techniques but they need to know how to teach others that content. They need to understand the ways in which learners come to know the content and how to support those learning processes (Shulman, 1986). As with expertise in other areas, it takes a lengthy period of practice and experience in the domain to become an expert teacher. Thus, when policymakers adopt the "quarterly report" business model as the model for educational accountability, they run the risk of making premature and erroneous judgments about existing policies and programs.

In summary, if we are serious about creating educational contexts in which serious efforts are made to support the learning and development of the Other 3 Rs as well as the 3 Rs, we need to rethink how we design those environments, what the targets of our efforts are, and how and when we evaluate whether we are accomplishing those goals. Rigorous research—at both macro- and microlevels—will be required to understand how learning happens in designed environments, expected time frames for acquisition, and how to interpret what we observe for individuals who may be cognitively, culturally, linguistically, and physically diverse. Only through such a process can we truly ensure that no child will be left behind—cognitively, socially, or emotionally.

REFERENCES

Bloome, D., & Egan-Robertson, A. (1993). The social construction of intertextuality and classroom reading and writing. *Reading Research Quarterly, 28*(4), 303–333.

Bransford, J. D., Brown, A. L., & Cocking, R. R. E. (2000). *How people learn: Brain, mind, experience, and school.* Washington, DC: National Academy Press.

Brown, A. L., & Campione, J. C. (1996). Psychological theory and the design of innovative learning environments: On procedures, principles, and systems. In L. S. R. Glaser (Ed.), *Innovations in learning: New environments for education* (pp. 289–325). Mahwah, NJ: Erlbaum.

Carney, K. E., Oney, B., Goldman, S. R., & Pellegrino, J. W. (2004, November). *Interpreting the How People Learn Framework: What lies in the overlaps?* (Working paper). Chicago: University of Illinois at Chicago.

Cochran-Smith, M., & Lytle, S. L. (1999). Relationships of knowledge and practice: Teacher learning in communities. In A. Iran-Nejad & P. D. Pearson (Eds.), *Review of research in education* (pp. 249–305). San Francisco: American Educational Research Association.

Cognition and Technology Group at Vanderbilt. (1992). The Jasper series as an example of anchored instruction: Theory, program description, and assessment data. *Educational Psychologist, 27,* 291–315.

Cognition and Technology Group at Vanderbilt. (1997). *The Jasper project: Lessons in curriculum, instruction, assessment, and professional development.* Mahwah, NJ: Erlbaum.

Ferrero, D. J. (2005). Does 'research based' mean 'value neutral'? *Phi Delta Kappan, 86,* 425–432.

Goldman, S. R. (2004). Cognitive aspects of constructing meaning through and across multiple texts. In N. Shuart-Ferris & D. M. Bloome (Eds.), *Uses of intertextuality in classroom and educational research.* (pp. 313–347).Greenwich, CT: Information Age.

Goldman, S. R. (2005). Designing for educational improvement that scales: Processes of inquiry in practice. In C. Dede, J. P. Honan, & L. C. Peters (Eds.), *Scaling up success* (pp. 67–96). San Francisco: Jossey-Bass.

Goldman, S. R., Reyes, M., & Varnhagen, C. K. (1984). Understanding fables in first and second languages. *Journal of National Association for Bilingual Education, 3,* 35–66.

Grant-Pillow, H., & Dweck, C. S. (2003). Clarifying achievement goals and their impact. *Journal of Personality and Social Psychology, 85,* 541-553.

Greenberg, M. T., Weissberg, R. P., O'Brien, M. U., Zins, J. E., Fredericks, L., Resnik, H., & Elias, M. J. (2003). School-based prevention: Promoting positive social development through social and emotional learning. *American Psychologist, 58*(6/7), 466–474.

Haney, W. (2000, August). The myth of the Texas miracle in education. *Education Policy Analysis Archives, 8*(41). Retrieved April 1, 2001, from http://epaa.asu.edu/epaa/v8n41/

Kohn, A. (2000). *The case against standardized testing: Raising the scores, ruining the schools.* Portsmouth, NH: Heinemann.

Lee, C. D. (2001). Is October Brown Chinese? A cultural modeling activity system for underachieving students. *American Educational Research Journal, 38*(1), 97–142.

Linn, M. C., & Hsi, S. (2000). *Computers, teachers, peers: Science learning partners.* Mahwah, NJ: Erlbaum.

Martin, D. B. (2000). *Mathematics success and failure among African-American youth: The roles of sociohistorical context, community forces, school influence, and individual agency.* Mahwah, NJ: Erlbaum.

McNeil, L. M. (2000). *Contradictions of school reform: Educational costs of standardized testing.* New York: Routledge.

Newman, F. M., Smith, B. S., Allensworth, E., & Bryk, A. S. (2001). Instructional program coherence: What it is and why it should guide school improvement policy. *Educational Evaluation and Policy Analysis, 23*(4), 297–321.

No Child Left Behind Act. (2001). Retrieved on February 10, 2002, from http://www.ed.gov/nclb

Norris, S. P., & Phillips, L. M. (1994). Interpreting pragmatic meaning when reading reports of science. *Journal of Research in Science Teaching, 31,* 947–967.

Palincsar, A. S., & Magnusson, S. J. (2001). The interplay of first-hand and text-based investigations to model and support the development of scientific knowledge and reasoning. In S. Carver & D. Klahr (Eds.), *Cognition and instruction: Twenty-five years of progress,* (pp. 151–194). Mahwah, NJ: Erlbaum.

Pellegrino, J., Chudowsky, N., & Glaser, R. (2001). *Knowing what students know: The science and design of educational assessment.* Washington, DC: National Academy Press.

Shulman, L. (1986). Those who understand: Knowledge growth in teaching. *Educational Researcher, 15,* 4–14.

Stokes, D. E. (1997). *Pasteur's quadrant: Basic science and technological innovation.* Washington, DC: Brookings Institution Press.

Valencia, R. R., & Bernal, E. M. (Eds.). (2000). The Texas Assessment of Academic Skills (TAAS) case: Perspectives of plaintiff's experts [Special issue]. *Hispanic Journal of Behavioral Sciences, 22*(4).

Wiley, J., Goldman, S. R., & Graesser, A. (2004, January). *Taking a critical stance and learning from on-line scientific information: Evidence from eye-tracking and think alouds.* Paper presented at the Winter Conference on Text, Discourse and Cognition; Jackson Hole, WY.

Zins, J. E., Bloodworth, M. R., Weissberg, R. P., & Walberg, H. J. (2004). The scientific base linking social and emotional learning to school success. In J. E. Zins, R. P. Weissberg, M. C. Wang, & H. J. Walberg (Eds.), *Building academic success on social and emotional learning: What does the research say?* (pp. 3–22). New York: Teachers College Press.

ABOUT THE AUTHORS

Mary M. Brabeck, PhD, is professor of applied psychology and dean of the Steinhardt School of Education at New York University. She is currently a member of the American Psychological Association's (APA) Board of Educational Affairs and is a Fellow of APA (Divisions 7, 35, and 52). Her most recent edited books are *Practicing Feminist Ethics in Psychology* (2000, APA) and *Meeting at the Hyphen: Schools–Universities–Professions in Collaboration for Student Achievement and Well-Being* (2003, University of Chicago Press).

Jeanine C. Cogan, PhD, is assistant director of the Other 3Rs Project funded by the McDonnell Foundation at the American Psychological Association (APA). Before joining APA, Dr. Cogan was founder and director of her own consulting business where she focused on research and policy analysis and had a diverse client base, such as the Harvard Eating Disorders Center, the American Sociological Association, and the Prime Minister's Office of Stockholm, Sweden. Working with other eating disorder leaders, Dr. Cogan was the founding executive director of the Eating Disorders Coalition for Research, Policy, and Action.

Carol S. Dweck, PhD, is the Lewis and Virginia Eaton Professor of Psychology at Stanford University and is a leading expert in the area of motivation and achievement. Her recent books include *Motivation and Self-Regulation across the Life Span* (with Jutta Heckhausen; 1998, Cambridge University Press) and *Self-Theories: Their Role in Motivation, Personality, and Development* (1999, Psychology Press), *The Handbook of Competence and*

Motivation (with Andrew Ellliot, 2005, Guilford Press), and received the Book of the Year Award from the World Education Fellowship.

Jacquelynne S. Eccles, PhD, is McKeachie Collegiate Professor of Psychology at the University of Michigan. She has served on the faculty at Smith College, the University of Colorado, and the University of Michigan. In 1998–99, she was the interim chair of psychology at the University of Michigan and is now past president of the Society for Research on Adolescence and a member of the National Academy of Education. Her research focuses on topics ranging from gender-role socialization and classroom influences on motivation to social development in the family, school, peer, and wider cultural contexts. Much of this work focuses on the socialization of self-beliefs and the impact of self-beliefs on many other aspects of social development.

Susan R. Goldman, PhD, is a distinguished professor of psychology and education at the University of Illinois at Chicago. She is also codirecting the Center for the Study of Learning, Instruction, and Teacher Development. Her current research activities focus on the psychological processes involved in how people understand and learn from text, discourse, multimedia, and conversation (face to face and online).

Catherine Good, PhD, is a postdoctoral research fellow in the Department of Psychology at Columbia University in New York. Her work focuses on the ways that stereotypes, achievement-related beliefs, and the environment influence stigmatized individuals' intellectual performance, sense of belonging, and persistence in the stereotyped domain, as well as the processes through which they do so.

Edmund W. Gordon, EdD, is the John M. Musser Professor of Psychology, Emeritus at Yale University and the Richard March Hoe Professor of Psychology and Education, emeritus and director of the Institute for Urban and Minority Education (IUME) at Teachers College, Columbia University. He is also Senior Scholar in Residence at the College Board. Professor Gordon is widely known as one of the founders of Head Start and for his significant contributions to research concerning the education of low status populations.

Tom Luce is Assistant Secretary, Office of Planning, Evaluation and Policy Development of the U.S. Department of Education. He was formerly chairman of the National Center for Educational Accountability and founder of Just for the Kids, a nonprofit organization that analyzes and employs student achievement data and best practices to spur student achievement. Mr. Luce was a founding partner of Hughes & Luce, where he practiced law for more than 40 years. He has been appointed to numerous major posts by state governors, most notably serving as chief of staff of the Texas Select Committee on Public Education. He is coauthor, with Lee Thompson, of *Do What Works: How Proven Practices Can Improve America's Public Schools* (2005, Ascent Education Press) and the author of *Now or Never: How We Can Save Our Public Schools* (1995, Taylor Publishing). This article was written by Mr. Luce in his private capacity. No official support or endorsment by the U.S. Department of Education is intended or should be inferred.

Richard Mayer, PhD, is professor of psychology at the University of California, Santa Barbara (UCSB) where he has served since 1975. His research interests are in educational and cognitive psychology. His current research involves the intersection of cognition, instruction, and technology with a special focus on multimedia learning and problem solving.

Brenda X. Mejia, MA, is a PhD student in the Department of Couseling and Clinical Psychology at Teachers College, Columbia University. Her research interests are focused on acculturation, multicultural mental health, and educational achievement of Latino and African American populations. For the past 4 years, she has been a research coordinator at the Institute for Urban and Minority Education (IUME).

Terezinha Nunes, PhD, is professor Educational Studies at the University of Oxford. Her research spans the domains of children's literacy and numeracy, and her focus of analysis covers both cognitive and cultural issues. Dr. Nunes was awarded a prize for her monograph, *Literacy and Poverty*, by the Brazilian Society for the Progress of Science. Recently she was awarded a British Academy Research Readership.

Robert Sternberg, PhD, is Dean of Arts and Sciences at Tufts University and former IBM Professor of Psychology and Education and director of the Center for the Psychology of Abilities, Competencies, and Expertise at Yale. He is most well known for his theory of successful intelligence, investment theory of creativity (developed with Todd Lubart), theory of mental self-government, balance theory of wisdom, and for his triangular theory of love and his theory of love as a story.

Rena F. Subotnik, PhD, began her position as director of the Center for Psychology in the Schools and in Education at the American Psychological Association (APA) in January 2002. Prior to her position at APA, Dr. Subotnik was professor of education at Hunter College, where she coordinated the secondary education program and served as research and curriculum liaison to the Hunter College laboratory schools (grades preK–12).

Lee Thompson, PhD, holds a law degree and a doctorate in history from the University of Texas at Austin. In addition to practicing law, she has taught at Stanford Law School and the University of Texas at Arlington and has been a visiting scholar at the Center for the Study of Law and Society at the University of California at Berkeley. She is coauthor, with Tom Luce, of *Do What Works: How Proven Practices Can Improve America's Public Schools* (2005, Ascent Education Press) and the author of *The Reconstruction of Southern Debtors: Bankruptcy after the Civil War* (2004, University of Georgia Press).

Mary E. Walsh, PhD, is the Daniel E. Kearns Professor of Urban Education and Innovative Leadership in the Department of Counseling, Developmental and Educational Psychology at the Lynch School of Education at Boston College. She also directs the Boston College Center for Child, Family and Community Partnerships. For the past several years, Dr. Walsh has been a lead partner in a school–community–university partnership among Boston College, the Boston Public Schools, and community agencies and resources with the goal of addressing barriers to learning and promoting academic achievement.

Gregory White, is the Executive Director of the National Academy of Education. Prior to this position, Greg served as assistant director of the APA/IES Postdoctoral Education Research Training and as program officer for APA's Center for Psychology in Schools and Education. Before joining APA, Greg worked as a director for grant-making initiatives focused on education and youth development for United Ways of New England, served on the staff of City Year, and has experience as a counselor for the Boston Public Schools.

Barry J. Zimmerman, PhD, is a distinguished professor of educational psychology and head of Learning, Development, and Instruction at the Graduate School and University Center of the City University of New York. He is known for his theory and research on social modeling and learners' self-regulation in a variety of contexts, including academics, sport, music, and health. With support from the U.S. Department of Education and the National Institutes of Health, Dr. Zimmerman has designed intervention programs to enhance the functioning of at-risk students and children with asthma.